Strangers Nowhere in the World

Strangers Nowhere in the World

The Rise of Cosmopolitanism in Early Modern Europe

Margaret C. Jacob

PENN

University of Pennsylvania Press
Philadelphia

10   9   8   7   6   5   4   3   2   1

Published by
University of Pennsylvania Press
Philadelphia, Pennsylvania 19104-4112

Library of Congress Cataloging-in-Publication Data

Jacob, Margaret C., 1943–
    Strangers nowhere in the world : the rise of cosmopolitanism in early modern Europe /
Margaret C. Jacob.
        p.   cm.
    ISBN-13: 978-0-8122-3933-1 (cloth : alk. paper)
    ISBN-10: 0-8122-3933-4 (cloth : alk. paper)
    Includes bibliographical references and index.
        1. Cosmopolitanism—Europe—History. 2. Toleration—Europe—History. 3. Europe—
Moral conditions—History. I Title.
HN380.Z9 M645   2006
306.094'0903—dc22   2005058499

In memory of Richard F. Hunt,
a cosmopolitan gentleman

Contents

Introduction

Being cosmopolitan in Europe during the early modern age meant—as now—the ability to experience people of different nations, creeds and colors with pleasure, curiosity and interest, and not with suspicion, disdain, or simply a disinterest that could occasionally turn into loathing. This benign posture, whether toward foreigners or disbelievers in one's own religion, did not come about—then or now—automatically, or even easily. It happens when circumstances or situations, times, and places exist that are propitious. In other words, such a varying stance in the world possesses a history, and this book seeks to recapture aspects of it. Focused on Europe from roughly 1650 to 1800, the chapters ahead take their definitions of the cosmopolitan from what those contemporaries said, as well as inevitably from our own lived experience.

We can recognize the early modern words used to describe the cosmopolitan as now being a part of our own idealistic vocabulary. Cosmopolitans, as French philosopher, Denis Diderot, put it in his encyclopedia of 1751, are "strangers no where in the world."[1] They accept the foreign hospitably, without necessarily agreeing with, or practicing, every cultural value associated with it. They enjoy people different from themselves, live next to them comfortably, or socialize and trade with them respectfully.[2] A gossipy journal of the 1770s in the Dutch Republic called itself, *De Kosmopoliet of Waereldburger* (The Cosmopolite or World Citizen). It surveyed theater and the arts, taking a particular interest in foreign languages and unusual dialects. It sought to treat nothing foreign or strange as unknowable or despicable. It also satirized the new sociability associated with the cosmopolitan, in effect making fun of its own ideal.[3] By the second half of the eighteenth century the word, and the ideal, had become commonplace.

Then in the 1790s the implications of cosmopolitan mores received a novel treatment and were given international dimensions. The German philosopher Immanuel Kant created a political agenda for the Western nations by proclaiming the cosmopolitan acceptance of all peoples to be a necessity. It would become, he said, the foundation for a perpetual peace among nations.

And he saw hospitality toward strangers as the tell-tale sign of cosmopolitan behavior. In the same decade other, anonymous, writers agitated for political reform at home and addressed the British in the voice of "the cosmopolite."[4] Their writings forcefully associated cosmopolitan values with the impulse for political reform. As we shall see in the chapters ahead, they were right to see the linkage, to assert that certain political conditions—long associated with democratic republics—made cosmopolitan mores happen more easily. By the 1790s a century of experimenting with constitutional systems of governance in Britain, and the growing realization on the Continent that monarchical absolutism was doomed to failure, made cosmopolites certain that democracy, and the revolutions that were then promoting it, lay in their interests. In societies where nationalist pressures mounted by the year and would soon lead to the Napoleonic Wars, a few visionaries longed to transcend those profound rivalries.

I am not suggesting an early, until now unnoticed history of the ability to think about other people ethnographically. I am not wishing us to pretend that the same Europeans who could on occasion mix amicably at home with the foreign or dream of perpetual peace did not also practice the slave trade abroad. But I am saying that in certain early modern circles and settings, with motives that could range from millenarian Protestantism to the desire for profit, some Europeans approached those distinctly different from themselves hospitably, with a willingness to get to know them, even to like them. From at least the sixteenth century such an expansive person was termed a *cosmopolite*, best defined as a citizen of the world.

Vagaries will always surround the word, and all we can do is provide a few examples of its usage. From 1600 to 1800 writers in search of universal fellowship and human rejuvenation, sometimes through medicine and alchemy, signed themselves "cosmopolite." Others who decried the treatment of minority religions, in one case the massacre of French Protestants during the wars of religion, shielded their identity under the anonymous label, cosmopolite.[5] As early as the 1640s in English, the cosmopolitan came to mean someone who identified beyond the nation. At the same moment in French, the cosmopolite offhandedly appears as a "habitué of all the world." All these wordsmiths probably had different causes and agendas in mind, particular to their moment. They did, however, bequeath to us a useful vocabulary. Their opponents, ever watchful, saw the implications and drew them out to the extreme. They said that cosmopolites could not identify with their country and could not be good citizens.[6]

Now, early in our new century, we reject the indictment. Regardless of our national identity, we now see the cosmopolitan acceptance of strangers, foreigners—or just people who are exotic or different—as increasingly compelling, even necessary. Learned conversations occur among theorists about how best to achieve a vibrant cosmopolitanism.[7] Cities afford daily experience of people whose customs and skin color announce their differences, and most of the time—and most people—strive to be accommodating, even hospitable. Yet tensions also mount in European cities as their original inhabitants react bitterly to the foreigners in their midst. At moments these reactions to foreigners, especially of Moslem background, resemble the tensions of white and black Americans who have struggled for a century and more to cohabit urban spaces peaceably. Having a historical perspective on past experiences of the different and the foreign may put some of these struggles in perspective.

Yet even when being successfully cosmopolitan very little is known about why and how the ideal arose in the West. Why did early modern theorists or pundits seize upon the notion of cosmopolitanism as a form of virtue, one that would make Europeans hospitable to foreigners, comfortable among people of different religions, or simply eager to socialize outside of kirk or kin, among relative strangers? Clearly commerce made people imagine a wider world, but mercantile life is only part of the larger story of how and why some Westerners began to think in cosmopolitan ways.

An interrogation of places and people from the seventeenth and eighteenth centuries helps us better understand how a cosmopolitan idealism became thinkable, if not fashionable. A few places to launch this inquiry are fairly obvious: both science and merchant life have long been associated with inculcating a cosmopolitan affect. As we shall see, both associations have merit, but need qualification. Such nuancing is possible because a different kind of history, one here focused on practices and social experience, qualifies what once had been taken as truisms about why some Europeans began to think in cosmopolitan ways. International commerce helped but, as we shall see, the potential of mercantile exchange to instill cosmopolitan mores rested on many variables. Science too contributed, but the most avowedly cosmopolitan voices in its early modern camp were often alchemical—not the first practitioners who come to mind when we think about the scientific.

Such varying conditions and unexpected participants cannot be accessed by writing yet another intellectual history of the cosmopolitan ideal. There already exist excellent accounts of writers and philosophers, largely from the early modern period, who wrote idealistically and learnedly about the cosmopolitan.[8] Rather, the goal of the pages ahead lies in presenting practices, behaviors, social habits, mores from the quotidian long past, that may offer insight into the circumstances that made the cosmopolitan sometimes more, other times less possible. Sometimes contemporary witnesses spied what the eye of the historian sees and used the terms "cosmopolitan" or "cosmopolite" to call attention to what they were doing, or advocating. Alchemists were particularly fond of invoking the term, of crossing any border in search of their illusive treasures. But even when sources do not invoke the word, this book labels as cosmopolitan social practices that others at the time may not have called by that name.

Beginning in a small southern French city, Avignon, the chapters ahead classify some behavior from the past—in the absence of a better term—as cosmopolitan. Avignon afforded that opportunity because the city's clerical magistrates, representatives of the Inquisition, found certain activities—the mixing of Christians and Jews, Protestants and Catholics, or the breaching of class lines—so unacceptable that they left rich records of their efforts to stop them. Perhaps the terms "cosmopolitan" or "cosmopolite" are best understood within the setting depicted in the opening chapter. The deliberations of the Roman Catholic Inquisition sought to impose a clear alternative—the majority report in some places—that placed subjects behind the barriers erected by confessional loyalty, or social place, or national identity. The defenders of orthodoxy and the power of churches and kings thought that border crossing might threaten their authority. They believed that opposition politics could arise more easily when social experience spilled beyond the confines of confessional community, or kith and kin. They had been right to worry. As the final chapter will show, by the 1770s a cosmopolitan affect did indeed knit together the many participants who made up a growing, international and republican conversation. It spelled trouble for empires, monarchs, and their states or colonies throughout the Atlantic world.

In 1790 French revolutionaries stormed into Avignon, and the new National Assembly in Paris finally incorporated it into the French state. Then future generations forgot about what Avignon had been like (and by implication what France might have been like if left) under the control of the Roman Catholic Inquisition. From the Middle Ages until 1790 it had governed the city and some surrounding territory for reasons that had to do with events centuries earlier in the history of the papacy. Leaving records in this southern provincial setting, these crusty anti-cosmopolites might have been missed, just as we might ignore their many early modern counterparts who once held or aspired to power.

An older historiography about early modern Europe, written after World

War I, had not been so forgetful. Writing in the aftermath of imperialist war, European historians saw the importance of cosmopolitanism. Nearly a hundred years ago when those historians wrote, cosmopolitan behavior seemed much more difficult and problematic than it does today. Living in the wake of the virulent nationalism and imperialism of the nineteenth century, Europeans then knew the dangers of nationalism, at home and abroad. They looked for ways to achieve cosmopolitan mores and affects because they implied peaceful ways of dealing graciously with foreigners who might become enemies. The great historian of French letters Paul Hazard even located the earliest French usage of "cosmopolite," when in 1560 the humanist Guillaume Postel urged his prince to become one by seeking a universal peace, especially in religion and with the Turks.[9]

Inspired by those now dated historical accounts, but less enthralled by the power of competitive nations, in today's world cosmopolitanism has taken on meaning closer to home, a way of living in our own multiethnic towns and cities. Thus it becomes clearer that in the early modern period it could also mean transgressing within a traditional society of orders, titles, exclusionary kith and kin, religious barriers and prohibitions, gender norms and affectations, and as always, it meant thinking past national identities, being accepting of foreigners at home and abroad.

It is harder to spy cosmopolitan behavior when writing in only one national history. Sometimes to find the transgressive the historian herself has to cross spacial or national boundaries. Even when beginning and ending in Britain, as this book does, it was helped by voyaging and living abroad. Because so many histories stick to events in one nation, or to the formation of its national identity, they tend to miss alternative life experiences, ones that point away from privileging the nation. Being comparative in our archival focus may privilege past lives that—like the comparative historian's perambulations—gazed beyond the nation. Using a historical method that requires border crossings offers certain explanatory advantages. We see that cosmopolitanism can have a variety of meanings: the embrace of foreigners, the crossing of religious barriers, as well as the ability to step away from family taboos and regional parochialism.

For centuries nationalism dominated the consciousness of most Europeans, and it often obscured the cosmopolitan practices that lay beneath the surface in urban settings throughout the Euro-American world. Since 1945 Europeans have struggled to put that legacy behind them and to embrace a pan-European identity. In the same period foreign migration to every Western country—the cities of the United States have also witnessed the same pattern—has meant that everywhere we turn we see ethnic, racial, religious, and linguistic diversity. One theorist involved in the ongoing discussion around cosmopolitanism describes large cities everywhere in the world as now possessing "multicultural enclaves [that] are harbingers of new faces of citizenship . . . no longer based upon exclusive attachments to a particular land, history, and tradition."[10] We see the effects of this new identity in everyday social interactions, in the classrooms, or workplaces, or dinner tables of Los Angeles, to name a familiar setting to this author. While the current levels of racial and ethnic diversity may be unprecedented in the urban West, rising to the challenge presented by diversity and embracing cosmopolitan mores, has a past. Here we will examine evidence of behaviors, mores and practices we may legitimately label (sometimes avant la lettre), cosmopolitan.

First we will focus on the mingling of Christians and Jews, aristocrats and commoners in Avignon. We will then move on to examine the cosmopolitan implications found in the clubbing of genteel alchemists and naturalists busily distilling plants or making air pumps. Next the book turns to the jostling of foreigners in stock exchanges across northern and western Europe, searching always for the conditions that made those moments hospitable and not contentious. Then we will turn to the ritual fraternizing of masonic "brothers" in privacy, even secrecy. The freemasons have also always been associated with the inculcation of cosmopolitan mores. We want to know what truth lies in the claim. We will end with liberal Protestants and republican revolutionaries of the 1790s, young radicals who thought they could remake the world, and in the process invented the bohemian. All are here invoked to unveil practices that lay at the origins of modern, Western cosmopolitanism. Although it only surfaces as an articulated ideal largely after 1750, the chapters ahead demonstrate that some experiences antedate the ideal, possibly making it more easily imagined by late eighteenth-century philosophers.

The mingling, jostling, clubbing, and fraternizing here described constituted situations where, willy-nilly, people behaved in relatively cosmopolitan ways. To make such a benign statement about how expansively early modern Europeans on occasion could act toward one another, toward strangers and foreigners, requires a reorientation in thinking about aspects of European history. It asks that we briefly take our gaze off the rise of the national states, off the wars and tensions to which their progress gave rise. We should see cosmopolitan mores in situ at the same time as the wars—perhaps only in a few places, but there, nonetheless.

Each chapter offers episodes—case studies as they are known in the historian's trade—that give some insight into how and why, and under what circumstances, relatively cosmopolitan behavior appeared. In Chapter 1 we will witness the devout fathers of the Holy Inquisition as they tried to keep people anchored by the exclusive embrace of the one true faith; inadvertently, they help us locate the transgressors. Thus throughout the book, without ever having wished to be so helpful to the historian, alarmed censors, inquisitors, and spies leave evidence of border crossing that points toward the cosmopolitan. The boundary police can be found in Protestant as well as Catholic Europe, as the Societies for the Reformation of Manners in Britain will show us. In that same opening chapter cosmopolites spring up, simultaneously and seemingly at will, in Avignon, in England, in the Dutch Republic . . . wherever organized social life outside the home can be observed.

Anchored by our acquaintance with the antipodes of cosmopolites and their enemies, we must then turn to alchemy and science at the critical moment when modern scientific practices first coalesced, in the decades after 1650. Chapter 2 presents Protestant visionaries in London, like Robert Boyle, who laid out the experimental method based upon mechanical assumptions. His counterparts also appear; French naturalists in Paris who anchored the newly founded Académie des sciences. Somewhat surprisingly, we find in both places that alchemy informed their experimental practices. Within a few decades it would come to be dismissed as magic. In very different national contexts these mechanists and alchemists made science a more open enterprise, one geared to the search for reform and human rejuvenation. The group activities so inherent in the practice of science began early in its history. In complex ways the need for experiments to be witnessed made the social setting of natural inquiry more congenial than most for the emergence of cosmopolitan mores. A specific vision of humankind—often of alchemical origin—provided idealism in both places.

Chapter 3 turns to very public venues, to the currency and stock exchanges, long extolled by visitors as fascinating microcosms, social spaces that threw strangers and foreigners together in ways predisposing them to be cosmopolites. After 1700 Western Europe experienced a marked advance in international, indeed global commerce, and luxury tastes developed that valorized foreign patterns and designs.[11] A globalized universe became conceivable, even consumable, as never before. Just as the Western consumer economy pulled ahead of all competitors in the global market, so too there appeared the first articulations of the cosmopolitan as an ideal.[12] Predictably the historical records of exchanges, found in Antwerp, London, Paris, Lyon, and Marseille, tell a more convoluted story than the simplistic notion of freedom sometimes said to be the essence of commercial life. The cosmopolitanism practiced on their busy floors may be described as real but fragile, hard won only after decades of practice. Whenever exchanges functioned under regulations imposed by an absolutist state, be it Spanish or French, their open practices were also more easily put into retreat. A walk on the floor of early modern exchanges makes visible, but vexed, the cosmopolitanism proclaimed as being there by poets and pundits.

After 1700, genteel and curious seekers did not need to be scientific or alchemical when they searched to broaden their social horizons. A new cultural and intellectual tone had emerged among the educated. Profoundly related to and partly caused by the cosmopolitan behavior here described, the Enlightenment rested on new social gatherings resolutely apart from the courts and the religious confraternities.[13] Chapter 4 examines one of the newest and most exotic forms of eighteenth-century sociability. We have arrived at the masonic moment.

Eighteenth-century allies of the new science—particularly in its Newtonian form—freemasons have often had their enemies from the eighteenth century onward. No one in the twentieth century hated them more than the Nazis. French archives recently returned from Moscow—the Russian army took them in 1945 from the Nazis who had stolen them in Paris—shed new light on how to read the social limits and permissions that freemasonry offered its disparate members. Like the immensely public exchanges, the very private social enclaves formed by lodges showed cosmopolitan impulses by degrees, in some places and not in others. Always they sought by rules and constitutions to turn lodges of relative strangers into society and government in miniature.

But when strangers assembled in order to behave as "brothers," issues became fraught, and the tensions seen in other sites of cosmopolitan mores surfaced dramatically. Masonic lodges struggled over who should be admitted into their intensely urbane, but private world. We will examine the detailed records of one lodge in Bordeaux, where the agonizing about membership continued throughout the eighteenth century, and where—at least when it came to the admission of Jews—the cosmopolitan impulse faltered. A lodge that had crossed social barriers enough to be composed of English and French merchants struggled—without success—to be even more open. Lodges in London and Amsterdam admitted Jews. Yet meeting privately, even secretly, bonded by shared and internationally known rituals, the Christian "brothers" of Bordeaux, although themselves from different nations, could not bring themselves to embrace Jewish members, even visitors.

Finally, one aspect of freemasonry, namely its claim to be secret, requires attention. In masonic hands the claim amounted to an affectation, possibly even a way of seeking attention. By the 1720s and 1730s just about everything found in lodge practices (rituals, passwords, dress, and manners) had been exposed and scrutinized in print. But in the 1790s, as politics in so many parts of western Europe turned deadly, imitators in need of secrecy found something in masonic practices that became almost the sine non qua of modern subversives, revolutionaries—and terrorists. The modern birth of the secret society as an agent of political action—and directly imitative of masonic practices—turned the possibility of the cosmopolitan in powerful and new political directions, potentially sinister. Chapter 4 will close with Irish revolutionaries who by 1800 gave birth to the form of politics dependent upon secrecy. In the process they made the practices of eighteenth-century freemasons seem quaint. Caught in the thicket of British persecution, Irish radicals formed secret societies; they gave birth to a darker side of the radicalism and republicanism of the 1790s.

Chapter 5 returns more optimistically to the revolutionary moment of the 1790s. In that decade British radicals and romantics aspired to new personal identities. Moved in the direction of democracy, inspired by revolutions abroad, they defied inherited emotional boundaries and sought to live without the constraints that had governed male and female behavior in previous generations. They identified as citizens of any revolution, anywhere, and all required personal transformation. In the search to become worthy citizens of a new era, they slipped out from under the net of traditional social mores. In effect, they invented the bohemian. The cosmopolites of the 1790s inherited a generation of republican political agitation combined with liberal Protestantism that as early as the 1760s had crossed oceans and channels. Their goal of becoming citizens of the world made them men and women better fit for other, less repressive seasons, when revolutions and wars did not threaten the established authorities so profoundly. Yet more than any of the others in our cast of characters, the eccentric radicals of the 1790s seem familiar; we can imagine them in our midst, in one of our own immensely diverse, polyglot urban centers.

Although the radicals of the 1790s seemed more familiar to us than the alchemists who long preceded them on the path we have identified as cosmopolitan, there was no preordained evolution. Every impulse toward expansiveness had its detractors, its obstacles; every chance to open up to the foreign and the different could be thwarted. In Antwerp in the sixteenth century it was possible to be murdered on the floor of the stock exchange. In London during the Restoration the state saw to it that Quakers were barred from operating businesses at the Royal Exchange. In Lyon right up to the French Revolution a statue of the Virgin Mary sat at the center of the exchange, a warning to Protestant merchants that they were less welcome than their Catholic counterparts. Every episode reveals that we cannot understand the emergence of the cosmopolitan ideal in our modern consciousness without first seeing a set of early modern social experiences that had been contested, fragile, easily put in retreat, but—and this too is important—the cosmopolitan possessed revolutionary implications for who governed in the very states or colonies wherein the behavior slowly, fitfully took shape. Just as present-day theorists have imagined, the cosmopolitan did in fact augur a new radicalism. So too, as we know in our time, it would then also be a tentative impulse.[14]

Urging that we take new approaches to European history—ones that require thinking across national boundaries and confessional fault lines—seems a valid response to the expansive changes that have occurred within Europe and the West in general over the past half-century. The unprecedented crumbling of the economic borders within Europe, the new globalism seen in the people and mores of Western cities, these, alone, should force us to rethink aspects of European history. Yet despite such developments over the period of the last sixty some years—from when the European Union was first formed, right up to today—we have remained enthralled by the history of the formation of the nation-states. They still organize the curriculum of nearly every history department in the country. To be sure, a few other topics have fought for attention. We now also write about gender relations, or class tensions, or racism, slavery, and xenophobia—all valid, all worthy, even urgent topics. But we have also lost the narrative of other past practices that might inform current tensions and debates.

Of course, the cosmopolitanism of the Enlightenment owed debts to the classical world. It is indeed the case that Zeno, the stoic and social outcast, and Diogenes, the cynic, writing in ancient Athens, provided a rationale for a community above the state, for rational people becoming "citizens of the world."[15] Even earlier, Homer may have seen that a rough similarity between nobles and commoners implied the possibility of universalist ideals, among them human equality.[16] As we shall see, by late in the eighteenth century, the notion of human equality came to imply the necessity for cosmopolitan border crossing.

But a great deal of human and Western history had unfolded between Zeno and the Enlightenment, between Diogenes and Kant. Indeed not much attention went to the ancient ideas about cosmopolites until they were revived in the eighteenth century. In ancient Greek society where slavery at home was commonplace, as was a haughty notion of Athenian superiority, such globally civic thinkers were probably more outliers than fashion setters. They did not live in significantly large urban settings where international commerce was commonplace. Perhaps in the early modern period such theorists were also outliers—as they sometimes seem to be today. But that does not mean that the behavior they sought to valorize is without a history.

To fill the temporal vacuum stretching from the ancient writers to the late eighteenth-century moments of high idealism about the cosmopolitan we need to take another look at early modernity, looking through different lenses, asking different questions from those posed by the traditional history of ideas, or by the national histories. We need a history of cultural practices, of de facto mores, not simply high ideals. We need to dwell upon *praxis* or *experientia*, not upon theory, *episteme*, or *scientia*, to use terms familiar to that age.[17] With the aid of historical evidence, much of it archivally based, a new argument emerges about the antecedents of the modern notion of the cosmopolitan: long before Kant wrote, some early modern Europeans were having new experiences we may legitimately describe as cosmopolitan. They may not have reflected upon those experiences with the depth of insight we associate with the great theorists, but that makes their practices, or habits of being social, no less real or interesting. Historical evidence suggests that in the eighteenth century the cosmopolitan became a viable ideal because, even amid wars and national rivalries, select places existed where another, more benign experience became occasionally possible. Small enclaves flourished where social, religious, and national boundaries were routinely crossed and seeds of an expansive social experience took root. The cosmopolitan ideal proclaimed by Enlightenment writers matured partly because of the fecundity of those experiences.[18]

Finally, laying emphasis upon the emergence of cosmopolitan mores may give new insight into why the democratic revolutions of the eighteenth century offered such potent messages, then and now. Put another way, because we have lost sight of cosmopolitan practices experienced by a wide range of people in the past we lack convincing explanations for why later in the eighteenth century reform and revolution became infectious, first gripping the American colonies in the 1770s, then in the late 1780s causing upheavals in the Atlantic world, in nations as different in political structure as the Dutch Republic, the Austrian Netherlands, and France. Why did so many people, speaking disparate languages, in such differing political conditions, come to the conclusion that urgent change was necessary? A preexisting set of assumptions, vocabularies, and experiences, identifiably cosmopolitan and present for a century or more, made the international republican conversation happen more easily. For the words "all men are created equal" to have any substantial meaning, people, then and now, have to experience the foreign or the unfamiliar, be struck by how radically different other people can be, and yet decide that some universal statements are still applicable. If humankind is to respond to issues of tyranny, or ethnic and religious hatred, then history suggests that something like a "cosmopolitan consciousness," that is, "the repeated local understanding of one's connectedness to the whole" is required.[19] In the chapters ahead we find examples of how, out of lived experience, such a consciousness may have taken shape within early modernity in the West. Something, some compelling interest, often of a commercial or nascently scientific or intellectual nature, called for border crossing, for mingling in coteries outside of congregation, kith and kin, ultimately across national borders.[20] Fitfully, the mingling led to thinking, and articulating, the cosmopolitan ideal, now seen as a mainstay of liberal and tolerant social experience, a goal for peoples everywhere.

Chapter 1
Censors, Inquisitors, and Cosmopolites

Cities are, and were, the natural habitat of the cosmopolitan. In the course of the eighteenth century urban size grew. By 1750 Dublin and Amsterdam were at about 200,000 people, London well over 500,000, Berlin and The Hague had about 35,000 souls, while Avignon in the south of France barely housed 25,000. While all these other cities were presided over by lay magistrates, Avignon was ruled by Catholic clergymen. It existed as papal territory by virtue of a historical accident. Although in no sense a nation, this ecclesiastical state nonetheless policed mores and focused in particular on religious boundaries that it wished to enforce. Some Avignonese did in turn transgress, but in ways that might have gone unnoticed by state authority elsewhere, say in Paris. Thus, while we have the papal inquisitors of Avignon to thank for this unexpected glimpse at cosmopolitan behavior in the city, we do not want to imagine these watchdogs as utterly unique. Everywhere in early modern Europe the guardians of authority sought in some manner to shape mores and behavior, and none of that pressure was intended to further the goal of making people more cosmopolitan.

Amid the cloak of anonymity and the mingling permitted by urban trade, men and some women in all these cities found themselves in situations with unprecedented possibilities for talking, card playing, drinking, clubbing, or just mixing with relative strangers. In different cities we can see the socializing, the convivial and respectful mixing of people with vastly different backgrounds, often accompanied—and this became increasingly important—by some kind of structure or set of known rules and specific intellectual interests. To catch the nuances and varieties of cosmopolitan behavior, and what made it so threatening to the authorities in some places and not others, we need cases to study where it was highly suspect, spied upon, and when possible persecuted.

We especially want to observe cosmopolitan behavior in a place like Avignon, where national identity figured little, if at all, in the strictures of those who disapproved. The activities of the Roman Catholic Inquisition in

Avignon as it suppressed the cosmopolitan will concern us in some detail shortly. They are important precisely because they occurred in French territory (ungoverned by the French king), and not in Spain or Italy where the Inquisition is generally assumed to have worked effectively to stifle dissent or to inhibit many forms of secular fraternizing throughout much of the eighteenth century. As a consequence, Spanish social life outside the home centered on pious associations or confraternities fostered by the baroque Catholicism so popular there.[1] But Catholic Europe could also be a study in contrasts.

Avignon was different from both Spain and France. On the northwest side of Avignon the Rhone river—about the width of a New York City block— separated it and its province from all of France. The differences between what got persecuted in papal Avignon—as opposed to France—have much to tell us about the relative freedoms that could emerge, or be stifled, in any early modern European setting.[2] But lest we think of Avignon as the only hotbed of repression, the security interests of a variety of churches and states, regardless of the structure of their authority systems, first need to be addressed briefly. All could work to inhibit cosmopolitan border crossing.

In every Western country or colony the secular authorities had views and laws about what could be said and, most important, put into print. In absolutist countries, where central monarchical authority worked often in tandem with the Church, generally control operated more efficiently than it did in republics or constitutional monarchies. But throughout both Protestant and Catholic Europe censorship of books, theaters and newspapers was the norm, not the exception, until well into the nineteenth century, and beyond. One historian has described books in France during the reign of Louis XV (he died in 1774) as "controlled with a severity and minutiae rarely equaled."[3] A survey of a few of the various forms of repression to be found in early modern Europe suggests the way the world might have been if all the protectors of faith, morality, and established customs had gotten their way. Giving some sense of the range of what—and who—bothered them might make the tension between censors and cosmopolites in Avignon easier to grasp.

When social contacts seemed overtly political and dangerous, even conspiratorial, secular authorities sprang into action. The French crown watched for aristocratic cabals; it, and oftentimes the local courts or *parlements*, also took a dim view of an austere and indigenous religious movement known as Jansenism and its explicit critique of the luxury of the French church and court. In addition, all activity by foreigners was worth knowing about, as was any deviance from expected sexual mores. From the seventeenth century until well into the 1740s, spies followed foreign ambassadors, observed Jewish merchants, investigated homosexual behavior, raided Jansenist bookshops, and generally watched for morsels of information that the authorities might reward. Although relaxed somewhat after 1750, the French system of spying was so elaborate and thorough that people were watched for hours, days, and months. Some reports included juicy details about sexual indiscretions, or letters opened, and spies from other countries being spied upon.[4] No other spy system in northern and western Europe could quite compare with the thoroughness of the French.

Of course every European state worked actively to suppress presumed threats to its power, especially if they entailed contact with a foreign power. In Britain, after the Revolution of 1688–89, the authorities watched for Jacobites, that is, supporters of the deposed king, James II. Exiled largely to France (where we will meet him in Chapter 2), he and the international activities of his followers, seen as treasonous, were closely monitored well into the 1740s. Even in the relatively open Dutch Republic the oligarchic regents who ran the towns and cities were ready to close down any assembly that seemed to favor the restoration of the stadholder and his court in The Hague. Imported in the 1730s by the British ambassador—who had close ties to the Frisian family waiting in the wings to claim the stadholderate—the Anglophile masonic lodge in The Hague ran afoul of the regents. For a time its assemblies were banished. Persecution of differences, or social mixing, when seen as encroaching upon political authority, was never the exclusive habit of absolutists.

In the Dutch Republic the decade of the 1730s produced a growing panic about economic and moral decline. In 1730–31 a homophobic panic gripped the towns and cities and well over two hundred men were arrested—some even executed—for what the age called "sodomy."[5] Less serious persecutions occurred in 1764 and 1776. For a time this mania had a chilling effect on all male sociability outside the home, army, or church. In the privacy of their lodges, freemasons lamented "the slander-sick public . . . the hypocrites, prejudiced writers . . . cursed Inquisition and booming preachers who announce persecution."[6] Indeed, the situation for any group suspected of homosexuality in the Dutch Republic was so extreme that foreign commentators discussed it with a mix of curiosity and shock.[7] Modern historians have seen the panic as part of a larger crisis that gripped the Republic as signs of its economic problems became increasingly visible. Evidence from London and Paris early in the eighteenth century suggests that, just as in the Dutch Republic, the fraternizing of homosexual men in cabarets and specially designated houses had become more commonplace. Most of the time those unlucky enough to be caught elsewhere got away with only fines or brief imprisonments. In all places, however, their activities were illegal and seen as signs of moral degeneration. But in the Republic the persecution was most intense, and for a time all male socializing became suspect, constituting a natural check on the possibility of cosmopolitan encounters.

Oftentimes magistrates who spied a threat in any country were backed by segments of the populace. When public lewdness was seen to be on the increase, even without the assistance of the state, the pious sprang into action. In the 1690s London, and many provincial towns, became home to a vast number of new religious societies for the reformation of manners, and their purpose revolved about the policing of one's own morality and that of one's neighbor. Overwhelmingly Anglican in membership, the societies did admit Presbyterians, particularly if they were clergy, and in that one respect they represented a move in the direction of social border crossing into the religiously cosmopolitan.[8] This outcropping of voluntary policing, or the felt need to suppress "vice," arose for a variety of reasons, and high on the list was the Anglican reaction to the loss of privileges once enjoyed by the Church of England and removed as a direct consequence of the Revolution of 1688–89. Prior to it, non-Anglicans were persecuted. After the Act of Toleration of 1689 it was no longer possible to stop Presbyterians or Baptists or Quakers from worshiping openly and eventually from establishing their own schools. These privileges were not legally accorded to Catholics or to those who did not believe in the Trinity. In practice, however, they too slipped through the door cracked open by the Act, although more so in Britain than in Ireland. By the 1730s anti-Trinitarianism infected some Protestant congregations. Modern Unitarianism, so vital to the reformist and cosmopolitan political life we will examine in a later chapter, traces its origins to those groups.

In Britain the pious took offense at others' new post-1689 freedoms and the heresies they seemed to promote. The proponents of godliness imagined themselves as engaged in a war: "there can be no Neuters in this War, betwixt the Prince of Light, and that of Darkness."[9] Interestingly, there was little support for a renewal of religious persecution *per se*, and the anger among the godly at the loss of control surfaced as a generalized moralizing, a belief that England was descending into license and lasciviousness. The Anglican pious, along with a few non-Anglican moralizing zealots, set themselves upon the task of rooting out public lewdness, swearing, adultery, in short to insure that "in the midst of a crooked and perverse generation" the faithful may "shine as lights in the world."[10] Interesting from our perspective, as we search

for the emergence of structures supportive of civil society, the reforming societies often possessed constitutions. In deepest Yorkshire, societies with rules
like "Constitutions of the Society for Suppressing of Vice within the Corporation of Kendal" sprang up to rescue the reprobate.[11]

The volunteer societies bent upon reforming manners imposed rules
to regulate and discipline the lives of their neighbors, and themselves. Good
Christians were urged to report and help prosecute Sunday traders, blasphe-
mers, prostitutes, and drunkards. In the forty years the societies flourished
about 100,000 people were brought up on such charges.[12] The societies also
came dangerously close to involving the state courts in areas that had been
traditionally reserved for the clergy to condemn and cleanse. The devout from
the lower classes often saw the societies as a form of hypocrisy, and one
barber-theologian broke into print to argue that sin had been ordained for
a good cause.[13]

Members of the new societies were urged to pray and to attend church,
but most particularly to keep themselves away from persons dissolute and
disorderly. Keeping to one's self and one's coreligionists ensured godliness.
Members were admonished not to linger—even in the churchyard—but to
proceed promptly to the service, and whenever possible to turn conversation
in the direction of the edifying. Drinking in public provoked a particular
disdain. Volunteers were told that there was no point in aiming for greater
happiness in this world.[14] The purpose of restricting social contacts lay in
taking people away from the world while revealing its evils and discontents.
Mixing with strangers might mean being hospitable to sinners.

Protestant socializing for the purpose of policing the ungodly is not a
form of sociability that can be defined as cosmopolitan, however Godly and
goodly it may have been. The social vision being articulated looked inward,
to a narrowly defined set of behaviors, and when outward, to the other world
beyond the grave. Yet some elements of civility were present: the crossing of
religious boundaries between church and chapel and the habit of constitutional formality, of somber clubbing and gathering with a higher purpose.
By mid-century the societies for reformation had largely disappeared. When
societies intended to police behavior surfaced again in the turbulent 1790s,
they focused on political radicals. While they assumed a linkage between
radicalism and immorality, they focused their energies upon persecuting the
political, leaving the immoral largely to their own devices.[15] In either period
the historian in search of cosmopolitan practices must look largely outside
of religious assemblies, while always remembering that the pious might be
ready to frown in disapproval at what we find.

Early Cosmopolitan Sightings

The societies for the reformation of manners swam against the tide, and they became notoriously controversial. In addition, the pessimism at the root of the attempt to "reform" society stood in marked contrast to the obvious optimism that could be derived from developments in the learning of the day. The 1690s in England seemed like a time of unprecedented intellectual excitement. The laws revealed in Isaac Newton's *Principia*, published in 1687, became a subject fit for Anglican pulpit oratory. Newtonian science provoked attention in a wide cross section of English society, and scientific lecturing and experimentation fostered a new sociability. As we shall see in the next chapter, even a full generation earlier, students of nature could also be border crossers. By the second decade of the eighteenth century quite ordinary followers of the new science observed that only "to these our Times" had been reserved the honor of "great improvements,"[16] and crowds of observers paid to watch scientific lecturers.

Some of the earliest cosmopolitan fraternizing that we see in Protestant Europe, in both England and the Dutch Republic, began around science, and literary, philosophical societies sprouted in towns large and small. In a town as small as Spalding in Lincolnshire with its five hundred families, more than three hundred men in total began by 1710 onward to frequent the new and local philosophical society. "Lit-phils," as they have come to be known, inculcated useful science, letters and politeness to be sure, but they had little to say about private morality. In early eighteenth-century Britain, excessive zeal for religion had come to be far more controversial than enthusiasm for science.

Protestant Europe proved exceptionally receptive to Newton's science. Across the channel in The Hague, one of earliest groups that sought to disseminate his science set up a secret club, and into it came the young Dutchman Willem 's Gravesande. He emerged as the most prominent Newtonian scientist in the generation after Newton (who died in 1727).[17] The members of this little society were all Protestants, and they called one another "brother." They also published a journal in French that disseminated the new science far and wide. The minutes left by the brothers reveal them to have been jovial, even risqué, and an attendant society, calling itself the Knights of Jubilation, with some of the same members, left a meeting record of its drinking exploits. In it the handwriting deteriorates almost by the sentence. The Knights met as "brothers," under "constitutions" or "statutes of the order" and were chaired by a Grand Master. All were marks of an early freemasonry imported from England.[18]

The example of these two societies of The Hague perfectly illustrates what is meant here by the cosmopolitan. They included a postmaster in Brussels with literary interests, French Huguenot refugees, a German bookseller, the chaplain to an English aristocratic lady resident in The Hague, and, of course, the journalists who made up "the corps of the society of authors who compose the *Journal Littéraire*."[19] An engraver in their midst, another French refugee soon to become famous, Bernard Picart, adorned the opening pages of French translations of English novels and tracts; he also produced invitation cards in Hebrew.[20] He then led a team of writers and engravers who produced one of the first histories of all the world religions (see Figure 1). It sought to treat all religions judiciously, and it has rightly been seen as part of the early history of anthropology.[21] As Figure 2 suggests, his images about the Inquisition helped to seal its reputation for torture. Picart and his associates may also be described as citizens of the world and, more to the point, their interest in ideas, science and journalistic profit united them across national and language barriers. They met together because of shared interests and they privileged secular learning, widely conceived. French gave them a lingua franca.

The interests of Picart's friends branched out into publishing more generally and also to the circulation of clandestine literature, much of it hostile to all religion. In 1719 a few members of the group that made up the Knights of Jubilation in The Hague brought into print, in French, the most outrageous text of the early Enlightenment, *The Treatise on the Three Impostors*. The text owed a heavy debt to Spinoza, indeed it just lifted a piece of his writing and reprinted it. Adding to his text, the *Treatise* labeled Jesus, Moses, and Mohammed as the three great imposters. The materialism at its heart owed a great deal to an irreligious reading of the new science. The local authorities in The Hague rose up, confiscating every copy they could find. The publisher probably destroyed the rest, and to this day only one or two copies have surfaced.[22] The text sought to clear away the fog caused by the three major religions and advocated that people simply worship nature.

As we shall see in Chapter 2, however it was read, science had a unique role to play in the rise of cosmopolitan social experience, in part because controversies about experiments or results seldom bothered the religious or political authorities outside of Spain or Italy, where Copernican heliocentricity remained disreputable. But all authorities, Protestant or Catholic, got upset when scientific arguments were used to justify materialism or atheism. Science also required observation, hence groups of observers. Few of them were as outrageous as the so-called "knights" who clustered around Prosper

Figure 1. *Religions of the World*. Engraving. Teyler's Museum, Haarlem, The Netherlands.

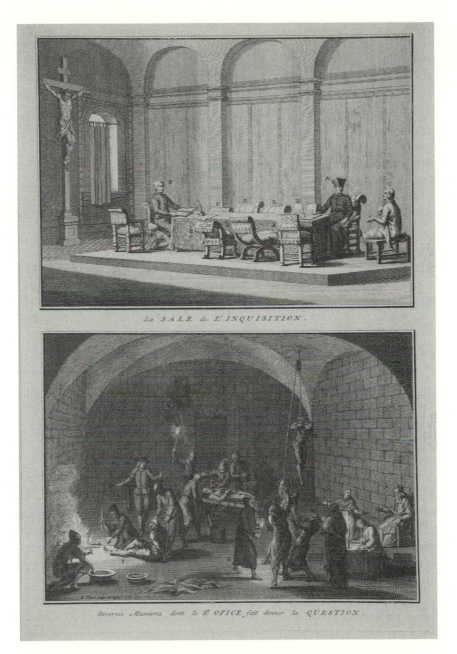

La SALE de L'INQUISITION.

Diverses Manieres dont le S.t OFICE fait donner la QUESTION.

Figure 2. *The Inquisition Room.* Engraving by Bernard Picart. Teyler's Museum, Haarlem, The Netherlands.

Marchand, their secretary. One of his closest friends, the freemason Jean Rousset de Missy, wrote a little tract advertising the contents of the *Treatise* on the imposters and in the process made both it and himself infamous. Not surprisingly, he also had a lifelong interest in science and freemasonry, and like so many members of this circle he hated French absolutism, admired English government, and worked on behalf of the Anglo-Austrian alliance. He also belonged to a lodge in Amsterdam that welcomed Jews.

In general, the deeply pious did not constitute the avant garde of the cosmopolitan—although few such border crossers were as indifferent to religion as Rousset and his friends. Where we can look into an individual life of the truly pious—as is the case with the Leeds wool merchant Joseph Ryder, who kindly left behind more than forty volumes about his interior spiritual life—we find social experience rooted entirely around home and chapel and a fear of people of a different religion because they might persecute or disdain.[23] Ryder flourished at mid-century in Yorkshire and was highly literate, even a writer of poetry. Yet his diary evinces not a scintilla of interest in the new science, or in secular learning in general. He seldom had a social experience outside of the company of his coreligionists. Across the Channel in France the same disinterest in crossing religious divides can be documented in Jansenist journals or in radically orthodox Calvinist circles in the Dutch Republic, where their leaders attacked freethinkers like Rousset and his friends.

In the 1690s a few English Protestants tried to reform manners and police the ungodly. Others took up science and joined literary and philosophical societies. In hindsight (which is always 20/20) we can say that by 1750 a polite and de facto cosmopolitanism would come to dominate the social life of Britain's educated and affluent upper classes. While the countryside required hospitality and generosity to visitors, the city expected polite visits from relative strangers, generally undertaken by coach with small gifts in tow.[24] Across the Channel by mid-century societies with the goal of being "useful"—rather like the lit-phils in Britain—had become commonplace in the Dutch Republic.[25]

We need a distinct contrast to the increasingly visible, polite, and cosmopolitan ambience of the urban eighteenth century. Such an alternative would help us establish what western Europe could have been like if, uniformly, governments hostile to social mixing among people of different religions had been in charge. Neither English Protestants, nor after 1689 their government, ever approached the thorough policing of social mores undertaken by the Catholic Church in areas where it firmly ruled. Of all the institutions dedicated to the maintenance of religious orthodoxy none had a more fearsome and well-earned reputation than the Holy Roman Inquisition. To this day in the popular imagination, say "the Inquisition" and the torture chamber springs to mind. In the English language during the eighteenth century common parlance had the Inquisition as a lawless institution where "prisoners are shut up in frightful dungeons, where they are kept several months, until they themselves turn their own accusers, and declare the cause of their imprisonment."[26] The viceroy of Sicily wrote to his old friend the French philosophe and Jean d'Alembert, after the Inquisition had been abandoned there, and described it as "a terrible monster."[27] When we search for the world the censors would have made, the Inquisition is as good a place as any to begin and end.

The Inquisition (Especially in Avignon)

In reality, the various inquisitions found in southern Europe were often more humane than the states wherein they resided and sometimes, when faced with people charged with magic or witchcraft, less gullible than their secular counterparts and the legal systems they employed.[28] The Inquisition in Venice rarely if ever executed those it deemed guilty. It handed them over to the state for service in the galleys, a life at sea so harsh as to constitute a virtual death sentence. Yet, as historians have noted, the various inquisitions could be obsessed with the Jews, and the reality remains that in Spain hundreds of them were burned alive or tortured by authority of the Inquisition in the course of the sixteenth and seventeenth centuries.[29] Also in Spain, it was well into the eighteenth century before the universities could openly teach that the sun stood at the center of our universe. In 1632 the Church had condemned Galileo to house arrest in Florence for endorsing the Copernican model of the sun and earth. By the mid-eighteenth century neither Spain nor Italy was in the forefront of scientific discovery or application, nor were they places we associate with the emergence of modern cosmopolitanism.

Although originally begun in thirteenth-century France to root out medieval heresies, the Inquisition enjoyed a long life in those areas or countries where the mid-sixteenth century Counter-Reformation against Protestantism had triumphed. The Spanish Inquisition exercised, and violated, the imagination of European *philosophes*, as we call the apostles of the Enlightenment, and they are largely responsible for our contemporary perceptions of the institution. The Inquisition of which they spoke may be imagined as a southern European affair, a backwardness filled with Spanish and Italian surnames. But as they well knew, the Inquisition also spoke French—while keeping its records in Latin—and operated in only one European site north of the Alps, in Avignon, papal territory until 1790, when the French revolutionaries seized it. One of the first acts of the revolutionary government was to close down the Inquisition. The Grand Inquisitor excommunicated these new and hostile authorities, then fled across the Rhone to the safety of Villeneuve-les-Avignon. When the revolutionaries entered the headquarters of the Inquisition they found no prisoners and only one instrument of torture, an iron pear probably used as a gag.

During the eighteenth century the Inquisition in Avignon operated at a greater pace than the rather sluggish performances of its courts in Spain, Venice, and Naples during the same period.[30] In Italy, aside from Rome, the secular authorities had a say in what their local inquisitions could investigate, but Avignon lay directly under papal authority and its Inquisition reported back only to the Sacred Congregation in Rome.[31] We want to examine how the Inquisition in French-speaking Europe worked, who were its targets, what role it played in the city and the vicinity, and by inference what social behavior in France might have been like had inquisitorial power extended nationally. The modern reader of the Inquisition's records is struck by its particular zeal to prosecute and physically punish behavior that, in retrospect, can best be described as cosmopolitan.

One purpose of examining the Avignon records lies in how they reveal an authoritarian—and specifically clerical—vision of the way traditional society should behave. Uniformly, and for well over the more than one hundred years of the surviving records—far from complete, thanks to the work of burning them undertaken by the French revolutionaries—the Inquisition sought to preserve the purity of religion and to enforce the social borders that maintained it. Yearly, the priestly authorities in communication with Rome fought a campaign to keep Christians and Jews segregated from one another, to spy on and curtail the activities of all whom they deemed to be "heretics," to confiscate books that had come from Protestant Geneva and were deemed "heretical," to enforce Catholic customs such as not eating meat on Fridays or during Lent, to maintain the chastity of unmarried women, and to ghettoize its Jewish population, who were expected to wear yellow caps or markers for easy identification. The anticosmopolites were busy folks.

In 1704 Father Lacrampe, the Inquisitor General, published a new set of laws. They required Jews (there were about 350 in Avignon) not to have openings in their houses that looked out onto Christian houses, gardens or streets, and prohibited Christian wet nurses from providing milk for Jewish infants.[32] The frequency with which these restrictions were renewed suggests what other sources confirm: they were frequently ignored by Christian and Jew alike. Unlike its counterpart in Spain or Italy, by mid-century the Avignon Inquisition also paid particular attention to local masonic lodges, and it undoubtedly had more of them than could be found south of the Alps or the Pyrenees.

In Avignon sociable gatherings that went late into the night with much drinking and eating were spied upon, and offenders—except noblemen— were hauled before the Inquisitors. During the first decade of the eighteenth century, times were hard in Avignon and in France more generally. Louis XIV's aggressive wars to the north, and after 1685 the revocation of the Edict of Nantes, brought renewed persecution of Protestants amid the reappearance of famine in the countryside. In addition Avignon's important textile industry was beginning to suffer from the competition of other centers like Lyon and the protectionist policies of the French king. In this atmosphere of economic decline, persecution, war, and rumor of war, some men decided to have a good time, to eat, drink, and be merry, and a bacchic society took root in French territory, in a town just outside Avignon.

The Inquisition sat up and took notice: "there is a wretched hamlet in the province of Occitan, and a new country house near the Rhone apart from this city of Avignon where certain bon vivants and hooligans have created a Bacchic Society, whose laws are particularly outrageous."[33] The report went on to assert that the society had invented rituals "for the ridicule and offense of our Most Holy Faith" and that it had become a debauched and dubious "new army." They had elected a *magnus Magister*, bailiffs, and commanders.[34] Occasionally this impious fraternity gathered within the walls of Avignon, and many members of the first families of the city and surrounding countryside, of both noble and nonnoble birth had joined, the report continued. Their membership entailed a certificate, and the Inquisitor told Rome that he was sending along a copy. The imbibers actually threaten "our rule and our own safety."

What should we do in these turbulent times? the inquisitor begged in his letter to Rome. Six years later the bacchic society was still going strong and its members, according to the Inquisition, included clergy as well as laity. It was still being watched with "all care and all caution while still avoiding publicity."[35] A publication purportedly by the society opened with news in 1703 and continued into the 1730s. It also said that the society had a grand master, brothers, statutes, and branches all over Western Europe. But by the 1730s the *Nouvelles de l'ordre de la boisson* could have been investing the drinking society with fashionable masonic overtones.[36] None of the claims about branches appear in the records of the Inquisition. Yet the mention of the clergy in Inquisition records about the society possibly sheds light on why the inquisitors took particular interest in a priest who was an eater of meat.

One Father Despech practiced his ministry in the local Church of St. Peter, and he presented himself before the Inquisition with a remarkable confession: he "had eaten roast meat in Lent and on other forbidden days for approximately two years, together with many other young men whose names he submitted. Likewise he had eaten wild partridges, rabbits large and small, and capons, sometimes in his own home, sometimes in gardens and in other secret locations."[37] At this distance we might think of this priest as overscrupulous or, out of cunning, confessing to a lesser sin to avoid the accusation of something greater. We might wonder why his story matters, what eating meat could possibly offer us as a glimpse of cosmopolitan behavior in a city where every effort was being made to prevent it.

The records tell us why we should be interested in this carnivorous priest. The inquisitor made clear that he listened very intently to this confession especially "given that many people have come to the papal city from regions near to the cities of the heretics, especially in these disastrous times of war against the impious heretics and fanatics in the province of Occitan." To the west of Avignon the province did not even speak French and may very well have been a haven for Protestants, among others.

Now the concern with the bacchic society and priest's meat eating begins to make more sense. Precisely in 1704, the king of France had reinforced his army in Languedoc and the Cévennes in an attempt to root out Protestants who had revolted in a messianic movement led by prophets known as the Camisards. As early as the 1690s they were prophesying the demise of the French king, and by 1702 they were in open revolt. After military defeat in 1704, the millenarian leaders fanned out into Protestant Europe in the hope of rallying converts to their cause and to bolster support for the war against France then raging in northern and western Europe. They preached on the streets of London, and among their scribes had been Fatio de Quillier, one of the closest friends of Isaac Newton. In the ensuing atmosphere, Europe began to look like it was returning to the fractious religious warfare of the sixteenth century.

Loose living with food and drink—especially in violation of the letter and spirit of the Lenten laws—could easily be associated in the clerical mind with crossing the border into the heresy of Protestantism. It would seem that the good fathers of the Inquisition were really now on a hunt for heretics.

This particular case of the meat-eating priest struck even closer to home since Father Despech's Church of St. Peter was one of the most important churches in Avignon, located right under the nose of the inquisitors. They wanted to find the accomplices of the meat eater. "I now hold seventeen accomplices and accessories to this crime whom I have judged to be unworthy of leniency, since they have confessed under threat. . . . I have thought it appropriate to investigate them vigorously, and have ordered the imprisonment of a certain lying innkeeper who is guilty of aggravated violation of the earlier edict [against meat eating during Lent]."[38] We do not know if any of the culprits were actually members of the bacchic society, but we do know that the Inquisition imprisoned them in the palace of the Holy Office and wished "to prepare no defense for them."

The meat eaters probably got out eventually, and the bacchic society managed to survive for at least five or six years. It may or may not be the same society, "the order of imbibing," that published *Nouvelles de l'ordre de la boisson*. It reported on discontents about wine taxes everywhere and even claimed that new chapters of the order were being founded in Paris, Amsterdam, and elsewhere.[39] Significantly for the story of cosmopolitanism in the West, we do at least know something about the founder of the bacchic order that so disturbed the inquisitors, one M. François Calvet de Montolivet from nearby Villeneuve. He studied the law, made a career in royal service as a tutor to the children of nobility, was a musketeer in the king's army in Flanders, and eventually became a local magistrate with judicial powers. In short, this was an educated man who had traveled abroad and in high circles, and the statutes of "l'ordre de la boisson" proclaimed that "in your August company you will only receive those people who always drink and eat well and who practice a joyous life."[40] Self-selected by their hedonism, the "brothers" rejoiced along with the "grand master" of the order and sought only the pleasure of the assembled. The terms of address should not allow us to assume that the order had a masonic character. Many orders and confraternities called their members "brothers," and by this date a grand or great master was not unusual. The Bacchic society seems to have had statutes, but no constitution, a word that existed at the time in French only to denote one's health or physique. Constitutions, the laws governing a society—the notion being an English import—were fundamental to masonic gatherings. In addition, nothing else about the society had masonic overtones. Indeed, dating from the first decade of the eighteenth century, it preceded the importation onto the Continent of masonic forms by at least a few years.[41] But in the eyes of the Inquisition the society of tipplers had other, more dangerous faults.

The inquisitors knew something about socializing and border crossing that we may have forgotten: putting relative strangers together to drink in groups, organized over time, meant that eventually they might get around to discussing politics. The only other record we have from the bacchic society is an anonymous and bitter poem dated 1709 about the miseries of Avignon. The people are up in arms, it said, there is no grain while famine stalks the land. They have been subdued by a "small army of the pope."[42] To the papal authorities watching all assemblage, it just made good political sense to keep this group clearly in sight. If the inquisitors knew the poem we have just cited, they would have been further alarmed. When people self-consciously pop their heads up out of the warren to which others have assigned them, they may think more critically about authority. Border crossers had to be watched.

The very next year the inquisitors were once again policing, on the look-out for people mixing with those whom they were supposed to avoid. Only now the offence occurred in August, and thus the issue could not have been a violation of the Lenten fast. Instead, on a Friday evening feast at which "certain noblemen, some of the most illustrious men of this city . . . and the Tribune of the Jews," as well as a priest, a lawyer, and actors and actresses from the opera, feasted and performed well into the night. Eating meat on Fridays was also forbidden, and once again when the rumor "of the activities that took place . . . was carried through the whole of Avignon" the father inquisitors took action. Witnesses were hauled before the court and "a true and sincere account of the fact—even if I have unanswered questions" was established that revealed "the nature and magnitude of the public scandal which the dissolute behavior described above, which was committed on a forbidden day, in a pontifical city, and close to Provence in France where there are many recent converts to the Faith." The only cause for pause, and the reason for the letter to Rome from which we are reading, concerned how to treat "persons of high standing in society . . . lest I should appear to deal with them either too harshly or more leniently than the gravity of the crime clearly requires." Other local noblemen were called into the proceedings to act as magistrates, but still advice from Rome was needed. No hesitation gripped the judges in the cases of the actors, "I had [them] . . . arrested, to prevent further trouble as they are dissolute wanderers and vagabonds whose faith and religion I find highly suspicious. If it were in my power, all of their race would be expelled from this city to which they flock year by year in these disastrous times."[43]

Many things were wrong about that Friday evening of social boundary crossings. Aside from excess in meat and drink, Christians and Jews from the highest reaches of their respective communities fraternized. Actors and actresses feasted, as well as performed. Everywhere in Europe they encountered prejudice and were judged to be lower forms of social life. The dim view taken of them by the Inquisition's prelates would have been widely shared, but not it would seem by the merry group being interrogated. A fairly raucous time had ensued and the Inquisitors even arrested the cook who had prepared the carnivorous meal. The account bristled with fears of heresy, as well as social and moral disorder. Even the military successes in the south where Protestants in the Cévennes were now converting offered little consolation. As heretics, they too were suspect. Rather than imagining priestly curmudgeons out to spoil the fun of the high living, we can find in the text left by the Inquisition the suggestion of a church that saw itself under siege, betrayed by everyone from the cook on up to the local nobility. Cosmopolitan socializing across class lines—possibly hand in hand with the heretical—had made its way to Avignon, and the fathers of the Inquisition were out to stop it.

As the century progressed theirs would be an uphill struggle. The fathers' constant fear centered on what would happen if "so great a scandal should become an incitement to others by going unpunished."[44] In the 1670s and '80s the Inquisition had good fortune in getting dozens to abjure their heresy. But by 1710 only between two and six people presented themselves for absolution, and there the figure stayed for the remainder of the century.[45] Clergymen plotted against other clergy whom they wished to have accused of the heresy of Jansenism, and they used local nuns to help entrap their victims.[46] Hardly harbingers of the cosmopolitan, Jansenists sought a highly purified and austere form of Catholicism and were critical about the power of the sacraments—and hence of the priest—to effect forgiveness and grace.

More interesting for our search for the cosmopolitan than the Jansenists, the Enlightenment had made its way to Avignon. In 1750 an Avignon priest confessed to writing verses that advocated "a pure deism."[47] Sometimes heresy could not be proven, as in the case of one François Bouyer, "accused before this Holy Office of uttering heretical words and blasphemous statements [who] was put to the torture for half an hour and more as measured by the hour-glass."[48] His torture probably consisted of leg braces into which wedges were hammered to increase pressure. They were very unpleasant, but neither unbearable nor life-threatening.[49] Bouyer had to be released because no confession could be obtained, but the very accusation of heresy could be a serious matter. Still others moved back and forth between Calvinism and Catholicism, as did Marguerite Laurence, who "began to fear that she had relapsed. She voluntarily appeared before me and humbly begged to be absolved."⁵⁰ The Inquisition had its supporters among the laity who sought out the ultimate forgiveness that it promised. Yet the carrot of forgiveness came attached to a stick. Reluctance to repent and come back into the Church fold could also lead to public and painful humiliation: "it was ruled that [Bouyer] should make an act of abjuration *de vehementi*, that he should stand before the doors of a church with a lighted candle in his hand and with his tongue squeezed in a wooden clamp [called in French a *bâillon*,] and lastly, that he should be exiled from the city."⁵¹ At this same moment torture was employed in Parisian jails when confessions were sought for everything from murder to poisoning and burglary.⁵² After the death of Louis XIV, heresy, or crossing back and forth between Catholic and Protestant, generally did not figure among the crimes the civil authorities in Paris pursued with any diligence.

With the power to torture and banish, the Inquisition watched for any move that might bring the faithful into contact with non-Catholics. In the summer of 1716 it was even prepared to risk an international incident when King George I of Britain stopped in the city along with an entourage that included many Anglican nobility. The chief representative of the pope, the lord vice-legate, wanted to know more about "the highest English nobility who adhere to the Anglican sect, and for whose benefit and instruction a certain preacher was to be on hand . . . perhaps for the purpose of indoctrinating them in the elements of their false creed in secret, in the palace of the King." Although the Inquisitor explained how difficult it would be "to infiltrate the palace of the King for surveillance," his job nevertheless required that "I shall use all due zeal to see to it that no rites of perverted religion are performed by any means, anywhere within the territory of this Ecclesiastical State."⁵³ George I might enjoy the weather and the wine, but he could expect no hospitality from the town's clerical authorities.

The story about King George and his entourage illustrates that notions of privacy and a concomitant religious toleration—in this case of a foreign prince—were simply not part of the repertory of Avignon's ecclesiastical state. The absence of such values suggests the necessity for their presence in settings where the cosmopolitan would flourish. Rather than seeing the arrival of a foreign, Protestant king as a chance to witness the exotic or the different, the authorities in Avignon saw the visit as dangerous, another instance when perverted religion and false creeds darkened the religious landscape. Although the Inquisitor's letter to Rome admitted that "after careful scrutiny and attention to their behavior and their way of life I gained no information that could possibly hint of scandal," nonetheless he saw to it that "the innkeepers [be] admonished lest any of them dare to serve meat to the heretics on fast days."[54] All behavior in public, and where possible, even in private and on the part of foreign visitors, had to reinforce Catholic beliefs. Such a conception restricted forms of social life to what best suited the goal of religious orthodoxy; processions and confraternities offered the best fit. Vigilance was required "lest any scandal should arise from their behavior and their habits of life which could work injury on our Catholic religion."[55]

We might be tempted to imagine Avignon as an insular place closed off from the larger world, even from France proper. The city of the popes was, in fact, one of the cities of Provence most frequently visited by eighteenth-century travelers who came for its beautiful landscapes and pleasant climate. From medieval times it had been a flourishing center of trade and had remained as open or commercial as any in southern France. And, of course, Rome kept its representatives throughout Europe informed about the dangerous heretics at work in other places, lest their identity, should they turn up, be missed. In 1720 an Avignon inquisitor wrote back, "I have received Your Excellency's letter dated last 16 May in which you deigned to inform me that there are certain heretics living in the territories of Bohemia, Saxony, Brandenburg and Frankfurt who are administering the sacrament of baptism not only illicitly but invalidly too."[56] The threat probably referred to the Anabaptists, one of many heretical Protestant sects to be watched with care.

No single group more vexed the Inquisition in Avignon than the Jews, and in that concern they mirrored the activities of the Inquisitors in Spain and Italy. The subjugation of the Jews by harsh social restrictions was intended to emphasize the supremacy and purity of the Catholic Church. In Avignon they were to keep careful records of their births, deaths, and marriages. The forced baptism of Jewish infants by Christians was expressly prohibited, but that was about the only favor the authorities fitfully conferred upon a minority they despised and sought to segregate socially and physically. Jews from the outskirts, especially from Carcassone but also Alsace, regularly traveled to the town and their business activities required that they bed down in hotels or hostels especially run for and by Jews. Right into the 1780s the Inquisition prohibited Jews from staying in the homes of Christians. Even staying in one of their own hostels without permission was a punishable offense and "in the year 1766 this 11th day of the month of September the Reverend Father Inquisitor commands [Martin], lieutenant of the *maréchausée*, to go and inspect the hostel called the Red Hat around ten o'clock in the evening, and to arrest all Jews whom he shall find lodging there without permission."[57]

Three Jews were found and imprisoned, and the owner of the hostel was forced to pay a fine. The lieutenant got paid for his trouble. In 1778 a Jewish husband and wife who leased a house adjacent to a church were told to vacate "and under pain of the penalties of Article 42 of the edict of Benedict XIV of blessed memory, by which they are bound." They are to go "and live in one of the ghettoes of this city or in this county, or to depart from this city and under pain of the penalties."[58] Anger could have been the only response had the good fathers known that in 1775 a Jew had been admitted to a local masonic lodge.[59] Yet Avignon did not have a monopoly on distrust for Jews. Also in the eighteenth century, by order to the *parlement* of Provence, they were ordered to leave Marseille within three days.

Note the name of the hotel mentioned above, possibly after the red hat that Jews in the town wore in preference to the yellow one mandated by the authorities. Again the Inquisition was fighting to maintain its authority as Jews preferred their own dress and liked to mingle and travel as need arose. They frequented billiard houses and other places of gentile amusement and faced fines if caught or imprisonment for repeated offenses.[60] In July 1789, undeterred by revolutionary events in Paris, the Inquisition demanded that young Christian women employed in the homes of Jews be dismissed immediately, and the records named them. Penalties were threatened, and these probably began and ended with fines. The inquisitors further demanded that the relevant edicts be once again posted in the synagogue. The campaign against employing Christians, even to light the Sabbath fire, had been going on since at least 1677, when the extant inquisitional records begin. But it was centuries old. In the 1670s, the first offense meant unspecified corporal punishment, the second brought with it a flogging, meted out to either Christians or Jews. In addition, Christians were not "to associate with Jews of the ghetto of Carpentras or of any other ghetto in this country or in this city of Avignon." Nor were they to sell to Jews or enter their synagogues.[61] Well into the 1770s and 1780s, the Inquisition was monitoring and prosecuting Jewish behavior, though by then the decrees from Rome had added the freemasons to the list of those to be restricted. When, in Chapter 4, we encounter a masonic lodge in Bordeaux composed largely of French and English merchants, agonizing about whether to admit Jews, perhaps we can better understand the background and depth of the prejudice that had been inculcated.

During the first decade of the eighteenth century the punishments doled out by the Inquisition against the Jews were finely calibrated and intended first to inflict financial pain and then, gradually, the social and the physical. Fines of up to 300 écus for frequenting Christian places led the list, and if they did not work, the next punishment entailed being "in the public square ... with bared head and holding a lighted candle ... begging pardon for his offense in associating with Christians—drinking with them and eating with them."[62] Prison offered a third possibility. Yet another weapon in the arsenal was the hated and humiliating, iron collar known in French as the *carcan*, a post dug into the ground to which a prisoner was attached by a chain with an iron collar around his neck. One Jewish defendant threatened with it had been accused "of compromising women's chastity by means of impious and heretical speech."[63] Staying outside the ghetto could also bring the threat of its use as well as the ubiquitous fines, in one instance to be paid to "Jewesses of this city [and neophytes] who are to embrace the faith of Christ."[64] Finally the local Jewish community filed a complaint to the Sacred Congregation in Rome saying that their livelihood depended upon being away from home and that "the Father Inquisitor of Avignon ... every day casts them into prison and condemns them to pay extremely heavy fines ... very often he also incarcerates the culprit's entire family."[65] Either the records contain an error in transcription, or it took Rome three years to answer the complaint.

Back and forth the complaints flew. The Avignon authorities said that the Jews were, inter alia, "a wicked race." Their behavior had changed in recent years, and they "no longer perpetrate in a hidden and clandestine manner ... in times past, this treacherous race did not attempt to violate apostolic constitutions and edicts without a certain measure of compunction ... now Avignon has thrown off its old bridle through a burgeoning licentiousness that has grown up over time ... one must complain of the public traffic of the Jews through all the cities, towns and forts."[66] Social borders as well as spatial ones were being crossed by the Jews, and the anticosmopolites were out to stop them.

In its own defense and sent to Rome, the Inquisition made a series of assertions that particularly interest us. It painted a vibrant portrait of rapid commercial change:

Because this wicked race (always intent upon ruining Christians and mocking and violating every law ...) had set up domiciles in virtually every part and village of the county ... they have rented houses and set up workshops, profiteering and committing fraud and rapine to the ruin of the Christians whose labor they employ ... as a result of too much interaction between Jews and Christians of either sex ... with the result that Christians could not find housing, and indeed, all the houses in the best locations were taken up by Jews ... with stunning and astonishing boldness ... they have every day wrought new stratagems and found new loopholes to evade the papal decrees.

Nothing seemed to work, and "the Jews fear only the second penalty, which consists of the iron collar—a corporal punishment which is the only measure by which they can be restrained."[67] Leaving aside the details of the bickering, the edicts from the seventeenth century cited and rehashed, and the obvious bias with which the Avignon authorities wrote to Rome about the Jews in their midst, we are seeing in the portrait being painted a mixing of peoples that is already occurring and against which the Inquisition is waging a rearguard action. "The Jews go freely about arranging marriages and dealing in mules and horses, in wine and oil, grain and meat . . . all of which are sold publicly in their shops . . . they make use of the services of Christian women who are not all poor and elderly but often very young and attractive . . . entering the Jews' ghetto, I found a very great number of houses which have views looking into the homes of Christians . . . I commanded that the windows should be closed."[68] The sexual fears only compounded the agonizing of the papal representations. Things were so bad that a Jewish butcher was selling meat to Christians even on fast days.[69] Such commerce worked "to the scandal of religion."

Clearly the relative breakdown in the Inquisition's hold on its Jewish subjects, amid the pressures of doing business, had sufficiently emboldened them to the point that they were prepared to turn to Rome for assistance. In 1703 the Jews petitioned the Sacred Congregation, with considerable assistance from their creditors who stood to lose if they could not be paid, that Jews be allowed to stay overnight outside of the ghetto. The inquisitors railed that "the mere report that the complaint about their situation had been heard" empowered the Jews. They then "invaded the entire county and began to lodge overnight in its towns and villages with the greatest boldness to stay outside their ghetto in spite of the edicts of the Inquisition." The inquisitors heaped invective on them, claiming that the Jews bankrupted Christians, went about the town in fine clothing, and then, in a particularly telling phrase, "go parading in their finery through the town squares like noblemen of famous families, in whose company they walk about organizing games, dances, choruses and drinking parties." In the final insult Jews then hired lawyers "to petition the Sacred Congregation to gain their desired result—namely, permission for overnight stays."[70]

The age-old hatred expressed in the language of the Inquisition had more dire consequences than simply trying to stop Jews from spending the night away from home. In 1698 a Christian girl baptized a ten-month-old Jewish infant. Subsequently, by order of the Sacred Congregation, the baby girl was removed from the home of her parents, cared for by "a Catholic wet nurse until the year 1702," and then put into the city's orphanage. We know about this legal abduction because in 1709 the Inquisition was trying to force her father in the ghetto of Carpentras to continue providing for her upkeep; "the said Jew Muscat is a very wealthy man."[71] Not only did he have his child taken from him, he was expected to pay for the care of the abducted girl. Note that, by contrast, in the 1650s in Amsterdam, minors who wished to convert to Christianity from Judaism against the will of their parents were prohibited from so doing. At least the Sacred Congregation in Rome finally relented on the matter of Jewish travel: no fees were to be charged for the license to stay in an inn for up to three nights, but they were never to stay in a private home.[72]

More than a decade later the inquisitors besieged Rome with complaints alleging that "once it was permitted to the Jews to stay in public hostels, they became so disobedient to the order that they have set up homes and habitations for themselves in virtually . . . every village . . . they have rented houses for their overnight stays and set workshops, earning their profits and committing acts of fraud and rapine to the ruin of the Christians, whose labor they employ in base, vile servitude, to the greatest dishonor and contempt of our faith."[73]

The Sacred Congregation in Rome directed its wrath not at the Jews but at the inquisitors, who in turn defensively explained that they had been following the law. They also changed the subject and claimed that every Jewish household in Carpentras (with its large Jewish population) used Christian servants at the Sabbath.[74] Fines, the iron collar, and flogging were to be imposed, in that order, for repeat offenders. We do not know how impressed or angered the Roman officials were by this show of authority but we do know that in 1719 the Avignon officials finally were forced to proclaim publicly, after the Jews complained to Rome, "that all shall refrain from illicit dispensation of the baptismal sacrament . . . against the will of their parents." Perhaps by 1719, and prodded by Rome, a glimmer of enlightened thinking made its way to Avignon, at least on the subject of forcibly baptizing Jewish children. Over the centuries the papacy had wavered and waffled on the subject, saying that it was a bad idea to forcibly baptize anyone, but then doing little to stop the practice.

After 1720 the records from Avignon grow relatively silent on forcible baptisms, iron collars, fines and the evils of Jewish visitations among Christians. In the 1730s a Jewish bookseller was convicted on charges of selling books on fortune telling.[75] In the 1750s the Inquisition still demanded that a doorway to the Jewish cemetery be locked: "the purity of our Faith cannot permit communication points of any kind to remain open between the houses of Christians and the houses of Jews; neither can it allow Christians to participate in Jews' funeral services or any other ceremonies of theirs."[76] Granted many records may have been lost, but from what we now know about its alternative in France, there seems little evidence to support the contention that the Enlightenment was fundamentally hostile to Jewish tradition.[77] Indeed one historian even laments the passing of the seventeenth century's "baroque tendency to stress the centrality of the Bible and ancient Israel."[78] Yet everything from the eighteenth-century records of the Inquisition suggests a grimly slow movement away from practices like forcible baptism. It seems doubtful that few, if any, of Avignon's Jews mourned the passing of the baroque seventeenth-century customs of their Christian inquisitors or found the previous century in any way more accepting.

The records suggest that throughout the eighteenth century contact between Christians and Jews quickened. Then or now, the master-servant relationship should not be taken to imply the cosmopolitan, but the Inquisition's records tell us that considerable and civil contact occurred between Christians and Jews in private homes and public settings. The parties and games point toward an easy fraternizing. Commerce must be counted as one of the most important forces that promoted cosmopolitanism. It forced business associates to mingle, even to develop friendships—much to the horror of churches or religious societies bent upon maintaining an orthodoxy that ultimately would have made rapid commercial development untenable.

One traditional index for measuring the spread of cosmopolitanism comes from the number and nature of masonic lodges to be found in any town or city. Freemasonry arose in Britain where lodges were commonplace by the 1720s. Their spread onto the European Continent can be spotted as early as 1710 in the Dutch Republic, but by the 1730s the authorities in Catholic Europe were deeply suspicious about what membership in a lodge meant. They spied an alternative religion, and they also objected to the British custom of frequent elections. Lodges regularly elected all their officers. Since the seventeenth century, the Church had wedded itself to royal absolutism, and the English had revolted from that model in 1640, and again decisively in 1688–89. Elections implied government by contract among the people, and not by divine right. In addition, in every lodge different professions, social stations, and often religions, met supposedly, as the masonic *Constitutions* (1723) insisted, "upon the level."

After the 1750s the lodges in France tripled in number and numerous French historians from Daniel Mornet in the 1930s to Ran Halevi in the 1980s have used masonic growth to measure everything from the growth of democratic social forms to the spread of Enlightenment ideals of tolerance and cosmopolitanism.[79] The good inquisitors of Avignon would not have been impressed by their logic, or perhaps better put, they would have feared as true precisely what the historians have seen. If one were Catholic, masonic membership after 1738, when the papacy condemned the fraternity and excommunicated anyone who belonged to a lodge, carried quite a load of symbolic freight. Some men, not least clergymen, ignored the papal ban and joined lodges at will. By the 1730s lodges could be found in all major French cities, with Bordeaux as we shall see in Chapter 4, one of the earliest to support a lodge.

The Inquisition in Avignon never left the freemasons unobserved, or unpersecuted, right up to 1789. Professional men—and possibly women—were rather like their counterparts in the rest of France, and they formed lodges under the nose of the Inquisition and in defiance of it. They—including two Benedictine priests—told their fraternal brothers elsewhere in France about being hauled in to see the inquisitors, and in disgust they gave their lodges titles like "virtue persecuted."[80] Throughout the inquisitorial records from the 1740s to the 1780s can be found "abjurations" by men who had been freemasons, but who then presented themselves "on bended knee," and who renounced freemasonry as teaching errors that contradict Church doctrine. Repentant freemasons were expected to turn in other lodge brothers.

Clearly the Inquisition took its task of rooting out freemasons from the town quite seriously. So seriously that in 1786 it raided the meeting site of a lodge and confiscated all its belongings. The provincial Grand Lodge in Aix sprang into action, and letters flew across the Mediterranean to Rome.[81] The French freemasons spied in the Inquisition's actions the same recent repression that had been undertaken against the lodges in Naples.[82] Only a direct appeal to the papal court in Rome was thought to be sufficient to redress the grievance, and eventually the lodge got back its possessions. Its orator lamented the fanaticism that surrounded them, and in Jean-Jacques Rousseau's language mourned how rarely men were ever free.[83] Within a year, the Avignon brothers were so confident about their survival that they wrote to their counterparts in London about their mutual love for the writings of the mystic Emanuel Swedenborg, about the members of their order being spread across the face of Europe, and about how "in acting thus we shall fulfil the orders which Heaven has given us relative to you, and as we have received the same orders with respect to several other societies, who like you walk in the Paths of Christ."[84] Freemasonry mixed with mystical Swedenborgianism was a heady compound indeed, enough to make strangers seem like brothers and to have any set of authorities sit up and take notice.

The timing in 1786 of the Avignon confiscation of a lodge's possessions suggests that there, too, the authorities were alarmed. They would also have been aware of the growing agitation for reform emanating from Paris and other northern French and foreign cities. Indeed in the next year open rebellion broke out in Brussels and Amsterdam. Had the Avignon inquisitors known in 1786 that their days were numbered, that they would be out of business and the pope out of one of his territories in 1790, they might have been even harsher, or possibly more cautious and circumspect in their actions. Either way, given the record of control and intolerance, the heresy hunting and the chain of infamy, it is doubtful that anything would have saved the Inquisition as an institution after the outbreak of revolution in Paris in 1789. Declarations of rights for men and citizens give Inquisitions little room to maneuver, and perhaps the best that can be imagined entails a peaceful end, and if historians have their way, a careful preservation of their records.

In one area of life where cosmopolitan values might have been learned, the Inquisition took up the same sort of policing as can be seen in the rest of France. Books were always suspect to the watchdogs of social mores. All through the eighteenth century the authorities in both Paris and Avignon kept on the trail of "forbidden books" or "heretical books," and again throughout France and in Avignon, pornography was high on the list of books confiscated, followed by works on Jansenism and those promoting anticlericalism. The Council of State of the King, the police, the bishops and archbishops, the procurer general, and the *parlements* all had a censorship role to play. The one exception to the pattern of book censorship in Catholic Europe offered by Avignon's Inquisition and by the French authorities, interestingly, concerned science. As late as the 1690s French almanacs routinely placed the earth in the center of the universe, yet there is no evidence from the surviving records in Avignon that its priests, or their French counterparts, confiscated any work in science or what the age called natural philosophy.[85] In Avignon all foreigners were suspect. The good fathers sought to keep Catholic society pure and segregated from persons not of the same orthodoxy. But the Inquisition left science alone.

Religion and Cosmopolitan Toleration

By dwelling upon the zealots of both Protestant and Catholic Europe, this chapter may have given the impression that during the eighteenth century no Christian religion could promote the cosmopolitan or the enlightened. Among the laity, and even some clergy of both camps, enlightened positions were occasionally articulated and used to promote notions of toleration in alliance with reforming regimes throughout western and central Europe.[86] Liberal Anglicans were among the earliest groups to take up and promote Newtonian science. Early in the century ecumenism can also be found between a few Lutheran leaders in Germany and Puritans in New England. Both saw a common cause in addressing the needs of the poor in Halle and the conversion of the indigenous peoples of the New World.[87] Of course, such missionary activities were not without their imperial underside and were hardly at the forefront of the cosmopolitan. In the Dutch Republic Mennonites played a prominent role in literary and philosophical societies far in excess of their numbers. It is also the case that the eighteenth century witnessed considerable vitality among orthodox communities all over Europe.

Strangely, some present-day American-based historians who trumpet the religious vitality of the eighteenth century feel compelled to endorse the tired and tone-deaf assaults against the Enlightenment and its cosmopolitanism issued by the German philosophers Max Horkheimer and Theodor Adorno in *Dialectic of Enlightenment* (German 1947, English 1972), a work largely ignored until the postmodernists of the 1980s rediscovered it.[88] Horkheimer and Adorno were Marxists, belonged to the Frankfurt School of philosophy, and were forced to flee Germany in 1933. Exiled hospitably in Los Angeles, they came to see the liberal-rational political order, which they thought the Enlightenment had created, as in fact a pseudo-irrational, mythical form of early totalitarianism. They asserted that rationality never existed in a pure state and imagined that the proponents of enlightened living had claimed purity for themselves and their movement. They even imagined that much of the evils of modernity owed their origin, not to the habits of absolutism and the various inquisitions, but to the cosmopolitan mores endorsed by enlightened thinking. Issued in translation in the early 1970s, Horkheimer and Adorno's book made a mark among American thinkers enamored by the new wave of French thought represented most notably by Michel Foucault and Jacques Derrida. They too saw the Enlightenment legacy as at best problematic, and at worst, a cunningly veiled form of repression. None of the postwar French or German attackers of the eighteenth-century movement toward light could be described as remotely interested in or supportive of religion and its present-day proponents. But hostility toward the Enlightenment and its values can make for strange alliances.

By contrast to the negativity found among the Enlightenment's detractors, whether secular or religious in their inspiration, this chapter has tried to show the crimped social world the censors would have made and to suggest that it would not have been to our liking. It would have born little resemblance to the cosmopolitan forms of social life to be found in many modern urban centers throughout the globe. Being, however nascently, cosmopolitan in the eighteenth century required a "live and let live" attitude toward border crossing, which a deep commitment to religious orthodoxy seemed to discourage. It also required a receptivity to new ideas, and by 1700 among the newest could be found in the writings of the natural philosophers. It is surely ironic that Horkheimer and Adorno, two twentieth-century philosophers in the Marxist tradition—which prided itself on being scientific—turned against the Enlightenment, where historically science was first cradled and expanded. Science will figure in the pages ahead, but not the kind of science that twentieth century philosophers might have imagined when they used the word. It is time to take a look at early modern science as actually practiced and to find sources for the cosmopolitan idealism that it could foster.

Chapter 2
Alchemy, Science, and a Universalist Language

We take for granted the relatively open and cosmopolitan nature of early modern science. From the time of Galileo onward, the appearance of the new science in Europe entailed the formation of clubs, societies, or academies attended by men who would otherwise be strangers. They seem to turn up whenever and wherever interest in natural philosophy surfaces. In Galileo's time the Lincei in Florence, later the Royal Society in London and the Académie des sciences in Paris, and then the Academy of Sciences in St. Petersburg provide dates when in each place interest in the new science took hold: in 1610 in Florence, in the 1660s in Paris and London, in 1725 in Russia. Some historians and economists have argued that aristocratic patronage accounts for the appearance of this open, "public science" in early modern Europe.[1] That interpretation ignores the practices of science and the natural philosophers who did it; it also does not take all the evidence into account.

In seventeenth-century England no significant aristocratic patronage underwrote the work of the early, subscription-based Royal Society. In the same period, when the new academy of science in Paris started up under royal patronage, its proceedings were secret. Only foreign competition, late in the century, forced the king's ministers to open them up. There are more compelling answers than patronage, however useful, to the question of why Western science became open and cosmopolitan. Finding them means going back to the moments when the relative openness started. The patrons sought access to ways of knowing the world that belonged to the practitioners, and they, not the patrons, gave scientific life a cosmopolitan outlook.

When in the 1720s Peter the Great self-consciously sought to copy the behavior he had observed in Paris and London, science was already largely public, open, and increasingly cosmopolitan. Treating him as our anthropologist, we can use his observations to help explain something we often take for granted. Why did the intensely social configuration of the small society composed of relative strangers, usually accompanied by some foreign members, become so integral to the growth of Western science? Peter saw such academies as "nothing if not a society (gathering) of persons who assist each other for the purpose of the carrying out of the sciences." Then tellingly, he said that experiments needed to be verified in the presence of all members because "in some experiments many times one demands a complete demonstration from another, as, for example, an anatomist of the mechanic, etc."[2] The one could not quite understand what the other was trying to say without seeing it demonstrated. The complexity of the natural world required specialization, and it, in turn, required social interaction among relative strangers to get a hold on what needed to be communicated. When we place emphasis on the local practices of science, as many scholars have in the past twenty years, we need to remember that the local often included international observers and contacts.[3]

Something else also happened in these social settings. In the early modern period habits were put in place that powerfully shaped the self-policing character of scientific inquiry. In effect, quite early in the formation of modern science, the doers of natural inquiry operated in groups that could conceivably include those who would become their most vigorous competitors. As the late sociologist of science Pierre Bourdieu puts it, such habits, once institutionalized, have come to mean that scientific work can be assessed through "cognitive and communicative . . . power relations" that are shared and that explain "how science can constantly progress" toward greater rationality.[4] The cosmopolitan effect had implications for the nature of civil society; just as important, it also helped to set the self-examining character of science as we know it.

There is yet another reason to examine science when seeking to understand the rise of modern forms of social interaction. Increasingly, people interested in the origins of democracy, or in the formation of social systems adept at resisting the authoritarian, focus on civil society. The term "civil society" is elusive and should best be understood as a metaphor for all the activities people undertake within social circles outside the home, generally informal but especially organized and sometimes formal. In civil society strangers with only a few common interests become acquaintances, sometimes friends. Civility and politeness make bonding possible. The cohesiveness, vitality, and integration of such groups, have come to be seen as barriers to the impulse for control coming from censors, state bureaucracies, and in the eighteenth century from kings and local clergymen. We now believe that science played a vital role in the formation of civil society all over the world.[5] Conversely the forms of civil society, the conventions of politeness, of gender expectations, of competitive group and peer dynamics also shaped science in ways that are still not fully understood and certainly not always conducive to equality of opportunity or excellence. Yet the legitimacy of the knowledge being generated depended upon its having a public presence, and that in turn opened a range of new possibilities.[6]

The very practices and languages of early modern science unwittingly played into the formation of a cosmopolitan experience, at least for men. The borders of natural inquiry, as distinct from other forms of learning, were fluid, disciplines were unformed, yet specialization can be seen in groups of no more than ten or twenty practitioners. The fluidity of borders, between mechanist and anatomist, between botanist and alchemist, required social interaction, and so too did experimental demonstration. Inadvertently and slowly, within coteries where interest in nature dominated, cosmopolitan social mores were invented and strengthened. National borders were crossed, so too social classes—within reason—because specialized knowledge was constantly being conveyed to those slightly less expert than the conveyor. There was nothing *inherently* cosmopolitan or open about the practitioners of science themselves—indeed national rivalries, competition, and social nastiness were commonplace in early modern scientific circles. But natural inquiry, more than any other single new cultural phenomenon of the era—more than reading, or coffeehousing, or clubbing—constantly threw male strangers, and as we shall see, a few female ones, into new and sustained social contact over problems that experiments with nature presented. Long before the modern laboratory became essential to scientific work, group experience, complete with differences bridged but rivalries also enhanced, had become commonplace. This was especially true when medical and alchemical topics came up for discussion. What could be more compelling than the challenge of trying to find medical cures, or the elixir of life, or speculating on the elusive practice of attempting to transmute base metals into gold? The alchemical quest required border crossing; alchemy offers one of the keys to understanding the emergence of the cosmopolitan.[7]

To be sure, many factors were at work in shaping a cosmopolitan ethos within early modern science. But if the social character of scientific work was to be valorized and expanded upon, a specifically cosmopolitan ideology and a vocabulary about nature were needed. By the mid-seventeenth century there was no agreement as to what that vocabulary would be. Agreement emerged only gradually, generally by the 1690s. In the seventeenth century a variety of philosophical languages and practices competed. One was derived from Aristotle, another was alchemical and identified somewhat stereotypically with a sixteenth-century doctor, Paracelsus. And the newest arrival, and ultimate victor to emerge from the babble, was deemed "mechanical" and associated with Galileo, Descartes, and Boyle.

Each way of describing nature can be briefly defined. Followers of Aristotle, known generally as scholastics in recognition of the power over curriculum they enjoyed in the schools and universities, believed that the essence of matter lay in its "forms." An opaque term to us, it can best be understood when applied to human beings. The human soul, our form, gives meaning and life to the body. Form gives direction or purpose to bodies. By contrast, alchemy organized itself around the assumption that base metals could be turned into gold, but in daily practice alchemists largely addressed problems in metallurgy and pharmacology. The alchemical philosophy assumed a vital force, or spirit in nature, expressed in physical reality by three first principles, salt, sulfur, and mercury.[8] It also presumed the virtues of a quest for a universal medicine.[9] Finally the mechanical. A vision of nature first codified by Robert Boyle, it conceptualized matter as made of tiny particles, some said atoms or corpuscles, and their push and pull resulted in the motion of bodies. Bodies did not move because their "form" dictated falling to be in their nature. They moved because they were struck by other bodies. No contact, and there could be no motion. All the changes observed in nature could be understood by laws, or mechanical principles. Looking at the European intellectual landscape in 1650 no one could have said with any certainty which of these philosophies, and the practices they required, would become dominant. Note, however, that in Catholic Europe the authority of church and state solidly backed Aristotle as interpreted by his scholastic and clerical followers.[10]

All three philosophies of nature could be experimental, although the alchemical and the mechanical tended to flourish outside of the schools and universities where the scholastics taught, more by logic and rhetoric than by demonstration. For a time this babble of baroque tongues arguably inhibited the cosmopolitan, or at the very least made for confusion and contestation. Some philosophers such as Thomas Hobbes took refuge in mathematics precisely because it was less controversial, and hence less threatening to public order and the state. In the case of alchemy, where in its published form esoteric terms shielded its secrets from the vulgar, much diligence was required before its system could be mastered. Of course, it too had also always been controversial. The churches were hostile to anything that smacked of magic and the state authorities took a dim view of street-corner alchemy and astrology, among what the age called the "vulgar."[11] Yet alchemy possessed protean qualities and these enabled it to slip past social boundaries, and especially to travel internationally. We think of alchemy as secretive, magical, hence irrational. It could be all of those things while at the same time, paradoxically, being cosmopolitan. Devotees meant it when they took "Cosmopolitiae" as a pseudonym or made sure that *cosmopolite* appeared in their title. They saw themselves as wanting to publish in every European language because they aimed "at nothing, but the undeceiving of the world."[12] They claimed to want to search every country in the quest to find the philosopher's stone, the key to the elixir of life.[13] Their search to benefit all of mankind promised life itself, through an elixir that would "perfectly regenerate and promote . . . an endless life."[14]

Alchemy flourished at the courts of Europe and could be found in every country, among the Latinate and highly learned as well as among the semi-literate. Indeed, one of the most surprising conclusions presented by the study of the early modern languages of sciences concerns alchemy: it gave a specifically cosmopolitan and universalist set of values to the scientific enterprise. Of the three major ways of describing nature available in early modern Europe, only the alchemical provided an avowedly idealist message of renewal, rejuvenation, the crossing of borders and class barriers, in the search for the secrets of nature or the key to longevity. The diffusion and transmission of alchemy depended upon adepts who wrote, visited, and traded recipes across national borders, seemingly at will. It also relied on a vast storehouse of practices employed by pharmacists as well as artisans, people who made a living by using their hands. The practices gave them authority, and that made them, in their own right, "experts in the knowledge of nature."[15]

In contrast to the scholastic and the mechanical, alchemy offered the most universalist and idealist message emphasizing reform and salvation.[16] Janus-faced, it could do the bidding of highborn patrons and kings while at the same time promising wisdom only to the diligent and the pious. When under the influence of alchemy, the young student of nature and genteel Protestant visionary Robert Boyle built his "*invisible . . . philosophical college,*" as he called it, in order to "put narrow-mindedness out of countenance, by the practice of so extensive a charity, that it reaches unto every thing called man, and nothing less than an universal good-will can content it . . . [and] take the whole body of mankind for their care."[17] Boyle even believed that Europeans had new things to learn from the peoples of the world, however different, exotic, or in the term of the age, savage.[18]

A half century earlier in England, Boyle's cosmopolitanism could not have been so easily predicted. Around 1600 in London where a vast community of scientific practitioners lived and worked, the foreigners among them were invariably regarded as "strangers"—and competitors. The guilds for physicians and apothecaries tried mightily to exclude the strangers. One part in the story of the rise of the cosmopolitan among students of nature must include the gradual demise of guilds, a process clearly visible in most trades after 1650. Around 1600 family connections worked in the first instance to permit a circulation of knowledge about nature, and only gradually did London neighbors of different nationalities begin to talk together about nature. Protestantism offered one venue of commonality among English practitioners, French Huguenots, and Protestant refugees from Antwerp. There as we shall see in Chapter 3, by the 1580s the Spanish had succeeded in vastly decreasing the city's store of merchants and naturalists through outright religious persecution.[19] It did not help that the Spanish also flooded the area around the town in their zeal to conquer the rebellious Dutch. But persecution elsewhere did not guarantee a warm welcome in London. In late sixteenth-century England, even when Protestant and persecuted, foreigners were seen as strangers, odd and exotic, despite being very learned.

The gradual demise of the category of "stranger" in those London circles that focused on natural knowledge can be seen by the middle of the seventeenth century. Boyle's openness to the foreign and the international depended in part on his conviction that God's providence, as revealed in the political revolution he witnessed in the 1640s, called for universal reform and renewal before the final days of the world and the institution of a millenarian paradise. The study of the alchemical and the occult complemented a Protestantism that left "the universe saturated with supernatural forces and moral significance."[20] Alchemical adepts far less famous than Boyle, indeed often anonymous, urged their readers to "aim at the good of mankind, be as active as you can in the things which the integrity of your minds persuades you unto."[21]

By the 1640s, amid civil wars, foreign reformers flourished among Robert Boyle and the circle that would make up the emerging Royal Society. Boyle said that what should triumph were "the principles of our new philosophical college, that values no knowledge, but as it hath a tendency to use." The crossing of national boundaries in the service of usefulness, again in the words of Robert Boyle, entailed "a universal good-will."[22] As we shall see when we turn to the Académie des sciences in Paris such universalism would come fitfully and later there; it would be visible only by around 1700.

Part of the reason why the mid-seventeenth century in England saw an effervescence of science lies precisely with its foreign visitors. The Puritan revolution of the 1640s had inspired Protestant visionaries all over Europe.

The utopian ideals associated with the midcentury Protestant revolutionaries gave pride of place to natural inquiry, broadly conceived. Everything seemed possible: improved husbandry at home and in the colonies, especially Ireland, reformed education, the propagation of the gospel to "Jews, Turks, and Heathens," reformed medicine aided by alchemy. A general reformation—the analogue of the Protestant Reformation—seemed within grasp, and members of the Boyle circle saw themselves as its agents.[23]

Boyle shared his alchemical experiments with Samuel Hartlib, one of the foreign Protestants who sought to further the cause of revolution. In 1648 Hartlib proclaimed that "our happiness may be completed for our age in a full measure, and without interruption propagated afterward for many ages unto our posterity." Robert Boyle thought Hartlib possessed of a "Utopian intelligence."[24] Boyle told his sister that his "Chymical Practices" entertained his "moral speculations" and that he was at work on a treatise about the theological uses of natural philosophy.[25] By 1648 the victory of Parliament over the king had meant that in England the glory of God would be advanced by the reformation of the church and state. Hartlib saw that "God hath put into the hands of this Parliament sufficiently all the means and advantages that may enable them to discharge their duty."[26] The nation has been honored by victory, but not at the expense of the "communion of his saints also in all the reformed churches."[27] The mandate from God, Hartlib said, required the establishment of a universal kingdom, and simultaneously "this is a duty which should be mainly prosecuted by us . . . [we must] doe all this unto us above our neighbors."[28]

The late 1640s saw expectations of universal reform at a fever pitch. In 1647 Boyle believed humankind to be on the verge of finding a universal vocabulary, of "doing that in words, that we see already done in numbers." In the very next sentence Boyle turns to mechanical devises that may help discover "the weight of the air."[29] At precisely this time Boyle told his sister and Hartlib about the long hours spent at his alchemical furnace. The Protestant militancy of this circle, complete with the expectation of Christ's return to earth—augured by the many discoveries of a new philosophy—made universalism seem inevitable.[30] Others in Hartlib's vast array of international contacts thought that alchemy, in particular, would provide "a common ground from which all confessions could gain new insight into the principles of divine harmony."[31] New philosophies of nature were soon to be augmented by dramatic change in the polity. In 1649 the execution of the king, convicted on the charge of treason, made the establishment of a republic in England inevitable.

For Protestant seekers like Boyle and Hartlib the openness of the new republic exposed the limits and permissions set by their religiosity, its labile and contradictory qualities. On one hand the communion of all Protestants became the goal. An "office of communication," modeled on the cosmopolitan Royal Exchange and set in London, was imagined as "a center and meeting place of advices, of proposals, of treaties and of all manner of intellectual rarities." Boyle and friends would have "foreigners . . . made partakers of domestick, and such as are at home, of foreign strains; that all may in their several ability be set a work, and contribute unto the stock of learning, that which may be useful to everyone."[32] The English poet John Milton, also a part of this circle, was especially excited by the prospect of an exchange for ideas.

Cosmopolitan communication enjoyed a central place in the godly reformation, but access to it was qualified. Participants were assumed to be Protestant and pious. In 1651 as the new English republic took shape, Boyle

Figure 3. *An Alchemist in His Workshop.* Oil on canvas. Courtesy of the Bridgman Art Gallery.

feared that the Jews who were to be offered toleration as part of the mille-narian expectations of the Puritan state "may seduce many of those numer-ous Unprincipled (& consequently) Unstable Souls, who hav[e] never been solidly or settledly grounded in the Truth."[33] Just as the participation of Jews worried him, undoubtedly Boyle would have had deep reservations about even educated Catholics, whom he would have associated with royal abso-lutism. The biased treatment of Catholics in Ireland, where Boyle was born as the youngest son of the earl of Cork, should make clear the limitations that bound the Protestant version of the cosmopolitan.

Yet Boyle accepted that England needed to be some sort of relatively free republic and one capable of constant revolution.[34] In the same letter in which Boyle fretted about the damage Jews would do among the unstable, he gave voice to one of the first usages we have in the English language that points to the modern revolutionary impulse: "And as for our Intellectual Concerns; I do with some confidence expect a Revolution, whereby Divinity will be much a Loser, and Reall Philosophy flourish, perhaps beyond men's Hopes." The revolution would be intellectual and spiritual, ushered in by the new philosophical learning, both mechanical and alchemical. The genteel Boyle and his educated friends wanted spiritual and intellectual transformation, not social. The new philosophy to which they adhered had deep roots in artisanal practices, and its alchemical side also possessed dangerous undercurrents.

Dangers lurked precisely because the revolution lurched in both social and intellectual directions that Boyle and his followers feared. Real philoso-phy could be put to many uses. In the 1650s, during the heady days of the new republic, alchemy figured prominently in other circles, and suddenly a set of practices that promised rejuvenation turned ominous. In 1651 an anonymous "restorer of physics" laid out the stakes: having left the life of the courtier, the author said, "I began to feel those thoughts of natural phi-losophy . . . to give a fresh and sprightly spring to my soul . . . I fled to that Sanctuarie, the studie of the Occult, and almost unsearchable laws and cus-toms of nature in the Universe, the common country of all . . . to the general service of the world."[35] This student of the occult expressed the great and heretical danger that lurked in alchemy, the possibility of a return to pagan naturalism. "It was not an improbable assertion of some of the Philosophers, *That the soul of the World was in the Sun, and the Sun in the Centre of the whole.*"[36]

For such pantheistic views the heretical visionary Giordano Bruno had been burned at the stake in Rome in 1600. His search for a universal religion based upon hermeticism and sun worship had taken cosmopolitanism, allied with the new science, right into paganism and the heresy of naturalism. What need to worship God when the all-powerful sun could be a viable substitute? The anonymous "restorer of physics" had plenty like him. During the 1650s they championed the occult and found the lives of courtiers devoid of truth seeking. Even alchemists who proclaimed themselves to be pious spoke about the soul or spirit of nature.[37] Such language in the wrong hands moved dangerously close to a revival of paganism.

The Puritan revolution initiated the invisible college out of which would grow the nascent Royal Society. Modern science coalesced first in England during the turbulent 1650s. However progressive, Boyle and his circle nonetheless feared that the intellectual revolution they foresaw would also result in lower-class and sectarian heresy, in a return of pagan naturalism. Retreating to Oxford, away from the sectarian dangers found in London, they watched in dismay as radical reformers called for the introduction of alchemy and astrology into the curriculum of the university. They would serve to democratize its learning and bring it closer to that of ordinary people. Predictably the professors adamantly refused to alter their teachings.[38] The uses to which alchemy and astrology were put threatened their authority, and the landed elites as well as the highly educated, like Boyle (who was both), reacted vehemently. Those who wanted to restore monarchy (and succeeded in 1660) described books about "physick, Astrologie and the like" as being written by "indigent Vermine."[39] When the Royal Society was founded in 1662 under the leadership of Boyle and his circle, alchemy figured nowhere in its public proceedings.[40] When after 1660 the occasional alchemical work appeared in England, it was generally by a foreigner, dedicated to the king, or simply pious in matters religious.[41] Some writers continued to champion "chymical physick," and said that they searched for a universal medicine, "with the help of the Fire we understand the occult Hermetick and Helmontian Philosophy." But they never used the word, "alchemy."[42]

Many scholars have documented the political forces that worked to marginalize magic after 1660 and the restoration of monarchy. Seeing those forces comparatively, by looking at the role of alchemy in Paris at the same moment, as we will shortly, further complements their approach. In Paris, where no political revolution during the 1650s had threatened democratic or radical transformation, alchemy with its universalist and reforming message seemed unstoppable. In fact the survival of alchemy in official French scientific circles well after 1660 gives further weight to the argument that social and political fears forced it underground in England.

The leading force in the French Académie des sciences from roughly 1665 to 1675, Samuel Du Clos, had been both a Protestant and an alchemist. For Du Clos (who knew Robert Boyle)[43] the alchemical quest was another way toward the divine, another route when the traditional sacramental system of the old Catholic Church was no longer available.[44] The cosmopolitanism of reformist Protestant circles on both sides of the Channel led them to seek out other foreign Protestants for assistance in the quest for natural knowledge, albeit alchemical or mechanical. In the late 1680s Newton turned to the French alchemical writers for what he might have missed in his Latin and English reading.[45]

Indeed after 1660 private alchemical correspondence across the boundaries of the European states, and even beyond, was commonplace as the papers of Samuel Hartlib, among others, illustrate.[46] His contemporary, and for a time collaborator, Eirenaeus Philalethes, whom we now know to be George Starkey from the American colonies, signed himself as "citizen of the world" and gave his second title as "Cosmopolita."[47] In his alchemical writings he could claim ingeniously to be revealing "the whole secret"of nature and yet to be keeping it "artificially vailed."[48] On occasion alchemists, or those deeply influenced by the art, even ventured outside of Europe and displayed a willingness to take in non-Western notions of the body and remedies for its cure.

In the 1670s the Dutch physician Wilhelm ten Rhyne went to Japan at the invitation of the authorities there. Sharing his own medical knowledge across the abyss created by language and culture, he discovered the needle therapies derived from China. Ten Rhyne invented the term *acupuncture* to describe them, saw value in the technique for the treatment of arthritis and other ailments, and provided his Western readers with exact diagrams, complete with engraved pullouts of a Japanese man with the pressure points clearly marked.[49] The publication and dissemination of his work was significantly aided by one of those small social enclaves interested in nature. In his case it was the Royal Society of London.

Ten Rhyne's detailed description of the instruments and the techniques of acupuncture was the first of its kind. Although acupuncture would wait many centuries to become the legitimate practice it now is in the West, Ten Rhyne treated it with respect. Arguably his innovative approach owed a debt to the alchemy in his background. There was nothing in its philosophy of nature that would render Chinese notions of the body and illness unacceptable. By contrast, as Pierre Bayle noted at the time, mechanical understandings of the day applied strictly would reduce acupuncture—which required no direct contact with the injury by the needle—to the incoherent.[50] Ten Rhyne, like Du Clos, embraced aspects of the mechanical; he explained that the needle let "pneuma" escape from the blood. His book was endorsed by another Dutch doctor, the London resident Joannes Groenevelt, himself a renegade in conflict with the medical establishment in that city.[51] He became one of the most innovative physician-surgeons of the day, also with a penchant for secret remedies. Ten Rhyne dedicated his book to the directors of the Dutch East India Company who, along with his Japanese hosts, made his journey of discovery possible.

In the history of early modern science and the cosmopolitan, the nature of the social contacts throughout western Europe and beyond during the period from the 1630s to the 1670s was formative. One did not even have to be an alchemist to participate in the conversation. Correspondence across national borders organized by certain key figures like Father Marin Mersenne in Paris and Henry Oldenburg in London helped to make Descartes famous, put Hobbes in touch with Cartesian thought, and meant that, in general, students of nature from Sweden to Italy knew roughly what was happening and being discussed in the capitals. The growth of international commerce in goods and species had an intellectual corollary, and natural knowledge had become another commodity.

But commerce did not render local scientific culture in one place homogeneous with that in another. The forms that early scientific organization took, for example, in Paris versus London, were markedly different and only cosmopolitan by varying degrees. The case of Paris is instructive and reintroduces a theme to which this book will return many times. The institutions of monarchical absolutism—versus the looser social forms associated with cities and ultimately republics—worked fitfully, and then only under royal direction to institute and sustain foreign contacts. They would become cosmopolitan, not through royal decree or patronage, but largely through royal indifference.

Paris

In the 1660s in Paris the alchemical light that shone was filtered by the demands of royal secrecy. The French Académie des sciences came to exist in 1666 because Jean-Baptiste Colbert, the great architect of mercantilism, had convinced Louis XIV that he needed to have a group of natural investigators who would foster the interests of the crown.[52] Central to those interests were the maintenance and increase of the king's wealth as well as the protection of indigenous commerce and manufacturing. Foreign expertise required courting so as to be imported and made indigenous. The mercantile system assumed a fixity of wealth and a multitude of states in competition for it. Knowledge was part of the riches to be accumulated.

The earliest records of the new academy in Paris show alchemy, as well as the practice of secrecy, pressed into the service of the state. Meetings occurred in private twice a week, one day to consider mathematics, the other "physics." But in the 1660s "physics" meant alchemy, as well as medicine. The guiding spirits in matters experimental in those early years were two older naturalists, Gilles Personne de Roberval and Samuel Cottereau Du Clos.[53] They were among the four founding members in the division called "philosophy." By 1668 a mere twenty-two investigators assembled in the King's Library, and two of them, the famous Huygens and Cassini (currently the names given to a mission to Saturn), were foreign but essentially expatriated in France.

In texts to this day unpublished Du Clos laid out the terms and language guiding research. True to the experimental tradition within alchemy, he wanted the company to find by means of "l'analyse chymique" the underlying substances that compose all natural mixes, or combinations, found in the world. "Three of these substances are as we would say essential, l'esprit,

L' ACADEMIE DES SCIENCES.

Figure 4. *The Academy of Sciences.* Engraving by Bernard Picart. Teyler's Museum, Haarlem, The Netherlands. Picart did this rather fanciful depiction of the Paris academy making it appear to be open to all the world, which it was not. Other accounts do mention that the academicians seemed to talk at random rather as they appear in this engraving.

the oil and the salt because they participate in the essential virtues of the *Mixte* ... that is mercury, sulphur, and salt (which has no other name)." The three essential principles are proclaimed by *les philosophes hermétiques*, and together, but in ways that Du Clos explained as still mysterious, the three substances compose the philosopher's stone, the epitome of nature and the master of its arts.[54] "Rightfully these three famous materials can be given the denomination of the *principes hermétiques*." Note that the fundamentals of nature in the Paris academy were not the four elements of Aristotle, nor his forms—as was being taught down the road by the scholastics at the Sorbonne—but the three principles of Paracelsus. So guided, the academy spent months in alchemical distillations of everything from foxglove (a source for digitalis) to cucumbers.[55]

The orations of Du Clos to the newly assembled company also explicated Boyle's chemistry and physiology.[56] In those discussions he put alchemy and medicine, as well as the study of minerals, salts, waters, and the wines of France, at the heart of the intellectual life of the absolutist state. The proceedings of the first thirty or so years of the academy were deemed secret, not because alchemy with its penchant for secrecy reigned supreme in this period, but because as part of the apparatus of the mercantilist state, science belonged to *les secrets du roi*. But conveniently, the appearance of secrecy also lay at the heart of seventeenth-century alchemical practice. In some cases its adepts—particularly after 1660 in England—practiced the alchemical arts so secretly, or used code words so carefully, that only in the last twenty years have we discovered alchemy's importance for English scientists like Boyle and Newton, who would never have discussed it as openly at the Royal Society as did Du Clos across the Channel in Paris.[57]

As did so many alchemists, Du Clos told the academy—just as Boyle would have, had he been there—that his alchemy must be distinguished from that of "les Chimistes vulgaires." Vulgar chemists have appropriated its terms, he said, and insist that mercury, salt, and sulfur are the same as the elements of the Aristotelians. They do not see that they are the result of the primary union of the spirit of fire, that is, elementary particles (or bodies) that are spiritual and active principles.[58] Du Clos, like Boyle and so many of the new natural philosophers, did not want to be mistaken for a mere artisan—despite the similarity of their respective practices.[59] Du Clos also wanted to tarnish the vulgar with the scholastic brush, implying their backwardness. Where Boyle parted company with Du Clos was in their definitions of who should be counted among the vulgar and the backward. While Du Clos adored Paracelsus, Boyle blamed the Paracelsians for their secrecy and obscurity.[60]

In the 1650s in England the followers of Paracelsus had been seen to be allied with the most radical reformers. By contrast, in a French setting, Du Clos openly used the great Paracelsus because, as he said, "the work of penetrating and radically reducing all the mixed bodies is mysterious and secret. Various modern philosophers, following after a great number of very old Hermeticists, have recognized these three kinds of primitive substances exist in *ce genre de Mixtes naturels*."[61] Simultaneously, Du Clos did not hesitate to embrace one of the most important concepts of the new mechanical philosophy, the new doctrine of atomism, or corpuscularianism, which he knew to be novel and in contradiction to the teachings of the scholastics.[62] Boyle contributed to the introduction of atomism in the Paris academy, but true to its experimental and alchemical commitments, Du Clos noted that in his essays Boyle had not found it so easy to establish atomism "par les Experiences Chymiques."[63] The practicing alchemist and the mechanist had far more in common with each other than they did with the scholastics. The English alchemist and their contemporary Thomas Vaughan said that the scholastics engaged in "vain babbling."[64]

In his published work of 1680 Du Clos based his philosophical vision on reliable knowledge drawn from the senses and explained that "I have vainly occupied myself in reducing the mixes of various simple matters . . . to their first principles."[65] In a French book that he had to publish through the freer presses of Amsterdam, Du Clos laid out his commitment to Copernicanism and explained in detail his preoccupation with alchemical distillation. He argued in a naturalist vein "that Nature . . . is the Creator of substances, the first cause and principal, the internal principal, the ministerial director of movement." As in his presentations before the academy a decade earlier, Du Clos identified God as "the first of causes . . . the sole divine power" who made all the things of the world. At the same time, Du Clos designated nature as the soul. The spiritual fire offered nature the possibility of a complete perfection, and it was the source of all the transmutations aimed at perfecting metals. The schools, and therefore the schoolmen or scholastics, did not realize that the corporeal and incorporeal can be joined by this same spirit of fire (*l'esprit ignée*).[66] Du Clos's naturalist vision—in England by the 1650s it had come to be suspect for heresy—received integration with a mechanical understanding of motion in animals directly indebted to Descartes. Perhaps we can now better see how a far more powerful philosophical and mechanical mind, that of Isaac Newton, could embrace alchemy and find in it justification for his belief that gravity operated as a spiritual principal throughout nature.[67]

The English translation of Du Clos's 1680 French work completely removed his naturalism and his alchemy. Students could peruse his work on the waters of France and their distillations without seeing that beneath the text lay a commitment to alchemy.[68] Note, too, that one of the complexities of the alchemical tradition lay in its ability to hint at its first principles while laying out experimental protocols that did not necessarily invoke mercury, sulfur, and salt as the hermetic foundation from which springs all chemical knowledge. Du Clos's practices could be separated from his alchemical theory, as the English text shows, now that it has been compared with the original French. The English text also illustrates the empirical side of Du Clos. As he said in one of his talks before the Paris academy, "it is important to have many observations and experiments . . . natural things can be discovered by 'les sciences physiques.'"[69]

One of the problems with alchemical speech lay in its multiple layers, its use of straightforward description overlaid with allusion and allegory to signal—to those in the know—the tradition out of which a writer was speaking. Ultimately the complexity of its rhetoric and its reliance on myths and fables made alchemy incompatible with completely free and open exchange, with the first principles upon which cosmopolitanism ultimately flourishes. As long as the ethos of the alchemical tradition dominated the proceedings of the academy—and Du Clos was its key figure for about the first nine years of its existence—little energy would be directed toward opening the proceedings. This is not to say that foreign work was ignored. In the session in which Du Clos applied the basic principles of alchemy to making better explosives, he noted that Boyle's vacuum, artificially created by his air pump, shows that air is basic to combustion.[70] In the lifetime of Isaac Newton (born in 1642), the alchemists experimented—as Newton and Boyle perfectly illustrate—and they could talk to the mechanists, indeed embrace some of their central premises, like the atomic structure of matter or, in contradiction to the Aristotelians, the existence of the vacuum. Boyle's evacuated jar was said to have proved its existence.

When Newton became fascinated with French alchemy,[71] his guide into the French side of this pan-European practice was another pious Protestant from Geneva, Fatio de Duillier. He gained fame around 1704 when he transcribed the predictions of the French prophets. They roamed the streets of London announcing the demise of the Antichrist, namely Louis XIV. The aura of millenarianism hangs about the pursuits of so many of alchemy's radically Protestant followers like Newton. Time had to be measured, and it was running out. The work of finding the philosopher's stone and its applications was urgent and purifying, a preparation for Christ's Second Coming. We may not associate the alchemical with an opening of the world to strangers, but in their adherence to millenarian dreams so many seventeenth-century alchemists have to be counted in the story of the widening of Western culture, the opening of barriers to the strange, the foreign, and the exotic.

Before 1685 when he revoked the Edict of Nantes, Louis XIV had an accommodating, even inviting stance toward some Protestants. This king who sponsored the science of the day in his private library at first allowed foreign Protestants into the select company. His Paris company was not meant to be idle gentlemen, but rather to serve the interests of the state, and they were paid handsomely for their services.[72] The business of the state was to be their business. One of the observations that Du Clos made to the assembled concerned the role of sulfur in making a strong saltpeter. It was a highly combustible substance found in nature—often scrapped out of barns and cellars, and as he noted, "most abundant in earth imbued with the urine of beasts." Without an abundance of strong, well-dried saltpeter no state could make war because it was the substance that when lighted fired cannons. As a loyal servant of the state, Du Clos sought in his discussion of saltpeter to demonstrate the importance of one of his elementary principles, sulfur. Just as important, saltpeter was also a key to alchemical processes. In the same oration Du Clos referred to the effects that might be obtained by the application of fire and mercury to lead and iron, and hence to the holy grail at the end of the alchemical quest, the ability to turn base metals into gold. Rather than being so bold as to imagine the alchemist as having the answer to the mercantile quest (what better way to enhance the state's wealth than to forge it in a crucible?), Du Clos laid emphasis on the need for better saltpeter. Certainly Du Clos sought the transmutation of base metals into gold, and he discussed aspects of the Great Work, as it was called, at the academy.[73] He also devoted a lengthy treatise to the transmutation of metals that was never published. In the end, his heart probably lay with the medical possibilities of alchemical procedures. More so than Du Clos, the most famous Parisian academician—of Dutch origin and a mechanist—Christiaan Huygens contributed to the interests of the state and eagerly discussed cannon and their uses.[74]

Mechanics, and not medicine as such, proved more alluring to the absolutist state. In 1685, just after the death of Du Clos, a representative of Louvois, the minister who now oversaw the working of the Académie, came before it with this angry indictment of alchemy, and with a directive for future research:

I understand by useful research that which could relate to the service of the King and the State;—not the Great Work which also includes the extraction of Mercuries from all sorts of metals, their transmutation or multiplication, which Monseigneur de Louvois does not wish to hear spoken of—or else the investigation and examination of the mines and open-cast workings of France, as well as of all the sulphur-containing compounds used in war, or those able to desalinate sea water and make it fit to drink.[75]

The search for the philosopher's stone, distillation, and the transmutation of metals had finally taxed the patience of a state that had recently turned belligerent toward enemies it perceived at home and abroad. In one of the first historical examples of the state's intervention in the agenda of science, the king's representative complained about the time wasted on these distillations and begged that the company turn its attention toward material, rather than organic, substances: "The other research more suited to this Company and which would be more to the taste of Monseigneur de Louvois concerns everything that could explain and serve Medicine, these two things being almost inseparable because Medicine draws on the results and profits from new discoveries of physique [physics]."[76] The royal representative had gotten the message about the necessity for physical experiments; he just did not want them to be all about plants and their distillations.

Botanical experimentation and medical practice, rather than only the physical sciences, belonged to the alchemical search for the purity of substances through distillation as practiced by Du Clos and company. Indeed he has often been confused with a Parisian physician of similar name because he knew so much about anatomy and medicine, and he held the title *médecin ordinaire du roi*. For years, with Du Clos as director, the company distilled every conceivable vegetative substance, wallflowers with toxic properties, plants from Japan, *valériane sauvage* (the antispasmatic and sedative), fruits, artichokes, mushrooms, irises, coriander, and others.[77] The founding members, Bourdelin, Mouriercy, Du Clos, and Dodart, signed off on all experiments, some of which went on for months just on a single plant. The work was communal and the academy adhered to rules that purposefully inhibited individual research. In its early years the improvement of medical practices was probably its highest goal.

Eventually the attempts by distillation to arrive at the pure essence of things, and thereby to improve their medicinal properties, grew tiresome. Du Clos's credit fell markedly. At his death he supposedly abjured both his Protestantism and his alchemy. A French Protestant refugee journal coming out of the Dutch Republic recorded his abjuration and also the split in the academy over whether a work by Du Clos should be allowed to be published. His nephew claimed that Du Clos had come to see that he had wasted his time on the search for the transmutation of metals.[78] But remember the year was 1685, and Louis XIV had just instituted a virulent campaign of repression and imprisonment against all French Protestants. With Du Clos died the search for perfection and medical rejuvenation that reached out to adepts far and wide, at home and especially abroad. Yet distillation remained a vital part of practical chemistry nearly a century after Du Clos led the experimental life of the new academy. British chemists lectured on distillations of everything from aloes to vinegar and on the production of elixirs for ailments ranging from convulsions to wounds.[79]

As his alchemical search quickened, Du Clos left no stone or source unturned. The unpublished alchemical text he left behind bears witness to the border crossing: "on the resolution and volatilization of the perfect metal: Raymond Lull taught many methods for resolving . . . the perfect metal . . . Basil Valentine employed the water of saltpeter and sel ammoniac . . . Mr Boyle proposed the spirit of nitrite passed through antimony butter."[80] Indeed, Du Clos explained Boyle's entire experimental protocol in chemistry/alchemy to the academy.[81] In Du Clos's intellectual arsenal also stood the great German patron of alchemy, Emperor Rudolph, as did the ubiquitous Paracelsus. Their mutual quest entailed the search for a universal medicine, an elixir of life, as well as for the transmutation of gold, or in the words of Du Clos, "an elixir made with three elements of the philosopher's stone . . . the same elixir . . . that is proper for conserving the human body in its integrity."[82] In such a quest for longevity through a universal medicine any border could be crossed, any adept could be accosted for what wisdom he might possess.

Within the academy the search for improved pharmacy and medicine in general remained key to its early activities, as did chemical/alchemical experimentation in general. Yet gradually emphasis on machines, mechanics, and mathematics began to overshadow the medical. With the demise of Du Clos the alchemical language disappeared from the proceedings. The representatives of the state could only have been pleased. The language of the mechanical philosophy, with multiple debts to a variety of philosophies from Bacon to Descartes, Gassendi, Pascal, and Boyle, firmly took its premier place. In the French practice of chemistry the leading textbook of the 1680s, *Cours de Chymie* (1681) by Nicholas Lemery, relegated alchemy to the status of a fraud. It embraced "chemistry" along with mechanical explanations such as the shape of the atoms. As Bruce Moran has argued, the move was more rhetorical than practical in that what Lemery was doing in his laboratory looked awfully much like what Du Clos and other overtly alchemical practitioners had done. But in the new rhetoric lay a new consensus.[83] With everyone speaking the same mechanical language a larger, more encompassing conversation across the disciplines now became possible. And Lemery, as medical practitioner, also gave Louvois a dose of the practical remedies he had demanded, mixed with a smattering of lore and astrology.[84] Ultimately, in France just as in England—but for different reasons and in different political circumstances—the state found mechanical thinking more promising and, just as important, less threatening.

After 1685 Louis XIV had plenty of new work for his academy. Attention focused on the mapping of the heavens and the earth and, not least at the king's request, on improving the map of France. Greater emphasis than in the first two decades was placed on machines of every kind, on mathematical lessons and reports on everything from lizards to comets as seen in other parts of the world, in the French colonies of Martinique and Saint Dominque (now Haiti), in Siam.[85] Projects became grand, and in the early 1680s the academy talked about perfecting astronomy, geometry, and mechanics. Yet the members could also talk about the sun making its revolutions, seemingly to ignore the centerpiece of the new science, the Copernican notion that the earth, and not the sun, revolves.[86] At the same moment the academy discussed the weight of the air, a phenomenon that rested on atomic assumptions about the pressures and forces affecting all bodies, however invisible. In short, gradually a vocabulary was being put in place, more mechanical than it was anything else. The same process occurred in England at a faster rate in that by the 1660s, and largely for political reasons, alchemy had become a deeply private set of assumptions about how nature could be understood and manipulated, about how adepts could pry into its secrets and transmit them across every border.

The exiled Catholic king of England, James II, thrown on the mercy of Louis XIV by a bloodless revolution in England in 1688–89, might seem a strange fellow to illustrate the cosmopolitan possibilities to be found in the new status awarded the mechanical language of science. It was a way of talking about nature easily available to the learned, but nonscientific, as was the English king himself. Hardly a savant, James was still a Fellow of the Royal Society in London, and in 1690, now settled into his rather comfortable exile, he turned up for his first visit to the Parisian academy.[87] Louis XIV had built a new observatory for his academicians, and James wanted to see it. Fatefully, he may not have learned much about English politics, but the visit reveals he had clearly mastered a fair bit of the new science, and his French was excellent.

He may never have read (indeed few had) Newton's *Principia* of 1687 with its fulsome dedication to his majesty, but he had some idea what it contained.

In the course of a discussion with the academy about Huygen's discovery of the satellites of Saturn, and the many uses of the new observatory, the vexed problem of finding longitude at sea arose. The academicians and James II discussed the astronomical work of Flamsted and the Royal Society, the Jesuits, and the quality of Chinese mathematics. James noted the usefulness of knowing the eclipses of Jupiter's satellites for gauging distances on earth and hence for the reform of geographical maps. Comparisons ensued about the various systems for measuring planetary motion with Copernicus, Tycho Brahe, and Ptolemy discussed. Although a Catholic, the English king sided with Copernicus. James reported on the thinking of Newton and various others that the figure of the earth was not round, but the academicians assured him that the different length of the swings of pendulums seen in different places in the world—a set of experiments first done in France—was solely the result of climate and "the temperament of the air." They were not ready to accept the effect that gravitational pull would have on the earth and its relative density.

All the assembled professed to be interested in machines that can elevate heavy objects. The only language in serious play in these discussions with James II was mechanical and experimental: the weight of bodies, the shadows cast by the matter of the heavens, the effects of magnets, even the possibility that Newton's insight that the earth should be flattened at the poles because of the force of gravity on its center could be discussed, if finally rejected by the French academicians. The conversation with the exiled king of England tells us that, on both sides of the Channel, natural philosophers and their followers had arrived at a consensus about a common discourse about nature. It would be mechanical and experimental. Mechanical thinking suited state policy and objectives in both places and, most important, contained none of the hyperbole about reformation and renewal. But it did promise progress in the search for knowledge about nature.

Back in the 1660s, James's brother, Charles II, took the title of founder of the Royal Society of London and then left it to its own devises, financial and intellectual. By contrast, and in the same decade, the Académie des sciences was a creature of royal patronage, directly dependent on subventions from Louis XIV and charged with the task of doing his work. Machines intended for military use, and knowledge of military engineering gained on the battlefield, figure noticeably and particularly in the proceedings of the 1690s. This is hardly surprising given that international warfare raged, triggered by

French bellicosity.[88] The pressure of war may also have revealed to the king and his ministers that the academy was too valuable to be left relatively un-regulated, busily at work on its distillations. Thus in the 1690s an entirely new set of rules were drawn up that over time would tie the academy more tightly to the needs of the state, making it more noble and military in its orienta-tion.[89] At the same time the new regulations opened the academy to the out-side world and required it to begin publishing monthly proceedings, just as did the Royal Society in London. In that decade the academy had about four-teen members who were actively researching. With the possibility, indeed the necessity, of publishing original work, everyone had to get busy, or find out-side correspondents to fill the pages. After a brief flurry of activity in 1692–93, the academicians admitted that they were too few, and had too little contact with the outside world, to fill pages of a regular monthly *Mémoire*.

In 1699 the monarchy took matters in hand and the ever ebullient sec-retary of the academy, Bernard le Bovier de Fontenelle, said that the changes would make a totally new company, one that functioned more like a repub-lic.[90] Efforts were made to turn the academy in a more technological direc-tion with *mécaniciens* who worked directly with machines for manufacturing brought into the proceedings. They were also needed to work on the rivers and ports of the country.[91] Fatefully, the academy got the power to test all inventions and advise the crown on their utility and profitability. No such power extended to the scientific academies in England or the Dutch Repub-lic. By mid-century, French inventors bitterly resented what they saw as arm-chair philosophers with the right to kill their chance for a subsidy. We may see the renewed emphasis on technology from a different angle, from the pressure, partly due to the war-making needs of the state, to find out how things are made or done elsewhere. In the 1690s a few of the academicians began to compile notes for what can only be described as a projected ency-clopedia of the trades, of *arts et métiers*. In them we see the first glimmer of an interest in finding out about artisanal practices and foreign inventions. The latter interest would grow by the decade.[92]

Late in the seventeenth century the new French rules acknowledge what had been growing as practices within communities of natural philosophers in many places: rival parties and paradigms, individual as opposed to group experiment, and the necessity for arbitration to settle disputes with civility. All these new realities had to be addressed by an embrace of the cosmopoli-tan, by a vast expansion of the academy's membership, both domestic and foreign. Forty-one new members were added of whom six were foreign. Urgently the new rules called upon the academicians to "undertake commerce with diverse savants, found in Paris and the provinces of the kingdom, found also in foreign countries." Elections to membership would take into account if applicants had been "les plus exacts à cette espèce de commerce."[93] And they were to read works in mathematics and physics published wherever and to repeat experiments from them.

The king and his ministers wanted productivity, and they wanted the academy to be their eyes and ears on developments in the sciences throughout Europe. Just as had alchemy, until it finally disappeared, medicine receded further into the background. From 1699 the *Histoire et mémoires* of the academy mimic the *Philosophical Transactions of the Royal Society,* and one, or more, awfully bored academician was given the job of transcribing verbatim and translating the *Transactions* during its first two years.[94] The impulse at work here was more imperial than it was cosmopolitan. At issue lay the power of the state as enhanced by knowledge. The reform of the academy was undertaken at precisely the same moment that Louis XIV put a special tax on all foreigners resident in France since 1600.[95] He further bent every effort to stop the publication of tracts opposing the policy.[96]

In the 1750s Louis XV augmented the international obligations of the academy and insisted that it solicit and publish papers by foreigners. This was the same decade when ministers of the crown began to worry about foreign inventiveness and looked with increasing alarm over their shoulders to developments in Britain.[97] The inadvertently cosmopolitan by-product of the state's increasing interest in foreigners should not be confused with its essentially national and imperial intentions.

Finally, to illustrate the range of cosmopolitan experience that mechanical science could offer, one life—perhaps lived more fully than most—will have to suffice. Ehrenfried Walther von Tschirnhaus came from Saxon nobility. His father had studied in Italy and his mother was of German and Scottish origin. That sort of cosmopolitan background could be found in many noble families of the early modern period, but in the life of Tschirnhaus the study of nature expanded upon anything his family might have imagined as possible. In 1668 he was sent to the university at Leiden in the Dutch Republic at a time when it had become a center for learning Cartesian ideas and mathematics. It was the world that Ten Rhyne knew well. After various interruptions, Tschirnhaus made his way to London and fell immediately into the company of the Royal Society and, in particular, of Henry Oldenburg, its secretary. Letters of introduction from Oldenburg gave Tschirnhaus access to the Dutch scholar Huygens and the German mathematician Leibniz, both at work in Paris. All three worked together on mathematical problems; then

Tschirnhaus decided to spend three years in Italy where he worked with the natural philosopher and sometime alchemist Athanasius Kircher. Journeying back to Amsterdam, Tschirnhaus helped prepare for publication the works of his friend the heretical philosopher Spinoza. Perhaps Paris and its academy gave him his most secure home, and after being made a member in 1682 he went on to publish major articles in mathematics and a treatise on medicine. He ended his life back in Saxony where he developed porcelain factories, a European industry that he helped to found.[98]

Without dwelling on the question of the originality of his work, Tschirnhaus's life can tell us a great deal about the new cosmopolitanism. It required familiarity with the natural philosophical language of the mechanical—having the new mathematics coming from Descartes was desirable, but not essential—and it depended upon the social enclaves of science in the major European cities. It also required familiarity with alchemical languages and practice. With all that in place, and money in one's pocket, the natural philosopher who spoke French or Latin had a large world in which to play.

By 1700 almost nothing visibly remained of the philosophical contestation that lay at the heart of seventeenth-century science. For a brief time the alchemical had seemed to offer just as viable an alternative to the scholastic as did the mechanical. Indeed, distinctively, whether as spoken by Hartlib and associates or by Du Clos and company, alchemical language promised reform and renewal, a life improved, perhaps even at the millennium transformed. While all the competing languages of the natural order could work in the service of princes, the alchemical possessed the most subversive associations. People who tried to transmute metals into gold were ultimately working with higher powers than those offered by mere titles and patrons, although the latter were extremely useful. The practices of the alchemists may have been local—all experimentation or simply labor is—but their reach for the key to all wisdom knew no boundaries.

The idealism associated with the alchemical tradition worked in the early years of the new science to promote the search for universalist ideals, for notions about the improvement of man's estate that eventually became known as Baconian rather than as alchemical. The triumph of the mechanical philosophy ultimately swept all before it, and, along with scholastic ones, alchemical texts made their way into the dustbin labeled "discard." But before they met that fate, alchemical writings gave a humanistic and reforming impulse to the new sciences, another approach to the cosmopolitan. Alchemy may not have served the needs of the state as readily as did the mechanical, nor with its clues and secrets did it prove as easy to master as forces, atoms, and

weights. Yet the idealism about human rejuvenation and cosmopolitan border crossing remains in the enterprise of modern science and deserves to be
credited at its origins to alchemical and hermetic actors and texts seen by
1700 as quaint and obsolete. Alchemy got labeled as magic, and the secrecy
associated with it became dubbed irrational. But modern science retained
some of the heady idealism best characterized as cosmopolitan.

The penchant for secrecy and the search for lore and obscure wisdom
did not, however, die with alchemy. As we shall see in chapter four, in the
eighteenth century the cosmopolitan appeared in a new, masonic guise, one
that was deeply social, but also secretive and intensely friendly toward science. Late in the eighteenth century, there were freemasons who professed
the desire to revive alchemy, and with its help to invent a universal religion
of which the secrets of alchemy would be just a part. They too were mystics
and border-crossers, but by then out of step scientifically with their age, and
equally unprepared for the late century revolutions that made democracy far
more dangerous than alchemy or theosophy to the guardians of order and
the needs of monarchs and churches.

While alchemists and freemasons may seem eccentric cosmopolites to
the modern eye, there was little about mercantile life in early modern Europe
that leaves us as baffled. The market, then and now, required zeal and com-
petitiveness before it granted its participants even a modicum of success. But
it also required something less potentially hostile, and probably more pleasant. Social interaction with strangers, whether face to face, by letter—or now
on the Internet—can present cosmopolitan possibilities. But amid the vast-
ness of the early modern mercantile world, how do we get at the experience
of trade? One possibility lies in the life of the many stock exchanges that
doted the European urban landscape, and to which we will now turn.

Chapter 3
Markets Not So Free

One of the maxims of modern life tells us that commerce automatically makes people more open, more sophisticated, more accepting of strangers, and conceivably able, therefore, to imagine themselves as cosmopolites, citizens in a commercial world that breaches geographic and social borders. Buying and selling, lending and borrowing lie at the heart of the capitalist economic system that emerged in the West, first in Mediterranean urban centers around the fifteenth century, then in England and the Low Countries at roughly the same time. Trade in goods for money almost requires strangers. Barter generally occurs between people who know one another, if not by name, then by type, and hence by the needs particular to that kind of person. The thrill and danger of being in the market, supposedly armed with only money and goods, lies in its anonymity. Value becomes a labile negotiation when only a few of the variables can be known.

We have come to take it for granted that commerce between strangers requires rules of civility, a certain politeness allowing both parties ruthlessly to try to cut the best deal. The civility that is a prerequisite to the cosmopolitan had not always been so. If we look at the earliest exchanges in northern Europe we see that the physical and public marketplace only became civilized, and thus opened to the possibility of being a site for cosmopolitan mores, gradually and with the assistance of strong and local governmental authorities who had themselves largely gotten out of the habit of persecuting their citizens. When our contemporary theorists privilege a cosmopolitan allegiance over that accorded to the modern national state, we should not forget the historical role played by governmental authority in making any larger, cosmopolitan identity possible.[1] We must also remember that beneath the surface of the commercial and cosmopolitan, other, darker impulses and prejudices oftentimes lay buried, not forgotten, merely obscured.

In early modern Europe, as now, trade could occur anywhere, over vast and open spaces. But physical epicenters were needed. The temples of trade in the large, Western meccas of commerce stood at the exchanges, the markets for bills of exchange in goods and foreign currency. They lay in the center of cities like London, Paris, Amsterdam, Bruges, Antwerp, Lyon, Marseille, Berlin and Hamburg, where commerce occurred in everything, in cargoes, ships, stocks, and even, at a distance, human chattel. In northern and western Europe these sites began first in private homes, and then most famously in an open courtyard in Bruges in Flanders where, of necessity (given the weather), traders could also perambulate under covered walkways that extended the length and breadth of the yard. Outside of Italy, the Bruges exchange became the model first imitated by Antwerp, then late in the sixteenth century by the famous London Royal Exchange, perhaps the most written about and commented upon of all the early stock exchanges. In France as late as the 1730s the Italian exchanges were still seen as architectural models, to be imitated by French architects as famous as Robert de Cotte.[2]

We want to try to take the emotional temperature of life in these actual public markets to determine, if we can, the tone of social relations among the strangers and acquaintances there assembled. In cities where commerce could occur any place, at any time, only these exchanges, physical places with magistrates in charge, with watchers and keepers and visitors who left accounts, leave us with a set of records about experiences over several centuries. By the eighteenth century the exchanges, in particular the famous one in London, were hailed as symbols and realities of the cosmopolitan. In the new American republic, regulated public markets were regarded as places that could inculcate republican virtue, hard work, and discipline.[3]

The European markets—from the relatively free English and Flemish exchanges on one hand to the French markets tightly overseen by royal agents on the other—displayed varying degrees of cosmopolitan expansiveness depending upon both internal and external factors. As we are about to see, warfare, religious persecution, and, in the case of Marseille, mass bankruptcy compromised the exchanges and the cosmopolitan ambiance so vital to them. Hospitality could give way to anger, resentments simmering beneath the surface could sometimes explode onto it.

When visitors went to the major cities they seldom passed up the Bourse in Paris, de Beurs in Antwerp, or the exchange in London. Their physical space, layout, uses, and social configurations can tell us much about the preconditions around which cosmopolitanism may have emerged. It did so only gradually, and only after face-to-face commerce had been tamed and regulated. Indeed, the actual administration of the exchanges betrays suspicion and little glee at the wonders of the anonymous market haunt. The engravings we have of the various exchanges on both sides of the Channel (Figure 5)

Figure 5. *The Patience of the Trader Depicted*. Illustration from George Hoefnagel, *Traité de la patience*, sixteenth century. Courtesy of the Bibliothèque Municipale de Rouen. Photo by Thierry Ascencio-Parvy.

tell us that in Bruges, Antwerp, and London specially built buildings were given a geometrical structure, one more easily guarded. Merchants stood at appointed places so they could be more easily found. But note, almost every engraving we possess tells us that they also stood grouped by their nation or place of origin. Cosmopolitan mores induced by the market—such as may have put strangers at ease or even bonded them in ways unprecedented—never made them faceless or rootless as critics harshly maintained.[4]

Traders first became citizens of nations or city-states. In the Dutch Republic they might self-identify with their towns long before they would think of themselves as Dutch. Then perhaps out of unhappiness with their governments, or just because of travel and lived experience, they sought to imagine themselves as citizens of the world. But as we shall see in the French and Flemish records, religion, and the hatreds it could inspire, never entirely disappeared.

A French writer of 1576 gave a detailed description of the Royal Exchange in London, our first stop in this survey of the experience of market life, and he confirmed the national groupings revealed by the engravings. At the London exchange, in direct imitation of the Antwerp exchange, twice a day, as our French writer noted, "merchants who buy and sell all over Europe meet together in different sections according to nationality, from 11 to 12 in the morning and from 5 to 6 in the evening. Each nation has its own quarter, so that those who have business with them can find them more easily."[5] Two anomalies present themselves in this early account of the exchanges. The hours when trade could occur were severely curtailed. On both sides of the Channel that practice continued into the eighteenth century when in London eventually four hours a day became the not easily enforced norm. In Marseille the records tell us that the strict hours were intended to level the playing field, to give everyone the same chance to bid and deal. In addition, rather than imagining a free-for-all governed by the types of goods to be bought or sold, we need to imagine men generally clustered by their nations or, in the case of the Mediterranean cities of the Levant and Italy, by the place from which they came.

Thus if the cosmopolitan emerged in these setting it did so after a national or perhaps just a local identity had been firmly fixed. It is argued that the act of buying and selling may have required, and could certainly enforce, a national identity, and not necessarily a cosmopolitan one. The evidence from the floors of the early exchanges, at least for the Western merchants, partially supports the argument. Indeed Sir Thomas Gresham himself, the founder of the London exchange, had firmly implanted national loyalties for which he was amply rewarded by the crown and from which he profited handsomely.[6] In Marseille, however, where we can see the outlines of personal identities at work from the entire Mediterranean area, they could come from the many cities that made up what the French called the Échelles du Levant found in Smyrna, Alexandria, Constantinople, Cairo, Tripoli, Alep, Tunis, and Acre. Perhaps those inhabitants identified as members of the Ottoman Empire, or perhaps by their religion, in the case of the Jews. They were certainly not part of the nation as their northern European counterparts had come to know it, but they were serious players in the capitalist commerce of the region, in everything from coffee to grain. In Antwerp and Amsterdam merchants might just as likely identify themselves proudly by the Italian or Dutch city from which they originated. Western capitalism would not have started in the city-states of fourteenth-century Italy if specifically national identity were the sine qua non.

One manuscript sketch of the floor of the London exchange made by a visiting French engineer of the 1780s suggests that by that date national identities competed with professional as well as religious identities. The sketch of the floor plan shows the familiar groupings, "place hollandaise," "place des Indes Orientales," "place Française." But in the 1780s new groups have made an appearance: "the place of the Quakers," "the place of the Jews," "the place of the silk merchants," the drapers, druggists, and so on. Dating more or less contemporaneous with Kant's famous meditation on the necessity for the cosmopolitan, the sketch tells us that by then selling draperies may have given an identity as much as did one's being from the Dutch Republic, or France, or the East Indies.[7] The sketch also conforms to what we know about the Amsterdam exchange from an even earlier period. Guild identity weakened as merchants from all over received individual freedoms, and they might identify by their trade, their city, or their nation.[8]

The religious identities witnessed by the French engineer were probably much older, we may assume, and would only have been reinforced by distinctive and customary dress worn by Jews and Quakers in the 1780s as in the 1680s. Indeed London's Jewish mercantile community was well established by the 1650s, somewhat clannish by virtue of its religious strictures, but also possessed of vast international contacts.[9] When we consider the place of Jews in the cosmopolitan order associated with exchanges, we should remember the ambivalent status awarded them in lore about the origins of *la bourse* or the exchange. The most popular handbooks for learning how to be a merchant— available in many languages—claimed that the exchanges had originated first with the Jews, and the attribution had a deeply negative connotation.[10] In

England printed attacks on "aliens" singled the Jews out for special condemnation.[11] Yet despite what prejudices lay beneath the surface, in London members of the Jewish mercantile community married with non-Jews in numbers that were significant. We may take such behavior as indicating a greater, rather than a lesser cosmopolitan stance in the world.

Despite our discussing it first, the London exchange was not the earliest public exchange in northern Europe. That honor belongs to Bruges and then Antwerp, followed closely by Lyon. But the Royal Exchange and its management are extremely well documented and distinctive. Queen Elizabeth gave the exchange the title "royal." In fact, it was run first by a local parish and Sir Thomas Gresham, then by the private mercers' guild in close collaboration with a committee set up by the Lord Mayor of London. The same committee also administered Gresham College and eventually had a hand in assisting the Royal Society of London with repairs. In contrast to Paris, indeed all of France, the English monarchy had no say in what was resolutely a privately owned space and, at the same time, one of the earliest Western manifestations of the orderly public sphere accommodating foreigners. In London, unlike Amsterdam and Paris, the number of brokers was officially unlimited,[12] although in the former places plenty of brokers sought to get around the official limits.

But the social experience of foreigners did not necessarily loosen governmental policy toward foreign trade. Late in the sixteenth century with the backing of the government, English trading companies sought to regulate foreign competition to their advantage. Dutch merchants in particular complained of the higher customs duties being imposed and of their lack of access to London's halls for the selling of cloth.[13] By the 1620s the Dutch had established their own monopoly companies in the East and West Indies. In neither place, however, did the impulse to find monopoly advantage diminish the number of foreign merchants present at the exchanges. The economic policies of nation-states permitted, or limited, the growth of the exchanges and foreign access to them, but governments were never the determining factor in making the cosmopolitan happen.

At first the exchanges everywhere in Europe were very truncated, hardly the open, busy public spaces that they became by the middle of the eighteenth century. When administrative records for the Royal Exchange begin late in the 1630s, they do not suggest a place where much is happening except buying and selling of bills of exchange for two hours a day. From other records left by publishers, we know that, just as in Antwerp, some shops or "pawns" could be found at the London exchange in the earliest years. Gradually the shops began to figure more prominently in the interests of the committee that discussed and voted upon having them, their size, rent, and in the 1670s, their being allowed to have windows for displaying wares to the larger public, and so on.[14] Again literary evidence from the Elizabethan period onward describes a lively consumerism at the exchange, indeed far livelier than the two hours permitted for the exchange of merchant papers. Similarly the literary evidence from Elizabethan times does not suggest anything like the violence that can be documented in the municipal records about the Antwerp exchange for the same period. The records at the Old Bailey document thieving and pickpocketing in the vicinity of the exchange, but nothing more dangerous than that.

The shops and their windows at the London exchange tell us that the creature we have come to know as the consuming public has made its bustling appearance. So too have a few women, both married and unmarried, who are leasees of the shops. Perhaps as many as one third of the shops were leased by women, some of whom were widows or daughters of the original leasee. On occasion leaseholders argued that their specific trade was needed at the exchange, suggesting that once established there, they expected to be the sole practitioner in that small, potentially very profitable universe.[15] Clearly the shops did business more hours than the two—or later, four—allocated to trade on the exchange, and some faced outward, their newly allowed windows beckoning and enticing.[16]

Sometimes the shop's wares spilled out into the walkways of the London exchange, where fruit, and food in general, could now also be purchased.[17] In the alley outside the exchange, a part of its property, more food and baked goods here sold. Notaries of the public sealed deals, and booksellers like Elizabeth Nutt sold everything from plays to pamphlets. Barber-surgeons could be found who removed boils or pulled teeth. Beneath, or above the floor, lay cellars or floors leased out in the 1670s to the East India Company where the actual pepper and tea being traded on the exchange could be stored.[18] Lighting had to be provided by lanterns and candles, and watchmen were asked "to be diligent on their watch & thereby prevent the breaking open of shops or other injuries which may otherwise happen."[19] While the violent crime that plagued the Antwerp exchange never seemed to be a compelling part of the life of the London exchange, at least as the earliest minutes reveal, crime against property appeared from time to time. The picture for much of the seventeenth century gives the relative absence of crime—and by the presence of women—argues for a more or less peaceful and civilized place, where, by the 1670s if not well before, all the conditions were in place for the emergence of the relative freedom we associate with the cosmopolitan. Nothing in the London records, unlike the earlier Antwerp records, makes mention of significant tension between national groups, at least there was no public display of violent national or city-state rivalry.

By the 1670s the Royal Exchange should be seen as a commercial micro-universe within the larger London scene. Within its walls, and immediately outside them, merchants traded stocks, goods, as well as shares, but in the shops inside so too did tailors outfit, watchmakers repair, and fishmongers offer the catch of the day. The capitalist microcosm emerged as a reasonably ordered place—such as Voltaire described in the 1730s—only after it was tamed, and that required everything from a good, working clock to a sequestering of its denizens and their policing. The guild regularly appointed watchmen for that purpose.[20]

The Royal Exchange may be legitimately imagined as a microcosm that merged commercial transactions with the impulse to consume in an almost impossible to regulate environment. Rather than imagining the commercial as an automatic engine for starting the cosmopolitan express that leads inexorably to civil society, it would be better to see the money and stock exchanges for what they first were. They could be places of chaos and crime. Only gradually, and through the intervention of the governmental authorities and the freewheeling habits of consumption and the self-interest of merchants, did the exchanges become calm and safe enough for any reasonable social life to occur. The shops, and hence consumption, may have been the keys that unlocked that process, but nowhere in Europe would merchants thrive in an atmosphere of violence. In London shopkeepers routinely tried to make the exchange an extension of their home, to live in their shops and install beds.[21] The committee ordered them out, and probably they quit their beds, but certainly not their trading.

Ever present in the London exchange were the constable and porter, dressed in formal gowns, in pursuit of the ubiquitous nuisance, the "other," poorer economy of beggars, hawkers, fruit sellers, and pamphleteers who were to be sent to the workhouse but who seem never to be absent. The floor, side walkways, passages of the London exchange buzzed with "the idle" and "disorderly persons," many of whom were merchants in their own, less-respectable right. Booksellers in the so-called "Pawnes"—the upper tier of shops—of the exchange complained bitterly of the competition coming from the hawkers.[22] In 1689 the committee ordered them removed; thirty years later the hawkers were still there. In the rough-and-tumble of the respectable market "short loaners" also dwelt on the sidelines ready to practice what their enemies regarded as usury. Plays from the Elizabethan period, and beyond, also suggest that ladies of the night plied their trade in the shadows and recesses of the evening exchange.[23]

When commodities and commerce became too much to handle the almshouse or workhouse loomed. The committee that controlled the exchange also owned almshouses that abutted it and privileged a few poor people with a place therein. But life's travail did not end peacefully. There, as the goods stored in the cellars of the exchange shifted and burst through the windows, the infirm saw their abode threatened with ruin.[24] Occasionally, a merchant would be forgiven debt when his misfortunes were deemed worthy. Just as likely goods would be seized for rent.[25]

But just having a clock does not necessarily an impersonal order make. Indeed the exchange teemed with a liveliness closer to what we associate with a neighborhood than with a global market. In the early seventeenth century complaints mounted of debris littering the area around the exchange and efforts were made to stop the selling of fruit in the building and the dangerous use of fire by feather workers busily at work in their shops. In that same period the "abuse" of trading more than the two hours legally permitted was sternly reprimanded.[26] By the reign of Charles I the Royal Exchange was considered to be so important—and we may assume reasonably ordered—that statues of the king and his predecessors were installed, pictures hung, and shopkeepers taxed for poor relief in the nearby parish of St. Michael, Cornhill.[27] Symbols of order and gestures toward probity and virtue worked to reinforce civility.

Just a few years later, in the heady days of the English Revolution when all seemed possible—and Charles I and his army were on the run—Samuel Hartlib and other reformers, among them the poet John Milton, imagined an Office of Public Addresses explicitly modeled on the Royal Exchange. As we saw in Chapter 2, they longed to bring inventors into contact with investors and promote free trade and education in natural philosophy for all.[28] Given such inspirations, we might imagine that the relative freedom and cosmopolitan openness that Hartlib envisioned would simply evolve out of the life of the exchange, leading to a cosmopolitanism that would inexorably sweep all before it. But cosmopolitan dreams are fragile. Hartlib's ended with political defeat and the restoration of monarchy in 1660.

Given the tensions that the mixing and jostling at the exchange inevitably produced, after 1660 it still had to be carefully supervised at the same weekly meetings with a committee representing the city and the Mercers' Company, supposedly chaired by the lord mayor. The records from the 1670s reveal that aside from watching the market the committee was also engaged in political watching. During the Restoration the freedom upon which the cosmopolitan thrives was by no means a given. In 1679, and for the next two years, England was rocked by the Exclusion Crisis, an attempt—that failed—to stop the Catholic brother of Charles II, James, from ever ascending to the throne. The exclusionists assumed, with considerable insight, that James would seek to impose on his kingdoms the same form of absolutist authority, as well as religion, that the king of France enjoyed.

Out of the crisis emerged the two-party political system, with the Whigs fiercely opposed to James, and the Tories, royalist and largely in his camp. Riots in London forced Charles II and Parliament out of the city and to Oxford. The minutes of the Mercers' Company are entirely silent about all these events, but at precisely this moment, the lord mayor, Sir Robert Clayton, an aggressive Whig and a scrivener (in his case often setting up long-term loans), appears at all the meetings of the exchange, something his predecessors in the office did not regularly do. In the wider political world, the Tories won the day, and in 1685 James's crown was secured. But London and the small universe of the Royal Exchange became a Whig stronghold.[29] Thus began an association between the party and freewheeling commercial life that lasted well into the eighteenth century.

For an entire year, from June of 1688 to June of 1689, another moment of even greater political upheaval than the Exclusion Crisis, the revolution of 1688–89, a similar silence descends in the records of the exchange. The revolution removed the hapless James II from the throne by act of Parliament and put in his place William of Orange and his English wife, Mary. Their Dutch army had invaded in November. It waited patiently while William accepted the Bill of Rights, the Toleration Act, and the reality of a country now governed by the king in Parliament. Times were tense and hard. We know that in June of 1688 many shops in the exchange were vacant and the rents had to be lowered.

The pro-revolutionary political allegiance of the exchange's administrators stands out, not from any comments extant in the minutes, but from a single appointment, made when they resumed in June of 1689. At Gresham College, by this time a rather sleepy center for learning in natural philosophy, the lecturer in "Physick," that is, medicine, was forced to resign, and in his place, the mercers' company unanimously appointed the Reverend Edward Stillingfleet. He was the leading Anglican churchman of the liberal and Whig cause and a staunch supporter of William III and the revolution.[30] The mercers had allied the institutions they controlled with the revolution, presumably because its principles conformed to their own. After 1689, a Quaker who had been deprived of his shop in the exchange because of religious persecution effected against Dissenters by Charles II and the Anglican Church during the Restoration, "now [being] of a great age and in a low condition," had his lease renewed.[31]

Only after the revolution of 1688–89 did Quakers once again mix freely as equals on the floor of the exchange. Rather than seeing the cosmopolitan as simply an alternative to the nation-state, we need to realize that in the past at least—witness as we will shortly the Spanish in Flanders—repressive states made the emergence of the cosmopolitan all the more difficult. Having the state as an ally, or at least as a noncombatant, may vastly increase the chances of a lasting cosmopolitanism. As economic historians have noted, having the government "make a credible commitment" to the relevant set of rights is also essential "for economic growth to occur."[32] The revolution of 1688–89 had significant economic as well as social implications; it opened, rather than closed, opportunities for many.

In the eighteenth-century English literary apologists relished the universalist possibilities presented by the Royal Exchange. Joseph Addison and Richard Steele, writing in their famous *Spectator* in 1711, said that the conduct of "the private business of Mankind" turned the exchange into a "Metropolis, a kind of *Emporium* for the whole Earth." Factors, that is, the merchants who made deals for other merchants, they said, "are what Ambassadors are in the Politick World." Yet even Addison and Steele had to admit that the cosmopolitan had limits; in the swirl of international commerce, men stood amid their countrymen. "Sometimes I am jostled among a Body of *Armenians*: Sometimes I am lost in a Crowd of *Jews*, and sometimes . . . in a Groupe of *Dutchmen*. I am a *Dane, Swede,* or *French-Man* at different times." Nonetheless, the dizzying experience left the reporters describing the ultimate cosmopolitan ideal: "I . . . rather fancy my self . . . a Citizen of the World."[33]

Voltaire, of course, wrote the most famous description of the Royal Exchange, published in 1733: "a place more venerable than many courts of justice, where the representatives of all nations meet for the benefit of mankind. There the Jew, the Mahometan, and the Christian transact together as though they all professed the same religion, and give the name of Infidel to none but bankrupts. There the Presbyterian confides in the Anabaptist, and the Churchman depends on the Quaker's word."[34] Presumably Voltaire did not know that he could not have waxed as eloquently about his Quaker's word had he written before 1689. And neither Addison and Steele, nor Voltaire, tell us what they must have known in their hearts: citizens of the world had their enemies. In 1747 an anonymous poem put in words what some others, too, must had thought. It attacked the exchange for being a place where Jews, of all people, had liberties: "What Liberties have Freemen, when a Jew / Shall in the City's Heart his Trade pursue?"[35] Plays from Elizabethan times onward, with Shylock the most famous of all Jewish merchants, had commented upon Jews at the exchange, and they had been none too complementary about them.[36] The directors of the Bank of England were known anti-Semites until at least the early nineteenth century.[37] There was plenty of xenophobia to be found on the floor of the exchange, as elsewhere. We will see controversies about Jews and foreigners in Marseille as well. Yet from the mid-seventeenth century onward most sources suggest that a good third of all London merchants came from abroad, a pattern that remained true well into the eighteenth century.[38] And anyone with international business made an appearance at the exchange on a daily basis a high priority.

The picture we have of the cosmopolitan should not forget the threadbare child, from an engraving of 1758, seen rushing toward a charity box provided by the opulently clad traders from Portugal, Barbados, and the American colonies. The lives of all were governed by a centrally placed clock and its precision and beauty were highly prized.[39] In the universe of the London exchange time was truly absolute as Newton imagined it. It framed the proceedings and waited for no one. The dark side of the cosmopolitan, the discipline it demanded and the price to be paid if fortune or fecklessness made discipline untenable, was there also, to be seen if we read the minutes of the Mercers' Company, or put a critical eye to the engravings we have of scenes from the exchange floor (Figure 6). But while poverty and petty crime awaited the unprotected in London of the eighteenth century, conditions had once been far worse at the European exchanges. In Antwerp during the sixteenth century it was possible to be murdered.

Antwerp

If we go back in historical time to the earliest exchanges, in particular the one in Antwerp, a rather different picture emerges from the staid and relatively settled world found after 1600 across the Channel at the Royal Exchange. The London open air building with covered side paths for shopping and trading had been directly modeled on the *beurs* in Antwerp, which Gresham had witnessed in his travels. The word was derived from the proper name of a Bruges family—Van der Beurse. It had provided a gathering place for foreign merchants as early as the thirteenth century.

J.B. Cipriani delineavit-pinxque institutioni dicavit.

Figure 6. *The Royal Exchange.* Engraving by Giovanni Battista Cipriani. Courtesy of the Guildhall Library Corporation of London.

Antwerp had an exchange in 1485, and we know that some shops lined its outer walls because a jewel theft occurred there sometime between 1515 and 1525.[40] Antwerp only achieved its great importance after Bruges declined early in the sixteenth century. A combination of factors undid its popularity with foreign merchants: penchants for overregulation, for guilds, and for granting monopolies, among them the right to exchange money, which was given exclusively to the Flemish.[41] Not surprisingly, Bruges acquired a reputation for being unfriendly to foreigners. In particular, the Spanish merchants enriched by gold from the Americas found Antwerp to be more hospitable, and it had long-standing connections with London traders and agents. Bruges had also made the mistake of quarreling with the Holy Roman Emperor. By 1568 Antwerp had around 100,000 occupants and was well over twice the size of Bruges. In making conditions for the cosmopolitan possible, size mattered. Around 1,100 foreign merchants operated in the town as did over 270 publishers.[42]

A few decades earlier the city of Antwerp had also built a new, larger exchange to both the pleasure and dismay of the foreign merchants. Property values around the old exchange obviously were affected. In 1531 the open-air courtyard was laid out geometrically (Figure 7), and the magistrates intended quite purposefully to better police the new building. They wanted control over the traffic on the floor of the exchange, but also they needed to tackle the problem of crime. They forbade riots and the pulling out of knives.[43] Yet at the same time another statute forbade children and their cats from playing on the exchange floor, thus suggesting that the dangers were not so overwhelming that all but the armed feared to venture forth.[44] The Spanish emperor also used it as the place where government loans could be negotiated.

De beurs was built with floors, and the upper level, with over one hundred rooms, was meant to accommodate smaller merchants and the shops of artisans. Today it is possible to stand in the disused outdoor courtyards of the two exchanges that bustled in sixteenth-century Antwerp. Both were intimate, barely fifty by fifty feet. There are cloisterlike, covered walkways around the sides in which we can easily imagine vast amounts of business being done. Under the aisles shops abounded, where, among other items, paintings and jewelery could be bought and sold. This kind of easy commerce distinctively did not occur in France; there royal agents, and not shopkeepers, were the key players on the exchange floor. Contemporary accounts tell us that Antwerp possessed policies or statutes that were an example to the whole of the Netherlands.[45] The city policed but did not dominate the proceedings.

The town needed all the rules it could get. In the first half of the six-teenth century the impact of the Protestant Reformation in the Low Countries made for turbulent religious tensions. By the 1530s Protestantism set down deep inroads in the Low Countries, and the exchange served as a magnet that drew, as the records tell us, "illegal and heretical" gatherings.[46] By the decade of the 1560s the Catholic and Spanish king, Philip II, who owned the Low Countries as part of his empire, decided Protestant influence had to be stopped. But sending into the Low Countries both a vast army and the Inquisition led to open revolt. Only in 1610 did an informal peace return. The borders of the Netherlands and Belgium today are basically the outline of where the Spanish army was forced to stop. Antwerp and Bruges remained in the Catholic south, and Amsterdam became the major city in the newly emergent and independent Dutch Republic.

Yet quite apart from religious tensions, the Antwerp magistrates' records depict *de beurs* as a scene of richly textured, if miraculously ordered, chaos. Young and old played at dice and cards; children and possibly adults played bounce ball, and in 1533, just two years after the opening of the new *beurs,*

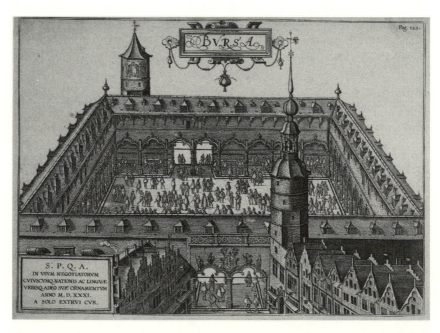

Figure 7. *Overdracht van Antwerpen.* By Piter van der Borcht, 1581. Courtesy of the Stedelijk Prentenkabinet Antwerpen.

the magistrates forbade quacks, second-hand sellers, bird thieves, songsters, among others, from darkening its door. Jewelers had their wares stolen. More commonly than not, merchants came to the Antwerp exchange with body-guards, and in 1562 the magistrates tried to insist that weapons—knives and pistols—not be carried into the building. Decades later a similar regulation would be required in Amsterdam.[47] In 1540 a Portugese merchant was killed at the exchange and in 1570 an English merchant, Thomas Malbaen, was murdered during the evening hour set aside for trading. In 1540 another Portuguese merchant survived an attempted murder probably committed by a Spaniard, if surnames can be trusted.[48] In 1551 an Italian merchant was murdered by another Italian; in 1561 murderous weapons were used in a brawl between a Genoan and a Milanese merchant. A group of Spaniards injured Englishmen, probably out of hostility to the privileges they enjoyed in the town.

Indeed the English privileges had been long-standing, and their com-pany, the Merchant Adventurers, largely traders in cloth, had fiercely guarded them, playing one Flemish or Dutch town off against another to secure favors. In 1550–51 the Merchant Adventurers obtained a new building from the Antwerp government, the "engelse beurs."[49] They got priority in the town hall when it came to complaints or suits. In 1553 the inevitable envy burst into open combat between Spanish and English merchants on the exchange floor.[50] When not actually brawling, traders put Latin libels on the walls of the exchange so that all the nations assembled would be sure to be able to read them.[51] Brawls were also common in the nearby inns and taverns. In gen-eral—although not in every case—the violence occurred between rivals from different cities or nations, that is until the Spanish army made its ominous appearance.

Injuries and murders were mentioned in the records as early as the 1530s, decrees against fighting and beating were issued in the 1540s,[52] and by the 1560s as the Spanish army and Inquisition turn up in its records, the chaos the soldiers brought to the floor reflected a greater chaos that had descended on Flanders. With the army came unruly soldiers and vagabonds and, in what was probably a futile gesture, all were forbidden to enter the exchange. Also with the Spanish came representatives of their Inquisition. In Chapter 1 we met their distant cousins of the next century, busily at work in Avignon keep-ing the faithful pure. Their habits had been inherited from practices honed by centuries of trial and error.

In the Low Countries of the 1560s many forces worked against the hos-pitable and the cosmopolitan. In that decade a document was drawn up by a member of a powerful local family of Spanish origin that sought to remedy the troubles in Antwerp, namely, to stop the spread of heresy and the accompanying image breaking. It gave a list of all the foreign merchants in the town, led by Thomas Gresham and his English colleagues. They were presumed to be Calvinists, the Germans, to be Lutheran, and the Spanish, Portuguese, and Italian, Catholic. What the list tells us—in passing, for this was not its intention—is that with the Inquisition present, the overwhelming majority of foreigners in the town were now from Catholic countries.[53] Accompanying it, a more sinister document named various local figures by their supposed religious sympathies and secret heresies.[54] As early as 1521 in Antwerp people were being branded, exiled, and dunked in the river for their supposed adherence to Lutheranism.[55] By the 1550s they were being burned alive for their beliefs. Mostly the heretic foreigners were banned, although in the 1580s English merchants were imprisoned by the Spanish authorities.[56] We can imagine precious little cosmopolitanism in a setting that had been poisoned by religious tensions and Spanish repression. At almost this exact moment a Dutch religious thinker, when meditating on the architecture of the Temple of Solomon, chose a design remarkably close to what could be seen at the Antwerp exchange: an open-air rectangle of a building with side walkways and an outer chamber where goods could be bought and sold. We can only try to guess what might have been in his mind, if he actually saw an analogy between the ancient worship that laid the foundations for Christian civilization and the bustle and danger of the exchange.[57] Or could he have fantasized that the exchange could be, someday, a place as peaceful as a temple.

For well over a century or more, the merchants and city authorities, until overwhelmed by the Spanish presence, struggled to instill a sense of order at *de beurs*. The first *beurs* had a clock on the premises as early as 1468, and all through the following centuries clocks at the exchange, like those of their French counterparts, were regularly maintained.[58] Indeed on a weekly basis the city magistrates issued rules and regulations to maintain order in the town, not simply at the exchange. By comparison to unruly children, dead horses, dogs and cats, and foreigners were only minimally regulated by the decrees issued by the town authorities. Only the inquisitors and their allies had taken a grim interest in outsiders. Indeed by one foreign account, written in 1599 and in French, after relative peace had returned to the town, "the strangers themselves have always been free by the *franchises* of the city . . . free [to go] about the town, the streets, the walls, the public and secret places."[59] They were not to stay in hostels if they were sick; and the sick and foreign beggars were discouraged altogether from staying in the town. Inexplicably, the records tell us that foreigners were not to buy butter.[60] Every effort was made to regulate what could and could not be sold in the bourse.

In the opening decades of the seventeenth century the Antwerp town records still contain ordinances against beatings, the use of knives, and the necessity of "den beursknecht," the servant of the exchange, to keep order. Yet at the same time in Amsterdam (in 1611) it was still necessary to announce "verboden om iemand te slaan," it is forbidden to hit anyone.[61] In 1650 the Antwerp *burgemeesters* required that they give permission to merchants before they could sell jewels, carpets, leather, paintings, and flowers in the bourse.[62] In the 1690s under the impact of war, once again all order broke down, and this was expressed by the authorities as anger that strangers were coming into the town effortlessly and enjoying the cabarets and hostelries.[63] By that decade, however, the glory days of Antwerp had since passed and its preeminence, thanks to the Spanish invasion and concomitant destruction, had passed to London and Amsterdam. Long before Addison and Steele waxed eloquent, mid-seventeenth-century Dutch poets like Vondel, Jeremias de Decker, and P. C. Hooft sang about the instruments of trade, "Papieren, wisselkanse, en munte, en beurskrakeel" to be seen in Amsterdam, where, as de Decker put it, "A churchman, then a Jew, a Turk and a Christian are gathered in a school of all languages, a market field of all wares, / A bourse, which maintains all the world's exchanges."[64]

It is little wonder that one of the first guides to operating on the floor of any exchange was written in Spanish in 1688 by a Jewish merchant and dramatist who knew the exchanges in both Amsterdam and Antwerp. It bore the title *Confusion de confusiones*. By that date, and by yet another account from around the same time and about Amsterdam, there is little evidence to suggest that the exchange there was actually dangerous.[65] The confusion to which Don Josseph (Peruso) de la Vega referred concerned the bafflement of buying and selling stock, the role of middlemen, the fluctuation of value, in other words the chaos of market life before anyone had thought to imagine an invisible hand. In the tract there is no mention of personal danger. Amsterdam could have been London, and risk had come to refer not to life and limb but to wealth, status, and livelihood. Perhaps a cosmopolitan stance in the world permits the bravado, sophistication, and type of courage that the ups and downs of commercial life require and encourage.

Yet commercial life offers no automatic access to the cosmopolitan. In Antwerp it was achieved only after a century or more of local governance that sought to impose order, and only after relative religious peace returned to the region. In London the royal authorities before 1689 thought nothing about taking a Quaker out of the exchange regardless of how useful his commerce might have been. Left unchecked and unregulated, or governed by authorities eager to persecute, as were the Spanish or the Anglican establishment, the exchanges need not have become cosmopolitan. Little about the life to be witnessed at the Antwerp exchange during the mid-sixteenth century would have called forth the glee of Addison and Steele, of Vondel or Voltaire. If the cosmopolitan means rising above the local and the parochial, then the parish needs first to be safe, well lit, policed, wellregulated, and run by reasonably tolerant people. Now early in the twenty-first century when we embrace the cosmopolitan rubric as the only cloak capable of enfolding ethnic diversity, we need to remember the struggle to impose civility over public commercial life, at least in northern and western Europe. However unwittingly, sometimes Voltaire could be glib.

The French Exchanges

The bourses I have examined in French cities were in some respects similar to those found in Protestant Europe: the omnipresent clock, the presence of guards or a concierge, a general hustle and bustle—at least as captured by the engraved scenes that survive. Most French exchanges consisted of an open plan, a square or rectangular building, often with multiple entrances, also indebted to the original Italian model.[66] In general, however, they did not have shops along their walls. And, in other ways, the French exchanges were profoundly different from what could be seen in either London or Antwerp. Those differences must go part of the way to explaining Voltaire's rapturous description of what he saw in London. In France the bourses belonged to the king's representatives in a municipality, and in many places their day-to-day running centered on royal agents of change. They were the creatures of the bourse who gave it a distinctive character and who rendered money, or species, into the central activity at its heart. More so than merchants or factors, they were meant to serve first the needs of the state, and then the public.[67] Although certain businesses, in particular, printing and publishing, flourished in the shadow of a French bourse, without the shops it was not a temple of consumption as was the case in London or Antwerp. Indeed, by contrast to London in particular, a French bourse was the model of order, regularity, discretion and even secrecy. There was also no major bourse in Paris, perhaps another factor in Voltaire's elegant, if glib account of what he saw in London.

"Bubbles" that burst, or crashes, were endemic in the development of early modern capitalism. Its history is littered with speculation that went wild on everything from tulips to specie.[68] In France, after the crash of the royal bank in 1720, brought about by the speculations in specie engineered by John Law, some thought was given to creating a central bourse. We know this only because an engraved plan of its open-air building, modeled on the existing exchanges, survives. Commissioned on 1 August 1720, the plan would have the Paris bourse be bordered by the rue de Grenelle and the rue des Deux Écus, and again, this idealized setting would have put shops on the second floor, well over one hundred of them.[69] Squarely, in the center of the plan, stood the "loges pour Mrs. Les officiers," the police who must enforce order. Policing the markets occurred in every national setting, but in France, given the crucial role of the official agents of change, their honesty had to be scrupulously enforced. Nothing came of the French plan. Instead, in 1724 an exchange, basically a large room, where nonmerchants as well as merchants could trade paper bills of exchange and cash in foreign currency, was installed in a gallery at the Hôtel de la Compagnie des Indes, and entered on rue Vivienne. It was opened for one hour at noon.[70] This is the same building that once housed part of what is now the old Bibliothèque nationale, generally entered from rue Richelieu.

Bills of exchange, wherever they were used, enabled the drawer to avoid having to transport specie, exchange currencies, and also to charge interest. Since currency fluctuated, the charging of interest in a Catholic country in that circumstance posed no moral difficulties. An exchange that carried an inherent risk permitted interest to be charged, whereas profit that entailed no risk smacked of usury.[71] In 1724 in the wake of the Law debacle, the crown sought to regularize the contracts of exchange by creating in Paris a single place for their execution, and it created sixty new *agents de change* who were supposed to be the sole brokers of such contracts. The exchange in Lyon, a free city, was never as tightly regulated although even there a broker or agents could charge a legally determined fee and presumably no more.[72]

By contrast to practices in England or the Low Countries, the French monarchy played a central role in large transactions that concerned just about any commodity. The office of *courtier de change*, or *agent de change*, was created in 1572 and its purpose had been to stop abuses and fraud largely in the sale of silk, linen, grain, even horses. In the 1590s the reforming king, Henri IV, established a set number of agents in all the principal trading cities of the kingdom and charged them with the task of dealing particularly, but not exclusively, with foreigners.[73] At that time Paris got eight agents and Marseille, four. In so doing, the king explicitly sought to imitate practices already in place in Lyon, Antwerp, Venice, and other places where interest, or the prices for goods being charged, was not to exceed what was permitted "par nos ordonnances." As subsequent edicts made clear the agents were to be servants of the king and were "never to traffic in merchandise in their own name, nor to charge commissions."[74] Instead they collected a small but set percentage on large transactions, at least that was the principle. They were to keep precise registers of all transactions, and the town officials—consuls—were to oversee those books. After 1638, at around the same time when the crown sought to check the practices of the agents, their office came to be inheritable.

By the mid-seventeenth century the honesty of the agents had become a matter of royal suspicion. In 1673 the agents who dealt with money and bills of exchange were separated from those who dealt with food, cloth, and substances of various kinds, and in most places that separation remained in place up to the Revolution in 1789. But after 1685, during the reign of Louis XIV, expensive wars required revenue, and reservations about the wily practices of the agents could not prevent the creation of more agents—who paid handsomely for an office that could be passed on in the family. The matter did not end there. Louis took away the offices almost as fast as he created them and then sold new offices for even more revenue. In the process the office itself became a financial matter, with a price to be paid for a guaranteed place in the king's bureaucracy, and the description of the office in turn laid almost complete emphasis on "change, banque, commerce et finances."[75] Handbooks of the period that advised foreign merchants on how to do business in France nevertheless praised the agents as a far safer way for friends, or even family members, to exchange funds, to use them as middlemen.[76] By 1714 at the height of royal bankruptcy, the agents were expected to pay the crown two sols for every livre transacted, and in Paris they were expected to attend Mass publicly, once a year as a corps. With the financial crisis of 1720 the agents were chastised for tumultuous assemblies that had occurred at the bourse, actually a street in Paris where the cafés were used for business. They were once again suppressed and new offices created.[77]

A major difference between France and Protestant Europe begins with the reality that there really was no bourse in Paris before the time of Napoleon. Instead until 1724, streets and zones—the area about rue Quinquampoix where could be found the Compagnies des Indes—did the work of the bourse. The city streets served in place of a central building that could be policed and organized. Finally in 1724, a room in a mansion near rue Richelieu stood in the place of the mighty edifice that Gresham had seen in the Low Countries and imitated. It was to be open for an hour a day, its entrance guarded by archers and a lieutenant general of the police; entry was to be restricted to those who had a pass (called *marques*), and, remarkably, in contrast to the rest of western Europe, women were forbidden entirely.[78] Protestants could not become agents of change, a rule that was reaffirmed in 1766. It was only in 1780 that a Protestant merchant in Marseille was allowed to join the chamber of commerce.[79] Transactions could not be interrupted, nor could prices be shouted out in a way that could invite haggling. And despite all the efforts of the crown to find out who owed what, or who possessed the most capital, the agents guarded their secrets jealously. Their clients had no intention of tipping off the state about the extent of their wealth.

The reform of 1724, and the room that became the legally protected Paris bourse, created new market conditions and permitted bills of exchange to be negotiated between buyers and sellers other than those who made the original contract. By the middle of the eighteenth century a lively market developed in third and fourth party buyers, in what was a form of speculation among essentially anonymous buyers and sellers. As bills of exchange could be negotiated among more and more distant strangers, an imaginary universe expands and takes on global dimensions. It is not accidental that anonymous books often used a globe on the title page or that bills of exchange could also be adorned with a comparable symbol. The globe symbolized that the user could be anyone in the world, perhaps even begin to imagine citizenship in such a spacious world.

While knowing something about the way bills of exchange could operate, we know very little about the actual administration of the Paris bourse. The records were lost in a nineteenth-century fire in the Hôtel de Ville. To get a sense of the life of a French exchange means leaving Paris. Before the sophistication of the multiple Parisian creditors of the eighteenth century, the bourses in French commercial cities to the south had taken on a cosmopolitan life of their own. The custom of having a place where merchants could meet and trade, or change currency, had spread into the south of France from the republics of Italy. Since the Middle Ages Lyon had been a free city and the entryway to southern France. Its wealth depended heavily upon the local production of silk, and in 1572 the crown recognized the importance of Lyonnaise commerce by establishing commissions or titles for the office of *courtier*, or agent of change.[80] In 1631 the consul in Lyon gave the merchants *un place de change* with a its own *corps de garde*. By 1637 an actually new building was in place; two years later it got a clock.[81] But unlike the neutral symbols of time, or the busts of kings found elsewhere, the bourse in Lyon installed a statue of the Virgin Mary.

Decades earlier Lyon had been a center of bitter contestation between Protestants and Catholics. If French Protestants made their way to the building they were meant to know that the power of the Catholic Church remained intact, at least in the temple of money, or *la loge du change*, as the Lyon bourse came to be known. When a chamber of commerce was finally established in 1703, all its members were also to be Catholic.[82]

Possibly coming out of the Italian, loggia, *la loge* carried with it the connotation of a place slightly private, a place where people live. One of the first descriptions in French of the changers and bankers who inhabited any bourse or *loge* (initially they were not supposed to be offices held by the same person) explained, "La première chose que doit observer un agent de banque est le secret."[83] In Lyon secrecy that "an agent of the bank must observe" did not imply the exclusivity found among the royal agents of change in Paris; the Lyonnais allowed all sorts of people to become *courtiers* of merchandise, or agents of banking and change who took 40 sols for every 3000 livres they negotiated.[84] The monarchy by contrast wanted to limit the number of agents of change.[85] The more traders, the better their secrecy, the less the crown could know about their assets.

But the freedom of the Lyonnais and of their bourse never sat well with the crown. Likewise by the 1740s the prosperity of the town had drastically diminished. It also needed a new exchange, and at the considerable expense of well over 120,000 livres, it was built.[86] The construction proved to be the last truly independent act undertaken on behalf of the bourse. In 1750 the king agreed to buy the building and to use its facade to announce triumphantly his dubious achievements during the War of Austrian Succession.[87] The statue of the Virgin remained in place in the new building, whose contents included many tables, suggesting that it was largely a place for transactions that involved specie and the exchange of money, as well as the drafting of contracts for the sale of goods. After 1750 it could have been closed at any time. Its cosmopolitanism, such as it was, stood represented by white statues of all the continents placed on the adjacent street.[88] Yet the royal reach could be limited. While the exchange in Lyon had become royal property, further to the south, at Marseille, the crown's control was a contested matter.

On the coast of the Mediterranean, Marseille looked out on what had once been the heart of the commercial West. Ships, from the Levant, from North Africa, and from Italy, lined its harbor. Citizens of the city sought and received permission to live abroad. The chamber of commerce created by Louis XIV authorized several hundred men in any decade to head out to the Moslem world, to seek their fortunes or act as agents for the crown in Alexandria or Tripoli or Cairo.[89] The chamber has been credited with promoting the extraordinary prosperity the city enjoyed in the late seventeenth century, one that would not survive the rise of the North Atlantic trade during the eighteenth. In the 1660s the magistrates authorized the establishment of a bourse to be located in the vestibule of the Hôtel de Ville.[90] There it remained until 1943 when the Nazis destroyed it as part of an effort to thwart an expected Allied invasion.

Nearly a decade before Voltaire put pen to paper about the wonders of the London exchange, an anonymous observer of the Marseille exchange waxed in rapture, "Our loge is a room where strangers can barely be distinguished from our representatives . . . our factors and couriers are our ambassadors, and they negotiate affairs, conclude treaties and maintain good relations within the rich society of men." In language so reminiscent of what Voltaire would write in 1733 that we can only wonder if he had read the account, the witness went on to explain the pleasure of seeing a dispute settled between an Egyptian and an Italian, of watching a negotiation between a merchant and officers of an Ottoman port, and simply of being delighted at the spectacle of such a large assembly of traders who had placed themselves in different quarters of the building. Almost breathlessly the Marseille witness told of entering through a large door and coming upon teams of Swiss, Germans, Genevans, Languedocians, French merchants from the Levant, Persians, Armenians, and Spanish; in short, he said, it became possible to imagine oneself as being from any nation. Then, less charitably, our visitor betrayed assumptions that lurked beneath the cosmopolitan surface: he remarked on elbowing crowds "of Jews or usurers."[91]

The Jews were the object of intermittent hostility in part because of the advantages of familiarity that they enjoyed in the Mediterranean trade. In the French case Jews who could speak Turkish or Arabic had a monopoly on negotiations between them and local traders.[92] The chamber of commerce was constantly being asked to assist merchants forced to compete with "the commerce of the prodigious Jews in the L'Echelle d'Alep," and it acknowledged "the very great jealousy against them."[93] In 1723 Marseille merchants bitterly appealed to the chamber of commerce to stop the French consul in the Levant from giving protection to the Jews in the region. It worked against French interests, they asserted, and noted that the English do not give such protections.

At this time Jews and other minorities, like the Armenians and Greeks, acted as brokers between European merchants and the Ottomans, and all could be seen from time to time in Marseille itself. The rivalries and tensions easily came to the surface; sometimes the authorities reflected them. In 1713 the king's representative wanted all the "hoteliers and cabaretiers" who lodged foreigners to come to the Hôtel de Ville, and report on their names, qualities, and place of origin.[94] The absolutist state watched closely the ebb and flow of commercial life, a check on its freedom that the lionizers of bourse life either did not know or chose to forget. Instead they spoke of how "the lodge is the temple where the god of money reassembles all of Marseille . . . where contracts both licit and illicit are brokered . . . credit is the entryway to the temple."[95]

Credit lay at the heart of the Marseille exchange, and its royal agents held the purse strings. An edict of 1709 had even permitted the *courtiers de change* in the city to act as bankers, but to do so with notes of credit not necessarily backed by specie in a vault somewhere or their personal wealth.[96] It is little wonder that the Marseille Chamber of Commerce, and the royal authorities, watched them with increasing concern. They were so worried about the kind of dealings that occurred in Marseille that at the instigation of the chamber the crown promulgated a national decree in 1730 that forbade bankrupts to enter the Marseille exchange until they had settled with their creditors.[97] Such decrees, probably in large measure futile, suggest a level of distrust, not only of the merchants but of the agents who advanced credit. It appears to have had little effect—so still the authorities watched. Beneath the surface of the Marseille bourse, like every exchange in Europe, lay a complex system of policing. In Marseille in the 1760s the Hôtel de Ville was protected by eight guards at night and sixteen during the day, as well as a captain, three brigadiers, a lieutenant, and a sergeant. The parlement for the region wished to secure "public tranquillity" against "seditious . . . and dissembling" people who lurked at the bourse and the surrounding cafés.[98] Concierges handed out tickets to merchants as they entered, presumably for the purpose of keeping out known bankrupts who were prohibited from doing business on the floor of any French exchange.

Hours when the exchange was open were also severely restricted, as was commonplace, but by mid-century opposition surfaced. A group of Marseille traders said that restricting the hours "is the arrangement for families and the necessity of sending the children *aux colleges* at a good hour. This reason would be without doubt invincible in a university but [not] in a city of commerce. [Maintaining the hours is puerile]." The critics described themselves as being "in favor of liberty . . . the welfare of all men, and the principal supporting commerce."[99] Wrapping themselves in language with an enlightened ring to it, some merchants had clearly tired of the restrictions that all the authorities—the magistrates, the parlement in Aix, the royal intendant—apparently had no interest in lifting. The chamber of commerce reacted angrily to the anonymous suggestion, and pointed out that the magistrates of the city are "the incontestable masters" over the exchange. Its transactions had to be carefully policed, notaries had to witness every negotiation, the agents of change had to bring notes of security before the police, every effort had to be made to prevent forgeries done by bankrupts.[100] At a time of crisis, such as occurred during a spectacular bankruptcy—the one that began with a rich merchant and a royal agent of change in 1774—the police had the power to suspend trading.[101]

Clearly, discontent had permeated the temple of money. In the 1760s other documents tell us that each day "over 600 heads of family" used the bourse, and that the floorboards were threatening to give way.[102] The parlement wrote to the authorities to demand that they prevent agitation at the bourse and the surrounding cafés.[103] Over ninety merchants petitioned for a new building. Still others opposed the move, probably because it entailed special taxes.[104] But the atmosphere of worry and complaint had deeper roots than the condition of the bourse's floorboards. Representatives of other exchanges in France wrote as early as 1759 to warn the officials in Marseille that bankrupts, "the disgraceful of commerce," have deeply distressed the commerce of France.[105]

Beginning in 1772, and reaching its nadir in Marseille in 1774, a real economic crisis gripped France. The culmination of the preceding Atlantic boom, the bust manifested itself at the foreign exchanges and as a credit crisis.[106] By 1773 there is a general recognition that little was being done anywhere to stop local bankrupts from reaching the floor of the bourse, and worse still, foreigners who were bankrupt, it was argued, had to be stopped and forced to register with the justice of the peace.[107] What is being suggested, had it been initiated, would have entailed angry denunciations on the floor of the exchange—once a bankrupt could be identified. Cities from around the country asked that the bourse officials everywhere be on the lookout.[108] Perhaps Voltaire had been right when he said that the only infidels in such a temple would be the bankrupt. If the authorities followed their own suggestions then, in bourse after bourse up and down the country, by the early 1770s men in dire economic straits were being angrily identified and hauled before the magistrates for the humiliation of being registered. Of course, the reasoning behind such pronouncements was deeply flawed, as a few commentators recognized. The logic of the market molded creditors around the interests of their bankrupt debtors. It was far better to have them in sight and to cut a best possible deal, rather than to walk away with nothing.

But the authorities in Marseille, like so many commentators in England, saw bankruptcy in moral terms and railed against those who might, in other circumstances, be seen as unlucky, rather than villainous.[109] They also wanted to impose a collective rather than simply an individual responsibility on men who were seen as willfully bad credit risks. None of these measures, at least in Marseille, proved to be sufficient. In 1773–74 cosmopolitanism, which in the past had operated to the benefit of Christians, possibly in some cases only to the advantage of Catholics, gave way first to an inhospitable suspicion and then to panic. No one was immune to the mistrust.

Up until 1774 the problems presented by the absence of credit and capital might be blamed on bankrupt merchants. But in May of that year one of the *courtiers de change*, a royal official, went under, and in his wake within five months over 150 merchants (out of about 600) also defaulted. These royal officials, a creation of Louis XIV, and the credit they dispensed had dominated the floor of the Marseille exchange.[110] No shops or hawkers interfered with their authority. Only the notaries stood in the way of a secret deal; they were expected to register it and presumably to know something about all the parties and their creditworthiness.[111] Since 1709 the courtiers had acted as bankers as well as the buyers and sellers of merchandise, and apparently with abandon they had extended credit and collected interest, to the point where a bankruptcy by one of their major creditors spelled doom.[112] Marseille also had a particular problem in that trade to the Levant took so long to complete that wealth embedded in a ship and its cargo could be uncollectible and unusable for a year or more. There was also a shortage of specie in the city, but the root of Marseille's problem lay with courtiers who had wildly overextended lines of credit to merchants.[113]

Our concern with the crisis of 1774 centers on the impact it had on the civility and customs of the bourse. At the height of the crisis a prominent merchant and former city official marched on to the floor of the exchange and in full drama denounced the courtiers and demanded their suppression.[114] Others argued that self-interest had become a vice: "The mobs in our stock exchange fight and destroy each other out of their individual interests and their prejudices." "Capitalists" need a motive for entering such a dangerous market, an important commentator argued, that only higher interest rates will appeal. He further noted the danger that if these ruinous practices continue, "a much greater part of our commerce will pass into the hands of foreigners," and France would pay a heavy burden if the situation in Marseille was not reversed.[115] Capitalists, traders, commerce, and courtiers were all parties to the edict of 1709, and now, it was claimed, the edict no longer worked to the benefit of either Marseille or France.

Some conclusions about the limits of cosmopolitanism in the face of massive bankruptcy present themselves, at least in the form of questions. When the stock exchanges displayed signs of a cosmopolitan openness, how dependent was that spirit on the limitless possibility of profit and prosperity? The breakdown of civility in Marseille points to a deep interconnection between these two impulses, the one for gain, the other for the civility and cosmopolitan interaction that eased deal making and the passage to wealth. Perhaps only the first made the second possible. Or could it be the case that as long as government-sponsored monopolists controlled a critical part of the market, and hence the availability of money or credit, the stability of its mores and customs would always remain fragile?

The courtiers were widely detested for their power and their imagined irresponsibility. Again, we see a linkage between sustaining a cosmopolitan ethos and a broadening of an imagined freedom in the market. Perhaps the fit between a cosmopolitan market and its preservation depended more heavily than we have recognized before this examination of Marseille on a belief that no single body, sanctioned by the state, could manipulate the market and get away with it legally. Certainly the anger at the courtiers became so intense that within a year the state had to suppress and reorganize the corps.

Somewhat reformed, the corps of Marseille courtiers survived right up to the Revolution in 1789. Perhaps they can be seen as forward-looking, attempting to introduce banks as credit lenders who actually owned part of a commodity's value. But it had been the French state that ultimately benefited from the excessive loans. Its chronic indebtedness made the courtiers key players who in effect collected taxes on all lending, as well as buying and selling, transactions. Where the king could own the exchange as was the case in Lyon, or where its agents could bring it profits at the expense of the overall health of the market, we see the possibility for disasters such as occurred in Marseille in 1774. At its root the crisis of 1774 had been possible because of the secrecy surrounding the actions of the courtiers. There was no place for merchants to discover who was in fact overextended. The open and cosmopolitan ambiance of the exchange masked a deeper reality. Mercantile elites did not want anyone knowing—especially not the tax-hungry state—how much they were worth, or how deeply in debt they had fallen.[116] Private reputation—not the reality of their situation—mattered above all else, certainly above the health of the public's interest. When the economic reality of an exchange turned grim, or when reputations were shattered for all to see, then exchanges within the absolutist state were places where denunciation and moralizing displaced a cosmopolitan peacefulness.

All early modern exchanges displayed moments of incivility and even danger. But by the 1770s exchanges throughout Europe controlled by local officials, and not by the king's representatives, worked more openly and more peacefully. The collapse in Marseille in 1774 set off a bell, clanging in the night, that the days where the king's corps controlled access to lending and borrowing were numbered. The French Revolution abolished the courtiers, and early in the nineteenth century Paris acquired a bourse modeled on what existed in the major cities of its northern neighbors. Merchants, factors and brokers now competed with no one enjoying the special protection of an inheritable, state guaranteed office. One of the divisions that had plagued the exchange floor in the old order gave way, and we may postulate that the French bourse had become more, rather than less, hospitable to all comers. It continued to be heavily regulated by the state well into the 1980s, and in 2003 a body independent of the state assumed regulatory authority over transactions at the Bourse. Strong national states and free, cosmopolitan markets only very gradually became inherently compatible.

Chapter 4

Secrecy and the Paradox at the Heart of Modernity (the Masonic Moment)

If the bourse during the eighteenth century gave expression to the mundane affairs of preoccupied merchants and traders, then the major literary and philosophical movement of the century sought to make them more thoughtful, to call them to higher, less self-interested ideals. The Enlightenment had origins in the religious and political discontents of the later seventeenth century. The new science also played a role in creating this new cultural agenda. By the 1680s enlightened critiques of authority or prejudice and superstition began in books, but quickly became a phenomenon associated with social life, with groups such as the cosmopolites we met in Chapter 1. Typically they coalesced around learned projects: scientific experimentation, the editing of journals, self-improvement defined as education through reading and discussion. The ensuing movement to enlighten initiated a new basis for human interaction, a search for tolerant interchanges across the cultures and religions of Euro-American society.

The search for toleration and self-education took myriad social forms, none of them more exotic and distinctive to the age than the new masonic lodges. In their midst, first in Britain, then by the 1720s on the Continent, could be found men, eventually women, who can only be described as unexpected. In a Paris lodge a Negro trumpeter in the king's guard mixed with a champagne merchant from the provinces; in London French Huguenot refugees met in lodges with minor government officials.[1] A long-time resident of Algeria, back home in London and self-identified as a freemason, praised Islam for its toleration and took Christians to task for their ignorance.[2]

The struggle for more cosmopolitan forms of social life entailed a repudiation of the privileges and practices of closed elites, in particular the clergy and, to a lesser extent, the old aristocracy. The lodges grew out of the early modern guilds of stonemasons who gradually were subsumed under the authority of the genteel, but mostly middling men admitted out of necessity for their ability to pay much needed dues. The free and accepted masons, as the newcomers called themselves, created new spaces where a different kind of social mixing became possible, more cerebral and having less and less to do with craft or work.[3] At every turn freemasons proclaimed themselves to be enlightened. They said that anyone would be welcome in a lodge—except a Jesuit.[4] Paradoxically they also embraced secrecy and discretion.

On the periphery of Europe where elite power often went unchecked—in Russia, eastern Prussia, or Ireland—cosmopolitan enlightenment struggled. Assisted by spies, the authorities of church and state everywhere watched, and as a result in such places robust civil society either faltered or took on increasingly more secretive practices. In Russia even the tsarina herself, Catherine the Great, used her literary skills to write plays attacking the freemasons, the most overtly Western and imported of the new social forms. These were widely read and performed, and while anonymous, known to be by Her Majesty.[5] Earlier, in Western Europe, during the conflict between the Protestant Reformation and the Counter-Reformation, secrecy had offered an opportunity for plotting or protection from persecution. After 1700 the religious hostilities became largely static, and secrecy took on new uses, generally, but not always—if we read and believe the spy reports—benign.

In so many places civil society embraced a protective, even playful, occasionally bizarre, layer of secrecy. The masonic form became the most famous: secret passwords, gestures, rituals and signs. But within the century, by the 1790s in places like Ireland, secrecy, often directly imitative of masonic practices, also became an essential part of political organization. Both playful and sinister forms of the secretive in social relations, with their promises and contradictions, and ranging from the 1730s to the 1790s, concern us now. In passing, we will also examine the mystical opportunities that the veil of secrecy permitted as French freemasons of the 1780s—among others—turned to the tradition of the magical arts in their search for a universal wisdom. It was as if alchemy had come back, not as a set of practices, but as a rather more cerebral mantra for change.

Given the power of the old elites nurtured by land and rural deference, cities with their anonymity—the larger the better—became the natural homes for new practices and mores. Enlightened circles preferred the coffeehouse over the confraternity, the salon as a celebratory site over the saints' days. The complexities and challenges of cosmopolitanism emerged most dramatically and paradoxically in the most fashionable form of clubbing, the new masonic lodges. Almost all forms of secretive political association in the modern world also first used the template provided by the lodges. Their habits of secrecy, once of guild origin, now imitative of court culture, at first created nothing more sinister than mystery and aura. Yet they offered a new urbane form of social grouping that could be reoriented toward political goals at variance with the interests of established authority. And, of course, by the 1730s printed "exposures" of masonic passwords, rituals, and codes had become commonplace. By the 1780s the freemasons themselves printed almanacs and handbooks that offered engravings of how to perform ceremonies, complete with the "secret" password of the year.

When enlightened clubbing among relative strangers became the fashion, secrecy also acted as an umbrella. The paradox of educated professional men, and some women, exiting the privacy of their homes to feast and to ritualize under the mantle of secrecy, best understood as exclusivity and discretion, seems at this distance almost bizarre. Why, just as the cosmopolitan became fashionable, so too did the rush to create rule-bound secret societies and exclusionary social venues? Men donned aprons and jewels, decorated chambers with ermine, installed "altars" with "tabernacles." They broke bread in an upstart organization that claimed a lineage back to the time of Solomon and his master mason, Hiram. Most important, the new masonic lodges repeatedly said that they wanted in their assemblies "brothers of talent and orators of merit."[6] Throughout the century masonic literature, much of it anonymous, would argue that symbols and mysteries, more than anything else, "produce in the heart and spirit of the individual sentiments that make them enjoy their work and duties," and all more readily enhance a feeling of equality among brothers.[7] Precisely because the new ideal of egalitarian cosmopolitanism posed so many challenges, internally to the older ingrained habits of clan and cult and externally from the suspicious authorities, the claim to secrecy created a "free" zone where a group of relative strangers tested new limits and permissions. They could imagine themselves as citizens of the world, and masonic almanacs and pocket companions routinely gave lists of every urban lodge in Europe (and their meeting times). Sometimes lodges in the Americas and foreign colonies were also listed.[8]

Two quite different places will provide the prime examples of the testing, as well as the tensions, within cosmopolitan fraternizing: Bordeaux and the much larger city of Dublin. In the first, French masonic lodges struggled throughout the eighteenth century with the implications of their commitment to cosmopolitanism, with the issue of whom they should admit or reject. In the second, during the 1790s, Irish reformers seized upon the masonic ideal as the model to be imitated by the new secret political societies they established. Their goals became the reconciling of religious differences between Protestants and Catholics, who once united in secrecy, would, it was believed, fight for profound change. Both French brothers and Irish reformers claimed that secrecy and discretion, accompanied by rules for behavior, focused the mind and fostered the bonds of society.[9] None saw secrecy as sinister—although we, in modern democratic societies, might. Ironically, the aspirations of most secret societies throughout the eighteenth century should be seen as nascently—if fitfully—democratic. In the Irish case, after the failed rebellion of 1798, the secrecy turned inward and became a way of life, the cornerstone for radical Catholic, and then Protestant groups, to be seen in the shadows of Northern Ireland to this day.

Secrecy and the Eighteenth-Century Lodges

Throughout the eighteenth-century freemasonry was—as it is now—a supposedly secret society. Yet paradoxically the lodges flourished in the eighteenth century among men—and women—who defined themselves as enlightened and hence decidedly open to people of different religions or professions. In any lodge people could be found who had no other reason for being present other than an interest in ceremony and the ideals taught by the masonic creed. In Bordeaux during the 1730s a Captain Patrick Dixon from Dublin fraternized with James Bradshaw, a merchant in the town, and they were joined by a local curate. All would have been familiar with the masonic *Constitutions*, first published in 1723 in London. It proclaimed religious toleration, brothers "meeting upon the level," rising in masonic wisdom because of merit, not blood or birth. Dozens of editions appeared in every European language, and strangers sought initiation who had little in common save their attraction to sociability in its masonic form. They sought personal improvement, and eagerly they practiced skills like voting in elections or giving formal orations before their brothers. They learned social behavior that was meant to be disciplined and refined, and they could be fined for breaches in conduct, both inside and away from the lodge.

In England and Scotland by 1700 the lodges evolved out of guilds where once only working stonemasons socialized and protected their craft from the unskilled or the uninitiated. Slowly they mutated into clubs for literate men attracted by the lure of the ceremonies, rituals, and an imagined history associated with the medieval guilds. Masonry, it was said, went back to the Temple of Solomon. Early in the eighteenth century in London the evolution was well underway. When the then aged and great architect Christopher Wren took the title of grand master, he probably met with friends, as well as master masons who worked with him.[10] Within a decade lodges began to spread out to the British provinces, and then in the 1720s to Ireland and Continental Europe, to Rotterdam, Paris, and soon Bordeaux, and by the 1730s to America. At the same time brothers, current or former, published "exposures" that explained the rituals to the uninitiated, or "the profane," as nonmasons were called by the initiated. By 1750, when there may have been about 50,000 freemasons in Europe, not much about the lodge practices remained secret. Yet brothers continued to value their "secrets" in the form of constantly changing passwords, new rituals and degree ceremonies, decorations, and dress.

The new public of the eighteenth century frequently met in private. That dichotomy remains central to much of modern social experience. The paradox at the heart of early modernity lay in its creation of a new public sphere that simultaneously championed the private, the interior, and the exclusive. The same public that read novels silently in the comfort of home also found "secret" lodges fashionable, even alluring. They were more typical of the age than might at first be assumed. The open-doored coffeehouses, pubs, or, in France, the cabarets stood as major exceptions to social gatherings that were more commonly semiprivate, even exclusive and sometimes bounded by secrecy.

The literary and philosophical societies required formal applications for membership and were confined to those so admitted. The royal academies for science—even the independent Royal Society in London and the Haarlemse Maatschappij der Wetenschappen in the Dutch Republic—were highly exclusive as to who could belong and attend. In London at midcentury coffeehouses existed where special slang was employed and largely understood only by their denizens.[11] Parisian salons, like the royal academies, were notoriously closed. Scientific lectures were the most open form of the new sociability, and, for as little as six pence or as much as two guineas, the public could attend one, or a course of lectures. The cosmopolitan emerged as an enlightened ideal protected by politeness, discretion, privacy, formality, dues, even secrecy. Eighteenth-century English literature presents multiple examples of characters obsessed with maintaining their privacy.[12] The popularity of such novels suggests that some of their readers may have found lodge membership a congenial escape from the tensions between the need for privacy and the demands of society.

When we consider masonic secrecy it might be tempting to see it as simply a medieval holdover from the original guild structure inherited by the lodges—where by 1720 nary a stonemason could be found. That explanation is too easy, and it certainly does not address the further mutation that masonic secrecy took in the 1780s and 1790s. Then groups like the radical Illuminati in Germany and the United Irishmen in Dublin self-consciously embraced secrecy in imitation of masonic forms, but they did so with decidedly political agendas. The linkage between the new socializing and secrecy may have also been somewhat overdetermined. Whenever the French authorities arrested booksellers for trading in the heretical and pornographic invariably they hauled in the odd masonic pamphlet. Within the precincts of the absolutist state, secrecy, when not part of the apparatus of the state, simply looked suspect.[13] Yet it made sense to practice forms of it, to be safe rather than sorry.

To contemporaries versions of extreme privacy seemed hardly out of the ordinary. Discretion and secrecy lay at the nub of court culture; there its purposes were obvious. Intrigue and jockeying for place behind closed doors made the courts all the more interesting. The forging of state policies required secrecy, then and now. While the enlightened had relations with various of the European courts, for the most part philosophes, freethinkers, journalists, and natural philosophers—however much they jockeyed for place—had their own decidedly nonnoble haunts. Yet in those venues—particularly in the places where antireligious or pornographic literature came into the world— secrecy was desired, even needed. A few months in the Bastille for writing or selling bad books would have convinced all in the trade of the perfect sense of secrecy.

What the daily practice of secrecy entailed we can never know for sure. According to masonic lore, brothers were to keep the identities of one another private, always to meet behind closed doors, regularly to invent new passwords and eventually rituals. Freemasons self-consciously defended secrecy as permitting freedom of expression and the fostering of brotherhood. Late in the eighteenth century Irish brothers, who saw in masonry a model for other types of overtly political organization, believed that secrecy nurtured and enthralled the senses, impacting particularly on sensibility and imagination. The radical William Drennan founded an entire political movement, as we shall see, based on the form of the lodge, and its power nearly undid British rule in Ireland, leaving a powerful legacy of secrecy in the service of rebellion. When in the next and final chapter we look at the international republican conversation that emerged in the Atlantic world in the 1770s we need to remember that while most of its participants were not freemasons, all understood the importance of discretion, if not secrecy.

Arguably, in the struggle to expand membership, secrecy also made cosmopolitanism easier. The daring and the bold found cover. For women to organize themselves as officers of a masonic lodge, for Jews to seek out fraternity with Christians, may have been easier because these gestures occurred almost entirely in a new public that was intensely private. What is remarkable about the private and discreet format of the lodges concerns how many improbable people were drawn to them, were eager to try their hand at a form of sociability imported from Britain, rule bound and, not least, costly. Masonic membership was never to be taken lightly. Without exception, lodges saw it as their right to police behavior, to outlaw licentiousness, drunkenness, and what was sometimes called, opaquely, blasphemy. Membership could work in a life as an alternative form of religiosity, and perhaps that is why by the 1790s reformers caught in dangerous situations, faced with official repression, were drawn to lodges, or to groups that imitated their structures.[14]

If we are to understand better how secrecy, or an extreme form of privacy, worked in the heart of early modernity, we need to examine at least one lodge in some detail. Help in understanding the vogue of secrecy comes from masonic archives not seen since 1940. With their aid I want to meditate on the multiple meanings and uses to which masonic secrecy could be put. In the process I want to complicate our understanding of the public sphere and early modernity, and the role of secrecy within both.

The Bordeaux Lodge

"Not seen since 1940" is not simply a tease. In 2002 I spent some weeks at the library of the Grand Orient of France, at 16 rue Cadet in Paris. There can now be found 750 boxes of French masonic archives recently returned from Moscow. Since 1945 they had been held in a secret archive. The Soviets tried to use these documents, and others, to barter with the Germans for the return of the Russian property that had been stolen by the retreating German army.[15] This story is poignant and germane to the issue of secrecy and modernity. On 14 June, 1940, the same day that the Nazis entered Paris, they burst into the building at rue Cadet and eventually took all its papers and archives. In short order similar confiscations occurred in Lille, La Rochelle, and Bordeaux, among various sites throughout the country. They believed that at the heart of the modern world and its corruption lay a vast Jewish-masonic conspiracy. In Berlin an institute was set up to search the records stolen from synagogues, masonic lodges, and liberal political parties in the Netherlands, Belgium, and France. The purpose of Nazi research was to find the starting point for the conspiracy that they said had brought about the

French Revolution and led to the decadent corruption of the 1920s and 1930s. We doubt that the Nazis had made much progress in their research when in May 1945 the Red Army came upon a depository that the Gestapo had hurriedly rushed from Berlin and hidden in a chateau in Silesia. It contained Jewish and masonic archives. In total, and from various locations, 140 tons of French documents—of which the 750 masonic boxes are a small portion—were seized and transported back to Moscow. The masonic documents undertook this secret journey as bartering chips or, just as probable, as part of the ever-seeing totalitarian state's desire to possess secrets for their own sake. Although no one knew that the Russians had them, the masonic archives were preserved in perfect condition. Their location only surfaced in 1992, and late in December 2000, under the specter of huge debts, the Russians began to return the archives to their rightful owners.

These archives, and their perambulation through Europe, have a lot to tell us. Throughout the twentieth century fascist political forces believed that the paradox at the heart of modernity, namely the secrecy associated with masonic fraternizing, the secret passwords, rituals, and signs, told the whole truth: the secrecy must have been about a cover-up of a hidden agenda to seize power while pretending to be ushering in an egalitarian transparency and democratic institutions. As we are about to see, secrecy did provide a certain safety throughout the eighteenth century, but the goals pursued under its mantle would have startled an earnest, unbiased inquirer, had such a creature existed at the Berlin institute founded by the Nazis. Secrecy worked where repression, aided by state spies, occurred on a daily basis. Unwittingly, by taking up the habits of secrecy, eighteenth-century advocates of the cosmopolitan gave hostages to the future enemies of democracy, many of whom would in turn use secrecy to their own advantage.

We can distance ourselves from the paranoid fantasies of the extreme right without for a second imagining that secrecy and exclusivity are unproblematic. To examine masonic secrecy as lived in the eighteenth century let us focus first on a rare document from what I shall call the Moscow collection. It is an extract made in the early nineteenth century from the minutes of the entire eighteenth century that then existed for the Loge Anglaise, founded in Bordeaux in 1732.[16] The original records have disappeared, but the summary made in 1817 has all the marks of authenticity in that so many of the entries are just what you would expect from any lodge.[17] What is very hard to find for any lodge are complete records for the entire century.

The Loge Anglaise believed itself to be the oldest properly constituted French lodge, and that claim is still probably true. The 1817 document was made for a new master and it summarized the major events or actions taken by the lodge, sometimes month by month from 1732 right through the French Revolution, and up to the year it was written. Aside from Paris, where masonry was imported by both Jacobite exiles and Whig ambassadors from Britain, Bordeaux was the most important city for masonic contact between Britain and France in the first half of the eighteenth century. The wine trade fostered those links, and the names recorded by the French-speaking lodge were alternatively French and English, Patrick Gordon, Wm. Barreyre, M. Boucher, and so on.

Most of the routine activities of the lodge entailed the admission of new members and the election of new officers. Sometimes such admission required discretion, as when on 25 September 1745 the lodge admitted one "Father Duquesnoy religieux célestin." The admission occurred just a few years after the 1738 papal condemnation of freemasonry. Ignoring the ban, a number of clergymen joined this lodge and many others, and discretion undoubtedly made their lives easier. Officially (as we saw in Avignon), the Catholic Church remained hostile to the freemasons and condemned membership as a violation of church decrees. With its dedication to absolutism in church and state the Roman church saw the lodges as alternative forms of religion. It also objected to the fact that lodges held elections so frequently. Clearly, some French clergymen simply followed their own conscience and basked in the conviviality the lodges provided.

As the Bordeaux records tell us, the clergy could also be willful brothers and a source of grief within a lodge. For example, the curé of Rions "was condemned . . . for his extraordinary indiscretion . . . to have led women into the lodge . . . and for having said that he would voluntarily pay . . . 3 frs for making it possible for them to see the lodge."[18] The curate faced a three-month suspension. Whatever the priest's motives and his relationships with women, the issue of women within freemasonry, as we shall shortly see, would not be easily resolved. Aside from women, other, far more powerful forces were also watching the lodge. In August 1742 the lodge had been instructed by the local intendant of Guienne to close itself down by order of the king. Punishment would ensue if the order were to be disobeyed. The lodge's ruffled response also appears in the minutes: "Given the implication of this order, the lodge decided to no longer assemble in the same place."[19] Clearly the authorities were watching the lodge, but in a cat-and-mouse kind of way. In this situation too much secrecy could be just as dangerous as too little. The lodge had to be sure that nothing threatening to the state or church occurred at its meetings or could be imagined as occurring. The repressive moment of 1742 coincided with the chief minister of state, Cardinal Fleury, and his Counter-Reformation stance. He was dead the following year. His intensely anti-British foreign policy would have made any lodge, but especially one full of English merchants mixing with French subjects, highly suspect. Certainly the freemasons did not much care for Fleury, and they penned many songs and diatribes aimed against him.[20] But other forms of subversive behavior, that Fleury probably never imagined, lurked under the mantle of Bordeaux freemasonry.

Subversion surfaced early in the life of *bordelaise* freemasonry, indeed earlier than in the life of any other European site, as far as we now know. A brother announced that women were holding their own lodge meetings in the town, "des Soeurs de l'Adoption." This would not do, the lodge decided, and in its wisdom decided to prevent them. Until this record came to light, the earliest known European women's lodge had been held in The Hague in 1751. There actors and actresses of the Comédie-Française had joined with local Dutch gentlemen to create a mixed lodge welcomed by the other, male lodges.[21] Officers could be both men and women, and as the 1751 record was written in French, the gendered nouns made the point: "Le Maitre" and "la Maitresse," and so on. The Dutch grand lodge approved of what was known as lodges of adoption, namely the creation of masonic social spaces into which women had to be adopted as they were not naturally born to inhabit them. In Bordeaux, by contrast, the issue of women's membership became instantly contentious.[22] Clearly some brothers, perhaps led by the local priest, thought that mixed lodges were a good idea; a majority disagreed. Thus began a controversy about the public role of women in civil society that continued until well into twentieth century.

Lodges for women signal an important social moment in the history of gender relations. These, like their male counterparts, were not simply social clubs. Voting in elections, dues collection, orations, officerships were an inherent and formal part of the public life of any lodge. By the 1740s in Western Europe women wanted to do such governing-like things, and some men approved, while others vehemently disliked public roles for women and the independence that went with them. Bear in mind that the freedom of women in public remained a fraught issue in the West until well into the nineteenth century. It was only then in Britain that the need even for public lavatories for women "was generally recognized."[23] Late in the eighteenth century women's lodges became all the rage in France, and while both men and women had voting rights, at least one lodge demanded that women could not meet without men being present and that pregnant women not be allowed to attend.[24]

Once again, auguring the future, the subversion of traditional social mores within the life of the lodges did not stop with women. Cosmopolitanism possessed an inexorable logic. Bordeaux held a thriving and reasonably integrated Jewish community of slightly less than 2,500 people out of population of about 50,000. In 1746 within a few months of the rancor about women being freemasons, the lodge faced the prospect of admitting Jews, "a proposition that is totally rejected." In the same year came a proposal to admit three "musicians of the theater" (*toneurs de instrument a la comedie*), and again opposition seems to have prevailed. Masonic cosmopolitanism in Bordeaux had its limits, and secrecy masked the limitations, as much as it permitted innovation.

The framework of secrecy also worked to shield from the eyes of the profane the enormous tensions presented by the notion of a voluntary association claiming, as did the lodges, that men can meet as equals and that rising by degree was a privilege based solely upon merit and wisdom. In contrast to the ideals of equality and merit, the lodge in Bordeaux—like so many voluntary associations throughout the history of modernity—kept wanting to limit its membership to men, or Christians, or simply the respectable, a category to which theater people did not belong at the time. Simultaneously, pressures were coming from every direction, from literate men and women who saw themselves as worthy of membership and capable of respecting masonic ideals, from local Jewish merchants who wanted to join with their French and English counterparts. Cosmopolitanism advanced slowly, and every step of the way provoked contention, in some places a willful desire to exclude.

Three years after the first skirmish about admitting Jews, one Cappadoce, as a Jew, turned up from Amsterdam in 1747 (again in 1749), saying that he had been admitted a freemason there.[25] Note that the Bordeaux lodge had discovered a few years earlier that its master was actually a Jew.[26] Clearly some European Jews had decided to take the possibility of cosmopolitan behavior seriously. Not only did the Bordeaux lodge take offense at the religion of its former master, it would also not admit Cappadoce. It refused to recognize him as *un frère*. He would not take "no" for an answer, and in two years asked again to be admitted. He was being recommended by the master of his Amsterdam lodge, the Loge de la Paix, who was probably at this moment (11 February 1749) Jean Rousset de Missy. On the second try, the Bordeaux lodge put its rejection starkly: "never will Jews be admitted among us." Back in Amsterdam, the more tolerant Rousset de Missy, a Huguenot refugee, had a long career as a journalist and promoter of clandestine works, and he was a self-described pantheist. The Loge de la Paix was very much under his paternal care.[27] Clearly secrecy in Amsterdam opened a wider berth than it did in Bordeaux, at least for Jews. In 1735 one Jewish name, Solomon Noch, appears in the founding records of Dutch freemasonry. Around the same time we know that Jews were admitted to London lodges.

At times secrecy did complex work. In general, the lodges expanded the new public by bringing strangers together around enlightened goals, and lodge after lodge proclaimed that "masons are citizens of the world."[28] No amount of cosmopolitan fraternizing would, however, erase even more secretly cherished prejudices. What mattered were the beliefs that men brought to social experiences they hoped would be enlightened. The gap between the ideals of toleration and integration, and the reality of social exclusion based upon religion or gender or social status, has been a constant throughout the history of modernity, whether early, late, or post. Secrecy could offer opportunities, but it could also cover over the social tensions rife among those who believed in equality—largely for themselves. The cosmopolitan remained an ideal, occasionally a reality in the eighteenth century, as today. Only then secretive social behavior seemed more normal, a practice common among courts and elites. The largely middling classes drawn to the lodges—with the possible exception of Russia where the aristocracy dominated the lodges—placed their ideals under the mantle of secrecy, however honored, often in the breach rather than in the observance.

Other forces made secrecy attractive. The reality of the deep inequalities generated by market and birth also bred the need for discretion and privacy. Within every lodge there was the persistent issue of poverty and the needs of brothers fallen on hard times. Lodges could be fonts of generosity, of sums given on an obviously limited basis and then only to those brothers known to them and truly worthy.[29] Throughout the century the lodge in Bordeaux went deep into its pockets to do what neither church nor state could, or would, do. On occasion it reached outside the masonic family and gave funds to local curés for distribution. Private money freely given required secrecy, at least as the terms of the gift were being negotiated. It did then and it does now.

Being discreet about charity funds given or received might have a logic to which we can relate, but the secrecy within secrecy found commonly in late eighteenth-century European freemasonry is perhaps the hardest of its many aspects to understand. Regularly, brothers and, of course, sisters were forming "clandestine" or irregular or "bastard" lodges that did not have constitutions from a formally recognized lodge. These served many purposes now largely lost to us, but this secrecy within secrecy receives some elucidation from the Bordeaux records. A brother had been frequenting "la loge Batarde de cette ville tenue par le S. Martin Pasquales, et sur l'affirmation, on lui a refuse l'entree du temple" (28 February 1764). The Loge Anglaise not only excluded the errant brother who had been attending "a bastard lodge in this city held by S. Martínez de Pasquals, and by acclimation, he had been refused entrance into the [masonic] temple." The lodge had even asked the mayor to look into the disruption in the life of the lodges caused by Pasquales.

The reference to Martínez de Pasquales gives entrée to the secret within the secrecy, to the curious turn toward the mystical that gripped many a masonic lodge late in the eighteenth century. Martínez de Pasquales was a masonic reformer of shadowy, but it was believed at the time, Portuguese Jewish origins who preached an occult form of masonry that was highly ritualized and mystical in its expression. He had lived for a time in Bordeaux and promulgated his version of masonic wisdom that long after his death in 1774 made deep inroads in the life of French freemasonry, indeed it could be found as far east as St. Petersburg.[30] He preached the hierarchy of created beings capable of transcending their place by spiritual union with the Divine.[31] Brothers and sisters of the 1780s found his teachings alluring, possibly because they were personally troubled in ways that we do not fully understand but that signal a discontent with the cosmopolitan experience inherited from an earlier age. Quarreling became endemic to the French lodges. Indeed French society in the 1780s, as seen through the prism of its lodges, displayed a degree of social unrest far in excess of what can be seen in other Western countries.

For example, in Bordeaux a "red lodge" was set up, and it brought an interest in the Rosicrucianism fermenting in the German-speaking lands. After the start of the Revolution in 1789 royalists specifically blamed the red lodges as "clubs de la propagande."[32] At the same moment a masonic priest in the Loge Anglaise was brought up on charges that go unspecified in the minutes. The following week seventeen brothers simply left the lodge and another five or six were excluded from it. Members from another lodge, the Etoile flamboyante aux Trois Lys, were refused admission. The very cosmopolitanism at the heart of the lodge had come apart, with English and French brothers at odds, and with the grand lodge in Paris largely powerless to heal the rift.[33] Within the national masonic temple lay deep divisions between the Grand Orient in Paris and many provincial lodges. These divisions stemmed in part from the effort by the Grand Orient to limit access to the higher degrees, or at the very least to oversee who would be entitled to rise in masonic wisdom. Social exclusivity formed the core of the agenda from Paris, but the provinces and probably many Parisian lodges, except for the most aristocratic, were not buying into it. A notation in the minutes of 27 September 1803 tells us that the Loge Anglaise simply stopped corresponding with the Grand Orient in Paris in 1785. Thus by the 1780s an atmosphere of dissension fueled by social discontent, possibly of nationalist origins, came to prevail and new and occult forms of masonry rose to prominence.

By the 1770s and 1780s the secrecy of the masonic umbrella sheltered new, private societies with distinctively occult, yet curiously cosmopolitan interests. It was as if traditional Christianity had failed to satisfy the striving and curiosity of the lodges and the turn toward the occult became palpable in the German-speaking lands but also, and especially, in France. At the center of the mystical movement lay a Parisian lodge composed of the crème de la crème of ancien régime society. By 1780s the *tableaux* for membership in Les Amis Réunis contained financiers, bankers, tax farmers, commissioners of the Royal Treasury, the intendant general of the post, and various other government officials.[34] Out of it sprang a remarkable society, Les Philalèthes, and its records—now further restored by the return of the Moscow archives—reveal the aspirations of powerful men searching for a vast and universal spiritual renewal. Les Philalèthes was never a lodge, but rather a regime, a system inspired by the teachings of Emanuel Swedenborg and Martínez de Pasquales, established for the purpose of human perfection. One of its founders was Savalette de Langes, the scion of a *noblesse de robe* family who had been active in *l'opposition parlementaire* that refused the reforms demanded in the early 1770s by the king's minister, Maupeou. At that moment the aristocracy using the *parlements,* or courts, served notice on the monarchy as to just how difficult it would be to challenge the traditional privileges that insured their financial exemptions. For his siding with the parlements, Savalette had been exiled and, probably as a consequence, his masonic activism increased annually.

In the setting provided by the lodges and their social off shoots, not only in Paris but also in Lyon, Strasbourg, Lille, among other towns, new and higher degrees were invented, and the ultimate forms of wisdom imagined as possible. Self-proclaimed masonic prophets, like Cagliostro, Martines de Pasquales, and J. B. Willermoz, became the pied pipers of this movement, which aspired to encompass all "les pays et regimes réunies a Paris."[35] For Willermoz, philanthrophy, especially on the part of the aristocracy, held the key to spiritual renewal while Les Philalèthes and Les Amis réunis wished to hold "un Convent fraternel," to be set up in Paris. Their documents tell us that they have put all their trust in "l'impulsion secréte, mais certaine, de la Divine Providence." In this instance, secrecy had sanctioned gnosis. The mystical wisdom found must be placed in the service of a total reform. The members of Les Philalèthes posed the question, "Has the masonic science possessed a rapport with the known sciences under the name of the occult science or secrets?" The answer presented itself. The assembled announced that they believed "in the rapport of masonry with Theosophy, Alchemy, the Cabala, Divine Magic, Emblems, Hieroglyphes, the Religious Ceremonies and the Rites of different Institutions, or Associations, masonic or otherwise."[36] They have discerned "a rapport between the usages generally adopted by the interior economy of the Masonic Society and those of which we have found the trace in the ancient works, which have conserved for us the usages of the primitive Church."[37] Wrapped in the mantle of secrecy, the brothers with occult interests wound up embracing every known form of ancient and modern learning and science—however far-fetched its foundation. They aspired "to develop the foundation of their opinion on the occult science . . . and to distinguish . . . which are the Schools of ancient Philosophy, and the other sources out of which Masonry has been enabled."[38] The goal became a total synthesis of all learning, a new, cosmopolitan "world religion that all the devout of whatever persuasion can embrace." Working within the disastrous financial context that many of these same French administrators helped to create, it is tempting to imagine them during the 1780s as embarked on a grand intellectual odyssey that would ultimately bring them to personal transformation, to a new reality not quite of this world, an alternative that could be embraced—and escaped into.

We may consider freemasons of the eighteenth century as in some sense apostles of modernity. They sought to cross the borders created by birth and blood, to embrace strangers as brothers, and to train themselves as civic men and women capable of speaking in public, voting, and deliberating. They tried to mix with other religious groups, sometimes, as in the case of the Loge Anglaise, with very limited success. As we survey their achievements and failings, may we not conclude that modernity possesses contradictory impulses, at once rational and irrational, both universalist and in danger of producing irrelevancies and intellectual cul-de-sacs? All those impulses are clearly present in the Bordeaux records. When posterity with its perfect hindsight lifts the veil of secrecy and finds something like Les Philalèthes, the contradictory impulses at work in modernity until well into the twentieth century parade before us.[39]

Yet there is another way of reading the records of the society and its occult aspirations. This would be to see les Philalethes as profoundly secular. In these records there is barely a wink in the direction of Christian orthodoxy. Instead, in search of a new truth the brothers have leveled the spiritual playing field in such a way that all sorts of beliefs and religious traditions—even mystical and irrational ones—can be accommodated under the mantle of sociability and secrecy. In such a spiritual universe, despite its Christian roots, might not all faiths—think of the Jewish brother from Amsterdam—find a berth? Conceivably. The mystical may not have been the kind of truth that Voltaire in Paris, or the Jewish reformer in Berlin, Moses Mendelssohn, had in mind when they preached toleration. Yet by its nature, I would argue, the spirituality of Les Philalèthes was harmless enough. It looks forward to the muddle of ideas that well-intentioned people, disaffected from traditional religiosity and possessed of little theological training, bring, even now, to their spiritual odysseys. In its universalism Les Philalèthes conjures up the vague religiosity or sentiments—or perhaps lack thereof—that have allowed people of many faiths peacefully to inhabit the same social space. In the heart of what in a few short years would become the "old regime" we have found the first stirring of what our own times will call the "new age."

Wrapped in the cocoon of well-intentioned mysticism did the French lodges ever escape long enough to confront the exterior world, and in the process drop the affectation of secrecy? Did the lofty exclusiveness of some enlightened circles ever give way to the reality outside? Clearly, in the eighteenth century, months in the Bastille for clandestine trafficking could be such a reality and, after 1789, so too was political upheaval. Rare among all forms of sociability to be found in France during the Revolution, the Loge Anglaise in Bordeaux has left records that span the greater part of the 1790s. Generally, in that decade only the Jacobin clubs were so audacious as to meet and leave written records of their conversations.

In November of 1788, as the national financial crisis deepened and the king was forced to accede to a new role for the parlements, the Bordeaux lodge responded to public events. Only rarely did the overtly political intrude into the life of the lodge: the convalescence of the king in 1757 was noted, the reintegration of the parlement of Bordeaux in 1775, and in 1778 and 1781 the lodge proposed that a mass be sung in celebration of the birth of two royal children, one the heir to the throne. In 1788 the reopening of the parlement in Bordeaux was celebrated by a banquet and speech making.[40] The orator proclaimed that "justice will get back all its rights . . . [before now] vain combinations based on foolish pride and human vanity . . . a vile egoism and sordid interest . . . have usurped the place of virtue and patriotic devotion."[41] A triumph for the magistrates and their "august chief" was hailed as was the maintenance of the rights of the province. We can contrast the *parlementaire* sentiments of the Bordeaux lodge with those found in a royalist lodge in Paris where officers of the crown reminded one another that while "masonry is an order in the universe," it is not an order in the state.[42]

We next hear in the minutes of the Bordeaux lodge from July 1790 that the Revolution must also be celebrated. They described the king as a "sensible monarch and dignified father of the French." The people must also be celebrated for their zeal, merit, and patriotism. In the nation the first anniversary of the Revolution called forth festivals that swore loyalty and harmony to the new order. In imitation of the Festival of Federation held on 14 July 1790, the Bordeaux lodges entered into "une pacte federatif" so that they need no longer be dependent upon the Grand Orient.[43] Clearly the Grand Orient with its aristocratic leadership had now been associated with the old order and some lodges wholeheartedly embraced the emergent revolution. In 1791 *la Loge Anglaise* had the first correspondence in its history with its sisters about candidates who had been proposed. Apparently a lodge of adoption had been somewhat integrated into its proceedings. A songbook of the year 1790 prepared for the use of all the Bordeaux lodges proclaims that "our country is free . . . the mason cherishes liberty without doubt, but the public peace is also the object of struggle."[44]

Clearly, the universal principles proclaimed by the Declaration of the Rights of Man and Citizen had implications for the practices of the Loge Anglaise. On 15 July 1790 an orator addressed his brothers on that very theme. Discord has appeared within the lodges and "the passions have been allowed to take too free access. . . . The practice of all the social virtues have been put in a troubled state by perfidious dissension."[45] The orator, M. Mailleres, urged the lodge to put itself under the same principles that now all of France accepted, and in particular to act upon the fact that in January 1790 the Jews of Bordeaux had been granted their civil rights. When news reached the city a near riot had broken out against their liberation.[46] Thus came the bold request, "a brother, a philosopher without doubt and a friend of humanity has made the following proposition: The Jews in a word are now active citizens. From this title they may hypothetically possess all the qualities associated with our mores, and will you admit them into our care or reject them?"[47] Fittingly, the lodge was being asked to replicate in its proceedings the universal principles proclaimed by the Revolution. Now we will see quite clearly how difficult, even inflammatory, those cosmopolitan principles could be when reformers sought their application. At that moment, the Revolution had gone too far for the Loge Anglaise. Its principles drastically expanded the limits that the lodge had set on its own cosmopolitanism. The political and revolutionary process had created a new, and avant-garde, set of principles for public and private life, and this single masonic exemplar of civil society, private, secretive, and with a history of prejudice, might, or might not bend. Ultimately the lodge rejected the implications of human rights for all citizens and refused to admit Jewish brothers. In the course of the eighteenth century, practices that had once protected the Enlightenment were now used to subvert the logic of its principles.

The Loge Anglaise still wanted to adhere to the Revolution, or to those aspects of it that suited its temperament. In October 1792 the departure of a brother to the frontier where "liberty will be defended" was duly noted. In the same month brothers were no longer to be addressed as *monsieur* but as *citoyen*. Events began to tumble into the temple as army victories were celebrated (27 November 1792), and in November of 1793 the name of the lodge was changed to include the phrase "of Equality." At the height of the Terror a delegation representing "the people" did the lodge "the favor" of visiting it. The very furnishings of the temple had to be replaced, the ermine suppressed, and in place of the old draperies and cordons of the officers appeared the patriotic tricolor. New pagan festivals started in the next month, and the winter solstice took its place on the masonic calendar of celebrations. The actual banquet had to be postponed in the absence of "les subsistances de première nécéssité." Finally, for fifteen months in 1794–95 the lodge did not meet because of the "force and vigor of the revolutionary turbulence."

Traditionally, we see the French Revolution as auguring the end of the Enlightenment as a distinctive movement with particular mores and conventions. In the case of freemasonry the date works well enough. What ended in the 1790s everywhere in Europe, for a time, might be described as the comfortable luxury of cosmopolitan gatherings devoted to literature or science, or the cultivation of masonic wisdom without reference to events in the outside world. Perhaps in the 1790s, along with the birth of democratic ideals, also emerged a truly modern, public sphere, one that only some elements within civil society were willing, or able, to accept. Private vices, like a dislike of the Jews, were not to be tempered, in this one instance, by the demands of public virtue.

During the Napoleonic years, as the attempt was made to turn back the clock on the more democratic innovations of the 1790s, the Loge Anglaise lost the right to recognize other lodges on its own. It had to be ceded to a provincial grand lodge. In 1806 the Bordeaux brothers put up a portrait of

Napoleon the Great in its banquet room, and the lodge's finances were deemed to be in a pitiable state. On several occasions the issue of admitting Jews into the lodge roiled the waters, and, once again, the lodge proclaimed that it would *never* do so. It acknowledged as how other lodges might be different and its remarks indicated that Jewish freemasons existed, possibly even in Bordeaux with its significant Jewish community. In 1814 *la Loge Anglaise* held a banquet to celebrate the return of the Bourbons to the French throne. This was a lodge that at least up to 1815 had come to regard aspects of the legacy of the Revolution as deeply problematic. Yet in the same period and under the sponsorship of the reformed grand lodge of France, new lodges were established in the Low Countries (then occupied by France) that challenged local social prejudices and pushed in the direction of the egalitarian.[48]

Clearly, no lodge would ever be able to embrace the damaging right-wing myth of a masonic conspiracy being at the root of the Revolution. The myth appeared as early as 1789.[49] But at some later date, when anti-Semitism became codified, the Loge Anglaise or some other lodge might have imagined that the Jews had something sinister to do with their own revolutionary emancipation, however much it had been justified as a result of universal human rights. The universalism of the Enlightenment, and then of the French Revolution, could always founder on the privacy permitted, indeed required, for the vitality of the public sphere. While secrecy, privacy, and discretion may protect civil society in perilous times, or shield it from the prying eyes of the state, or permit social experimentation, such habits could also provide a refuge for scoundrels.

One other element flourished within civil society of the late eighteenth century. National sentiments appear in the proceedings of the French lodges as well as in the Dutch lodges I have examined. Steven Bullock also has found republicanism at work in the lodges of the American colonies before 1776 and in the new republic. Orators told French brothers that "the health of the country has been your supreme law. Your personal interest disappears always before the national interest."[50] Perhaps only the power of the state was sufficient to intrude on the privacy so cherished in civil society. As nationalist interests grew in importance—even in the deeply decentralized but discontented Dutch Republic—voluntary associations succumbed to the lure of state ideologies. In town after town, Dutch lodges took sides in 1787 as unrest turned into revolution. In Britain the lodges of the 1790s were aggressive in proclaiming their loyalism. Early modern cosmopolitanism was fragile in the face of the lure of nationalism. Yet the very survival of civil society was perceived to depend upon the triumph of republican values. At the same time,

French, American, Dutch, Irish, even English republicanism could never be effectively separated out from national identity.

Secrecy and Modern Political Radicalism

In the 1790s the practice of secrecy—within the domain of cosmopolitan civil society—gave it new meaning. Its political potential was quickly recognized by reforming groups, paradoxically located in the vanguard of political change. After 1800 subversive societies, often employing secrecy to prevent detection, would vie with conventional ones for the loyalties of citizens. The anarchists led by Babeuf used masonic forms to organize their secret cabals. Where secrecy protected voluntary associations, the potential existed to unhinge the state or to engender in it the paranoid fantasies that fueled—and still fuel—dangerous and inhuman regimes. We have seen in Bordeaux that only personal, private beliefs render people truly tolerant and cosmopolitan, as well as watchful against arbitrary state power, or the prejudices that lurk in the heart. Clustering among the like-minded could promote enlightenment—or, as Les Philalèthes would have said, human perfectibility—only if personal belief in enlightened principles animated the assembled. Secrecy shrouds inner beliefs and in the final analysis, they will prevail over all publicly articulated decrees, even over legally sanctioned freedoms. At best, the brothers in Bordeaux should be seen as reluctant revolutionaries and cosmopolites who struggled to survive with their basic prejudices intact. For the most part they were private men who dipped their toes into the cosmopolitanism that freemasonry offered.

In other settings the importance of secrecy and masonic practices could also inspire. Their virtues dawned on reformers of the late eighteenth century, particularly on people caught in the grip of traditional, nearly feudal forms of belief and authority. On the edges of Europe landed elites and privileged clergy ruled largely unchallenged, and this was nowhere truer than in Ireland. Yet it was also there that enlightened principles of religious toleration were put to their severest test, and masonic forms appeared as the model that would transform the sectarian into the cosmopolitan. From Elizabethan times onward English Protestants had been given strips of land in designated plantations, largely in the northern part of the island. Most of those settlers were Presbyterians, many from Scotland. Lording over them and the entirely Catholic peasantry stood the old Anglican elites with their vast landed estates.

Far from the commercial vitality of a place like Bordeaux, we think of eighteenth-century Ireland as poor and Catholic, and its countryside was often just that. But Dublin with its expanding population of about 180,000 was nearly the size of Amsterdam, and in the 1790s the cities and towns of Ireland—places like Newry, Belfast, and Derry—became hotbeds of agitation that took on the might of the British colossus and the Anglo-Irish ruling elite. The central issue faced by Irish reformers lay in the gap between Protestants and Catholics, between the privileged and the openly discriminated against. Within the structure put in place largely in the seventeenth century, only Anglican, and not Presbyterian, Protestants enjoyed ascendancy. Not surprisingly, discontent festered among Presbyterians, who were often educated, the backbone of the professional classes. Only Catholics fared worse; they were denied the right even to be educated, and the elite among them sent their children to the Continent for schooling.[51] If Presbyterian and Catholic leaders could forge a meaningful alliance, a mighty and dangerous force would threaten British control over the colony. But how to do this?

Inspiration for reform came directly from America in 1776, and then from France in 1789. Irish republicans avidly participated in the international republican conversation of the 1770s and beyond. In the early 1790s large demonstrations erupted in Belfast as they did in Manchester and Edinburgh in support of the French revolutionaries. As one shrewd and alarmed Belfast observer of events in France and their worldwide political implications put it, "if we follow without restriction, the *theory* of human rights, where will it lead us? In its principle it requires the admission of women, of persons under age, and of paupers, to suffrage at elections; to places of office and trust, and as members of both Houses of Parliament." Speaking at an assembly to support human rights for all citizens regardless of religion, the Rev. William Bruce was clearly alarmed and urged caution against moving too quickly on behalf of Catholics, lest a transfer occur in "every power of government, from the most to the least tolerant, from the most to the least enlightened part of the state."[52] Bruce echoed the widespread uncertainty in Presbyterian circles about Catholics, and assumed with prejudice that Protestants were the more enlightened, tolerant, and cosmopolitan. They had more right to their rights.

Other Presbyterians in Bruce's acquaintance were electrified by the principles of the American and French revolutions and sought to carry them to their logical conclusion—none more so than William Drennan (Figure 8), and his sister and brother-in-law, Martha and Sam McTier. The Drennans belonged by faith and family to the circles of Dissent to be found throughout

Figure 8. *Portrait of William Drennan.* From a portrait in the Ulster Museum by Robert Hohe. Courtesy of the Ulster Museum. William Drennan (1754–1820) was a medical doctor by training, a cofounder of the United Irishmen, and a patriot. Of Ireland he wrote: "Oh Ireland My country! Shall I mourn, or Bless, / Thy tame and wretched happiness?"

the English-speaking world. Dissenters—Protestants who were generally Pres-byterians but never Anglicans—were systematically and legally excluded from the citadels of power, from government offices, from attendance at Oxford and Cambridge, even from local government, unless they were willing to take communion once a year in an Anglican church. Overwhelmingly, they showed a partiality to the American side in the Revolution that began in 1776, and the Drennans were no exception. Partly encouraged by the British govern-ment, Dissenters often made their way abroad, to America and to Ireland.

By 1750 in some northern Irish cities Presbyterians like the Drennans had become the majority, and they coexisted uneasily with the indigenous Catholic population and the so-called Anglo-Irish landowners who operated as the governing class throughout the colony. In the circles of Dissent little affection could be found for that "great empire that has thus outlived itself and is now degenerating into a state of political dotage. Great Britain in her dotage forgets her children."[53] Families like the Drennans believed that the future lay in their having access to governance and in granting Catholic emancipation. For much of the eighteenth century all Irish Catholics had been stripped of their land, denied education, and held under a set of rules known as the Penal Laws. These constricted their freedom to worship or to trade. Bitterness between Catholics and Protestants, particularly in northern Ireland, was endemic; remarkably a few liberal and enlightened Presbyteri-ans like the Drennans sought a way out of this predicament.

As an educated doctor with growing political interests, William Drennan ventured forth into more cosmopolitan circles than chapel life normally afforded. Finding himself practicing medicine during the 1780s in the mar-ket town of Newry, Drennan sought out masonic membership.[54] He told his sister that Newry was "a contemptible place," and boredom may have led him to the lodge door as did a growing disaffection from the many reform clubs that kept springing up and getting nowhere in the business of political re-form—at least in his view.[55] He may also have longed for the cultural life available in Belfast, where scientific lectures and plays were common. Sister and brother shared many affections, but none were more compelling for her than politics. In 1789 she wrote to him about the need to "*establish* Ireland in her fullest rights." In the same letter she noted the social snubs offered her by the local aristocracy from whose grand balls she was firmly excluded, and confessed, "I do feel it." [56] The Drennans were troublemakers, and William had an established reputation as a pamphleteer intent upon augmenting Irish self-governance. Fatefully given the year, in 1789 William Drennan moved to Dublin and almost instantly joined the circle of Irish radicals including

James Napper Tandy and the Emmet brothers. Robert Emmet would be hanged by the British government for his part in the rebellion of 1798.

By 1791, when the surviving correspondence within the Drennan family resumes, they faced the reality of growing Catholic unrest in Ireland. William Drennan saw Catholics as "savages" but also as people who had rights that had to be respected. Since the 1770s and the American Revolution, Dissenters like Drennan had been ardent Whigs. By 1791, in his view, the Whig clubs in Ireland had failed miserably to address the people's plight: "The one here literally does nothing more than eat and drink." The Whigs, he believed, had lost all fellow feeling for the people, and clearly Drennan had come to the view that democracy of some sort was the only course open to the Irish, both Catholic and Protestant.[57] At that moment his experience of freemasonry proved critical.

In the 1790s cosmopolitan idealists like Drennan had to address what he called "the commonality." In that crisis the social model that seemed most appropriate to the task came from the masonic lodges. Fervently, William Drennan wrote to his brother-in-law—not to his sister, for politics in this world or any other at the time was ultimately a man's domain— about his plan of action. First, a new and secret society needed to be formed into which Catholics and Protestants could be integrated: "I should much desire that a society were instituted in this city having much of the secrecy and somewhat of the ceremonial of freemasonry, so much secrecy as might communicate curiosity, uncertainty, expectation to the minds of surrounding men, so much impressive and affecting ceremony in its internal economy as without impeding real business might strike the soul through the senses."

Out of his lodge experience Drennan found a model of cosmopolitan socializing that could strike the heart, move the senses, inspire awe, and in the minds of nonmembers, induce uncertainty tinged with expectation. Its business would be deeply political: "a benevolent conspiracy" "a plot for the people" "no Whig Club" "no party title" "the Brotherhood its name . . . the rights of man and the greatest happiness of the greatest number its end . . . its general end, real independence to Ireland and republicanism its particular purpose."[58] Now in Ireland, late in the eighteenth century, the quintessential of eighteenth-century enlightened socializing had found new meaning. Faced with deep religious divisions, Drennan and his friends took up secrecy and ceremony as the way out of the religious and political impasse that existed in Ireland then—and to some extent now. The new secret fraternity, which became in 1794 the United Irishmen, needed to work "as speedily as the prejudices and bigotry of the land we live in would permit, as speedily as to give us some enjoyment and not to protract anything too long in this short span of life." [58] In the early 1790s, all over Europe, time seemed to move more quickly and to be moving inexorably in the direction of reform, if not revolution.

Drennan thought he had the formula for political success: publications "always coming from one of the Brotherhood, declarations, symbols and international communication." The oaths taken, like their masonic counterparts, would be "solemn and religious compact[s] that must be signed by every member. Then a symbol had to be devised worn by every one of them round their body next the heart. Finally, communication must begin with leading men in France, England and America so as to cement republicanism."[59] Secrecy lay at the essence of Drennan's plan, and he self-consciously told his brother-in-law why it was so important, "it gives greater energy within & greater influence abroad. It conceals members whose professions etc. make concealment expedient until the trial comes. I therefore think and insist on your not even mentioning it." When Drennan wrote those lines he almost certainly desired only reform in Ireland, not revolution. His brother-in-law worried that these ideas would "do mischief in the hands of hot headed people" nor did he want the Secretary of State on their case.[60] Many Presbyterians were by no means as fired up and confident as William Drennan. Acquaintances, like the cautious William Bruce, were even firmly opposed to the use of secrecy precisely because of the radical associations that by 1791 might be put to it. But Drennan, like Tandy and others, believed that some way had to be found to conciliate "the interests of Catholics and Protestants at present."[61] The aim of the United Irishmen would be to bypass those "aristocratical Catholics who think that the government will take care of them and to galvanize the democratic part of the Catholics in a deeply social alliance with Protestants."[62]

In Dublin, the United Irishmen began to take shape, but within a few years the authorities in Britain and Ireland shifted into high alert. Even the hierarchy of the Catholic Church feared the republicans, while at the same time many ordinary priests sided with the cause of reform.[63] Faced with the possibility of imprisonment, men like William Drennan drew back. He sat on the sidelines as Irish radicalism, spurred on by the possibility of an assisting hand from the French, became increasingly more vehement. Secrecy became ever more necessary, an essential part of the political fabric of opposition. The landed took fright and saw "the progress of democracy . . . indeed all through the North [of Ireland] . . . [as accompanied by] the systematic plans & resolutions of the committees & affiliated societies."[64] The authorities in turn added vengeance and martyrdom to the list of republican grievances, and by 1794 the secrecy imagined by Drennan as bonding had become life-saving. The violence of 1798–99 claimed over 30,000 lives and the forces of repression were swift and bloody.[65] Both sides experienced "universally the terror of being massacred."[66] Yet others, like Mary Ann McCracken, saw hope for both women and men: "the reign of prejudice is nearly at an end."[67] Out of the crucible of rebellion, led by the United Irishmen, came the bigotry of the newly formed and equally secret Orange Order and a profound retreat from reconciliation between Protestants and Catholics. The implications of that post-1800 retreat from the cosmopolitan haunt northern Irish history to this day.

Yet more than failure is to be learned from the experiences of the Drennans in Ireland and their less famous lodge brothers in Bordeaux. Secrecy, ceremony, symbol, and ritual belong to the story of the birth pangs of democracy and political resistance. Already in 1766 a masonic orator in Amsterdam told his brothers, "The main reason why freemasonry was so well received among the enlightened: the Natural state of humanity is therein restored perfectly, no disguise will be tolerated."[68] The dilemma presented by secrecy lies surely in our seeing only disguise, and not transparency, in its practice, especially when combined with arcane ceremonies and expensive rites of passage. Yet the evidence suggests that late in the eighteenth century the lodge had become a place where social egalitarianism could be proposed, the democratic sampled, even fostered. The key to the experiment lay in forms of behavior that blended the assembled, made them curiously anonymous in their aprons, robes, and badges. Esoteric symbols conjured up the universal, passwords whispered from ear to ear made differences give way to a cosmopolitan transparency. Once experienced, democracy could be, and often was, spurned. But its power could not be forgotten. For some people, just as Bruce feared and Drennan hoped, the theory of democracy would seize hold of the imagination and never let go. In their hearts they could secretly imagine themselves to be as good as their betters. Yet the habits of secrecy left another, but sinister legacy. In the hands of those who hate, or who would foster terror—witness Northern Ireland up to 1998—the practice of secrecy became the sine qua non of political and military activism with terrorist associations. Secret and radical political organizations may not be an exclusively Western invention, but in places like Ireland they first showed the world how powerful and dangerous they could be.

The lodges offered another experience of singular importance by the 1770s and beyond: regularly entertaining visitors from abroad. Take a prominent lodge in Amsterdam for which the signed visitors' book has survived.[69]

In the 1750s visitors turned up from other lodges in the city but also from Antwerp, Geneva, Stockholm, Bordeaux, Berne, Hamburg, Leipzig, London, and various Dutch colonies. A decade or so later, names to be famous by century's end appear as well, in 1774 Jean-Paul Marat, and Casanova, the infamous libertine. In Bordeaux over half the lodge meetings entertained visitors, even if one lodge that we now know well refused to admit them if they were Jews. Early in the 1780s the grand lodge in The Hague hosted a visitor from Philadelphia. Did they discuss the recent success of American independence? It is hard to imagine the subject being avoided.

The masonic habit of foreign visitations makes palpable the new cosmopolitanism of the lodges and points to the possibilities for international conversations they offered. These need not have been republican in nature; lodges were forbidden to engage in overt politics. But the Amsterdam lodge where Marat visited had a long history of reformist associations. It had been closed down as a result of the Dutch revolution of 1747–48. Reconstituted by the time of the revolution of 1787, many of its members were *patriots*, then forced to flee the country when the Prussians invaded to put a stop to the revolt. In 1795 when the French revolutionary army arrived in Amsterdam its brothers joyfully greeted those soldiers who were freemasons. Together, in triumph, they sang La Marseillaise. Thus, in its way, the Amsterdam lodge participated in the international republican conversation of the 1770s and 1780s, one that the cosmopolitan ideal had made all the more possible.

In most lodges secrecy amounted to nothing more than discretion and the fanciful memorizing of special rituals. They encouraging the bonding of strangers. But practices born in one era could be reworked for new purposes, and by 1800 the secret fraternal order of political men with a mission had appeared—in some places never to entirely disappear to this day. The 1790s witnessed new political impulses, and for those wishing to promote change in a democratic direction, for a brief moment the possibilities seemed limitless.

Chapter 5
Liberals, Radicals, and Bohemians

Visible in many settings and situations, cosmopolitan behavior suggested previously unimagined political and personal transformations. When our histories exclusively focus on enlightened philosophizing about the cosmopolitan, on what, for example, Kant had to say about the desirability of the cosmopolitan, they miss its role in an emerging international republican conversation that could also be internalized and intensely personal for its participants. The experience of imagining one's self as a citizen of the world infused actual political causes, pressing by the 1770s and more easily embraced when thinking beyond the nation. The logic unfolded: the habit of border crossings, be they over lines of birth and breeding, or religion, or national groupings, created a predisposition to imagine reform and possibly embrace the revolutionary impulse, even if coming from distant shores. For the first time in the modern West it became possible to imagine oneself as being part of an international phenomenon, commercial and scientific, of course, but also, and now in this chapter especially, personally transforming as well as political.

The cosmopolitan fervor of the 1790s had been long in coming and not entirely without precedent. From the 1750s onward foreign wars were experienced as increasingly global, and by the 1770s European refugees became a part of life. In the past having to take refuge had been a misery largely inflicted on the indigenous peoples of the New World, or a fate dished out to borderland colonists.[1] Increased migration, particularly of Europeans to the New World, also brought fresh participants and observers together in city after city, across both the Channel and the Atlantic.[2] In the British case, the imperial wars of the period made "real . . . the union between Scotland and the rest of Great Britain."[3] Information from throughout the Western world filtered into salons and lodges by print and letter, allowing some men and women to imagine themselves as less parochial.[4]

The sense of being participant in international movements for reform gave an unprecedented impetus to liberal and radical political aspirations.

From the 1760s to the 1790s, from watching developments in Philadelphia to marveling at the rapidity of events in Paris, reformers drew courage far in excess of what the pace of change in their own societies might have warranted. Putting an international conversation into social spaces created decades earlier in northern and western Europe and the colonies now made possible an unprecedented political momentum where vicarious witnessing could generate a new—sometimes false—sense of what was possible locally.

Through international contact every periphery could imagine itself a center. In the American colonies contact with like-minded opponents of ministerial and court authority in the mother country validated opposition politics while also bringing news. "We have heard of Bloodshed & even civil war in our Sister Colony North Carolina," Samuel Adams writing to another radical in Virginia, noted "how strange is it, that the best intelligence we have had of that tragical scene, has been brought to us from England!"[5] As we saw in Chapter 4, perhaps fatefully and unrealistically, the young instigator of the United Irishmen, William Drennan, living in provincial Newry, then moving on to Belfast, could also imagine himself—like Adams twenty years earlier—at the center of the international movement. When on the scaffold facing execution, his compatriot in the independence movement, Robert Emmet, spoke passionately about both the Irish nation and his "universal love and kindness towards all men."[6] Long after the imperial wars of the early nineteenth century made the idealism of the 1790s seem remote, Helen Maria Williams fantasized about going to America, where "[I will] pass my days in composing visions in praise of liberty."[7] But before inspiration came from abroad, in various nations the governing authorities had to be seen as inadequate to the task of reform. When they faltered, astute observers looked elsewhere for guidance.

The Closing of Alternatives to Republicanism

In the second half of the century many factors—some of them ostensibly contradictory—played into the disillusionment that preceded the shift toward practical reform with a republican tinge. In some places the policies of enlightened absolutists sowed unintended seeds. In the southern Netherlands during the 1740s and 1750s, the Austrian regime fostered reform wherever possible. Taking his directions from Vienna, Cobenzl's strategy aimed to break the authority of the old ruling elites, the landed nobility, and the ultramontane clergy. Inevitably the Austrian administrators in Brussels wound up enlisting the assistance of minor philosophes, men like Pierre Rousseau and Jean Rousset de Missy (whom we have met as the head of a masonic lodge in Amsterdam; see Chapter 4). Their religious and political views were far to the left, far more enlightened than anything the monarchy and its ministers had in mind, but they had the requisite journalistic skills.[8] Rousset also appealed to Cobenzl by noting that he too was a freemason.

As the career of this French Huguenot refugee Rousset de Missy illustrates, agents enlisted to do the work of kings can sometimes turn against their paymasters. By 1747–48, Rousset had evolved from being a client of the House of Orange and its British-Austrian allies—what has been called a "Dutch Whig"—into a fomenter of revolution, a zealot in the cause of reforming a corrupt republic. By 1750 he had been sent into exile.[9] The larger political causes that he championed, the reform of the republic, the Anglo-Dutch-Austrian entente against France, seemed lost. Only his beloved freemasonry continued to flourish.

As we also saw in Chapter 4, Rousset's politics lived on in his Amsterdam lodge. Decades after his death, in 1793, the lodge he had founded, with its gaze cast toward Paris and the execution of Louis XVI and Marie Antoinette, celebrated the demise of "the tryant Tarquin and his damnable wife Tullia." In 1795 the brothers rejoiced in the French Revolution, feasted with its invading army, addressing them as "liberators."[10] In 1787 many of its members had been forced to flee to Paris when Prussian troops invaded to put an end to the Dutch uprising. Most sites of sociability throughout the eighteenth century were loyalist, or at least conforming. But what was imagined as official corruption, in this instance the inability of the stadholderate to reform the republic and offer reliable support to its Austrian allies, occasionally pushed politically aware coteries into a posture of opposition that could continue for decades and transmit values from one generation to the next. In the 1780s we see glimmers of discontent also in philosophical and masonic circles in the Austrian Netherlands. In 1787 the colony was also in open revolt, and in 1795 Belgian democrats, like their Amsterdam counterparts, welcomed the French army.[11]

Although Britain had become a constitutional monarchy, and hence cannot be seen as the same species as the old regimes on the Continent, its political life also offered examples of official authority acting with unintended consequences and providing the impetus for socializing to turn radical and republican. In the 1760s the heavy-handed repression of the parliamentary reformer John Wilkes by ministers of party and crown fueled discontent that arguably would have remained dormant had Wilkes been allowed to take his seat and rail as he pleased. The fact that the high-living Wilkes proved open to bribery in return for staying exiled in France suggests that his understanding of politics had an opportunistic side that would be harder to find among British radicals a mere decade later.[12] In part the heavy hand of government created this creature; the populace and the clubs that rallied round him did the rest. But it was not accidental that among his most ardent followers were non-Anglican Protestants whose lineage, although no longer their sensibility, could be traced back to the mid-seventeenth-century Puritans. Wilkes may have been a freethinker and a rogue, but he represented a larger cause for reform. It had deep resonance with Protestants who identified favorably with the seventeenth-century revolutions that had undone absolutism in Britain. He also appealed to American colonists whose discontent with Britain had become palpable by the late 1760s.[13] Since 1689 and the birth of their religious liberty, many Puritans of both Old and New Worlds had mellowed and followed a pattern toward liberal, less Calvinist values, one that could be seen elsewhere within European Protestantism.[14]

Liberal Protestantism

For a new era of radicalism to take root in the second half of the eighteenth century—one that drew upon unprecedented transnational cosmopolitanism—many forces were required: print culture, growing urban literacy, and, most important, in northern and western Europe and the American colonies, the triumph in some quarters of a liberal, socially focused, more emotive, but firmly antifanatical version of Protestantism. By midcentury its benign face had traversed many national boundaries, and it could be seen among the middling classes in Birmingham, or Philadelphia, or Geneva. In the 1770s moral pronouncements of Protestant origins about virtue and the vitality of republics flourished in such liberal circles. This species of Protestantism believed in its own reasonableness, eschewed religious enthusiasm and any image of God as a tyrant.[15] Just as it crossed geographical and linguistic borders, so too the zealots it opposed were imagined as turning up in many guises, some as inquisitors, others as biblical literalists, and still others who thought they had an imagined voice from the Divine in their minds.

To be sure, self-satisfied liberal and tolerant Protestantism also possessed a deeply conserving impulse. Put in the benighted words of the Negro American slave poet Phillis Wheatley, everything could seem just as it should be, "All-wise Almighty Providence we trace/ In trees, and plants, and all the flow'ry race, / As clear as in the nobler frame of man, / All lovely copies of the Maker's plan.[16]

The supremely popular *Catechism of Nature* (1777) by the Rev. J. F. Martinet was read in many editions, both in the Dutch Republic from whence it originated and in England. Smugly, Martinet argued that God had made the whole world "a grand storehouse for man." He mentioned the gold and fruits from Africa as such bounty, simply leaving slavery out of the discussion. He offered the old physico-theology of an earlier generation refurbished for the affluent and, hopefully, pious. Yet within the sensibility of liberal Protestantism, however pleased it might have been with a myopic creature comfort, discomfort with affectation surfaced, with mores associated with the aristocracy, particularly of French courtly provenance. They were seen to inculcate "mean self-love . . . at the expense of the most important interests of society." The affectation associated with aristocrats, not republicans, figured, along with religious enthusiasm and indifference, as an evil that distracted from personal and social virtue.[17] Female voices rang out with particular clarity in the liberal Protestant chorus, and the evils of empire struck a cultivated note of high moral indignation.

The distinctively Protestant cast to the cosmopolitan republican conversation, however secular in its orientation, meant that the genteel language of morality and the language of political reform became inextricably united. In addition co-religionists networked across the Atlantic. The Congregational minister Ezra Stiles, in Rhode Island, had contact with over forty like-minded radicals in England. On 30 January 1749 when Massachusetts citizens were called upon to observe and mourn the hundredth anniversary of the execution of Charles I, the liberal Protestant minister Jonathan Mayhew rose in his pulpit to celebrate the distant Puritans who proclaimed that "Britons will not be slaves." Among the worshippers that day sat the young Paul Revere, soon to become an ardent republican and freemason.[18] Within the setting provided by the liberal Protestantism of the later eighteenth century, piety, social morality, and political principles fused, or, as Raymond Williams put it, "a conclusion about personal feeling became a conclusion about society."[19]

The writings of French philosopher Jean-Jacques Rousseau dropped into the emotional setting provided by liberal Protestantism, and in the 1760s and 1770s they electrified those drawn to reform. Rousseau dwelt upon the personal implications of political commitment, and the sources of his appeal across the linguistic boundaries were multiple and varied. Some people said that his books deserved to be burned, other raised their children according to his principles, perhaps best found in his fiction.[20] Emphasis needs to be placed here upon the moralizing quality of his political idealism and its compatibility with the transnational liberal Protestantism just described. Ironically Rousseau had his suspicions about cosmopolites, associating them with urban decadence or with other philosophers with whom he had quarreled. He also wanted to inhibit any impulse that he imagined would interfere with a commitment to the republic.[21] But whether Rousseau liked it or not, in 1762 at its publication, the *Social Contract* joined an already inaugurated, internationally cosmopolitan, and largely abstract conversation, much of it quite heated, about the nature of the best form of government, about republics, or the possibilities for reform as promoted by enlightened "despots." Rousseau's debt to classical republican thought was obvious, indeed he saw his birthplace, Geneva, as a once pure republic that had been corrupted by its elite.[22]

What is most important about Rousseau's vision, I would suggest, lies in the fact that unlike the earlier freethinkers, or for that matter Wilkes, Rousseau entertained no ribald and highly publicized hostility to religion per se. Indeed his youth had been saturated in the newer, far more liberal brand of Calvinism current in Geneva and elsewhere at the time. As a result, even liberal Catholics all over Europe could read him in preference to many of the other, far more irreligious philosophes.[23] In Italy Cosimo Amidei and Carlantonio Pilati, inspired by Rousseau, came to see that the work of reform had to be Europe-wide; it was not simply an Italian problem. Rousseau's universalist emphasis on purity and virtue, on the goodness of man, resonated especially well with religious liberals, but it also appealed to freemasons. They who had long used republican and moralizing language to describe the constitutionally imposed discipline and the egalitarian ideals of a lodge. As the Amsterdam masonic orator (quoted in Chapter 4) put it in 1766, "The main reason why freemasonry was so well received among the enlightened: the Natural state of humanity is therein restored perfectly, no disguise will be tolerated."[24] Visible from the 1760s until the 1790s, Rousseau's writings when combined with liberal Protestantism, provided continuity between the pro-American politics of Joseph Priestley in the 1770s and the democratic Unitarianism of Samuel Taylor Coleridge in the 1790s.[25] Rousseau painted the political as also deeply personal and transformative.

In Britain liberal Protestantism could inform personal piety but it could also have consequences in elections. By the 1770s Dissenters and liberal Anglicans made common electoral causes in districts from Bristol to the Tory-dominated Manchester.[26] They showed solidarity with the American colonists, expressed indignation with their grievances, and began a set of voting patterns that looked toward the great reform movement of the 1820s. The laity enjoyed liberal clerical companionship in these political endeavors and British radicalism had found its clerical adherents. Ordinary clergymen, generally non-Anglican Dissenters, routinely wrote their sons in school to discuss the details of news from America and how it "raised the spirits of the friends of liberty and America not a little."[27] They went on to decry "declamations . . . our High Church Doctors spewed out against the injured Americans." These same Dissenting clergymen were vital to the electoral efforts against the war in America, later in support of fundamental reform.

Of the many varieties of liberal Protestants none gestured more dramatically toward the cosmopolitan than did the Unitarians. First they made peace with the moderate and deistic version of the Enlightenment, then the old hostility to enlightened freethinking gave way. Unitarian clergymen took to describing Jesus in terms that were humanitarian and cosmopolitan, "Christ Jesus, that divine Deist and godlike friend to the human race."[28] Little wonder then that American deists like Benjamin Franklin gave assistance to Unitarians in search of a universal and socially anchored religiosity. The British radical John Thelwall, hiding from the authorities—to be found in the late 1790s in deepest Wales—noted that "if I could ever turn Christian again I should certainly be a Unitarian Quaker."[29] Both sects had compiled honorable records as opponents of slavery and advocates of the American Revolution.

With the aid of Benjamin Franklin, the English cleric David Williams wrote and published in the year of the Declaration of Independence *A Liturgy on the Universal Principles of Religion and Morality* (1776). We might describe it as ceremonies for cosmopolites. First put into practice at his Unitarian chapel in London, the liturgical message announced reform in language that recalled the Protestant enthusiasts of an earlier age. Yet the message relied upon the vitality of eighteenth-century practices, upon cosmopolitan invocations of "the humanity of this enlightened age." With his liturgy, complete with psalms, Williams "wish[ed] to try to effect a *Form of Social Worship* . . . which all men may join who acknowledge the existence of a supreme Intelligence, and the universal obligations of morality."[30] His morning service thanked God "for peaceable times . . . the administration of wise and good laws . . . every friendly and social enjoyment." In the evening the congregation of any or all would thank God "that we are placed in a social state," while the minister rejoiced "in the subversion of tyranny, oppression, and every thing unfriendly to the liberties of the world."[31] Not surprisingly, in 1792 Williams made his way to France along with Thomas Paine.[32] Also with a debt to liberal Protestantism, Paine's pen in turn could preach in the homiletic style made famous in the American colonies by clerics of the previous generation like Stiles and the Unitarian Mayhew.[33]

Several issues united these generations, and among the most important were slavery and women's rights. Emotive Protestant liberalism seemed drawn to distant causes, such as slavery, but also to the fate of sailors and captives.[34] Partly an outgrowth of this form of Protestantism, the humanitarian, an ideological stance of immense power and relevance to modern cosmopolitan politics, took shape in the 1770s. Of the many varieties of Protestants that embraced the stance, none were more important for the cause of slavery than the Quakers, and in particular their women preachers. They traveled in England and the American colonies denouncing the practice. In 1776 the Philadelphia Yearly Meeting resolved to disown any Quaker who held slaves.[35] By the 1770s slavery had multiple critics precisely in liberal Protestant circles, with Dissenters among the growing chorus of vociferous opponents. Arguably a cosmopolitan impulse with religious overtones—not nearly as common a hundred years earlier—made Africans into human beings who, like Europeans, should never be enslaved.

Inevitably seekers from foreign lands, increasingly disillusioned with the old regimes of the Continent and imbued with the writings of Rousseau, wanted to understand how the British proceeded. In the throes of Anglophilia a young Frenchman, Jean-Paul Marat, decided to see for himself how "liberty" fared in the land of its birth. Marat witnessed political agitation at first hand in England during the 1760s and early 1770s—during the so-called "Wilkes and Liberty" movement. Marat saw Wilkes imprisoned on charges that his supporters found to have been invented for the occasion. Like so many others, Marat turned to reading Rousseau, as well as to finding out why liberty, even in Britain, possessed so many enemies. Possibly under the impact of both Rousseau and the liberal Protestantism he encountered in England, Marat tried his hand at philosophy of a radical sort. In his mind radical philosophizing and personal opposition to what he deemed slavery of every kind were of a piece.

In *A Philosophical Essay on Man* (London, 1773), Marat's goal became the reorientation of materialism away from a crassly mechanical view of human nature toward one that emphasized the "soul" or emotions and passions. The following year Marat produced a devastating attack on the power of princes, on oppression and slavery, *Chains of Slavery* (1774). We can only wonder if Marat discussed either book with his masonic brethren when he turned up in Amsterdam and signed the visitors' book of Rousset de Missy's original lodge. *A Philosophical Essay on Man* would probably have remained forever obscure were it not for the fact that Marat became world famous as a leader of the French Revolution. In the essay he sought to give license to the expression of emotion and sensibility, to place them at the heart of the human experience. Twenty years later an emotive passion guided his politics and an equally violent passion drove his murderer, as Marat became a martyr to the cause of revolution.[36]

Marat in the 1770s fittingly captured the mood among British liberals and radicals. They had made reform, in particular the abolition of the African slave trade, a live subject for debate. In the movement against slavery, secular ideas associated with the Enlightenment were complemented, indeed augmented, by religious fervor of a Quaker and Methodist variety.[37] And there was no shortage of stories in print about the conditions of the slave trade and the brutality of the plantation system. Some were written by men who had been slaves. The international republican conversation could focus on concrete domestic issues like the nature of parliamentary representation, but it could also think globally and attack the human misery inflicted by European imperial expansion. There is no small irony in the observation that just as imperialism expanded so too did a cosmopolitan consciousness.

There were good, structural reasons for the late century disaffection toward slavery. The same century that produced the Enlightenment witnessed a hardening of slave laws and institutions, particularly in the British and French colonies. Plantation life had become socially respectable for the often-absent owners who reaped its benefits. In the British West Indies killing a slave was punishable only with a fine. In the French colonies the repressive Code Noir had been promulgated by Louis XIV in 1685, the same year that he began the persecution of French Protestants. In the course of the eighteenth century the situation of slaves in the French colonies had actually worsened, as more and more plantations were established and the black population came to vastly outnumber their white overseers, who ruled with increasing harshness. And slavery, as well as racial stereotyping, had plenty of apologists.[38] Yet remarkably, given the bias against Africans found in much of the travel literature, around 1780 an emotional sea change occurred in literate European circles.

No entirely adequate account has been offered for the emotional shift against slavery, but one piece in the puzzle must be the writings and testimonies given by blacks themselves. Travelers like Ignatius Sancho and Olaudah Equiano, both freed slaves who made their way to England, raised their voices to oppose the slave system. Many abolitionists entertained stereotypes about blacks, about the lethargy imagined as the inevitable result of the

African heat. Yet they also hated slavery, and inspired first by the American Revolution—then by the French—the abolitionists launched a moral crusade that slowly led to victory. At the same time disillusionment with the amateurish and stereotypical quality of travel literature caused reformers to demand a more exacting and scientific account of the world's peoples.[39] Some of the new accounts would harden racial categories, others would seek to write from the inside, from the values and assumptions of distant and foreign peoples.

By the 1780s the new American republic, no longer an imperial colony, rejoined the international conversation at the heart of the Enlightenment. One northern American state after the other—with New Jersey the last in 1804—abolished slavery within its domain. Southern plantation owners had to take care when they ventured north with their human chattel in tow. Thus a legislative body (the French in 1794 had been the first) had turned its back on centuries of the Western (and non-Western) practice of slavery. The effect on European liberals was inspirational. In Dublin Irish republicans saw American politics as the model for their own struggle.[40] In Belfast the republican newspaper of the 1790s, the *Northern Star*, denounced the attack on Priestley, the Unitarian supporter of the French Revolution. In the mind of the Irish radicals Negro slavery stood as yet another example of the British imperial oppression that Priestley had experienced.[41] In Scotland radicals compared "the negro's plight" to that of the Scots.[42]

For a brief moment from Philadelphia to Berlin, it seemed as if a cosmopolitan consensus had formed about a set of universal principles, the inalienable human rights upon which all enlightened people could agree. Yet the agreement remained a minority report. Not even all the loudest voices associated with enlightened opinion stayed the course on the subject of slavery. When British and French émigré radicals of the 1790s went to the new American republic quite a few (including Priestley's close associate Thomas Cooper) succumbed to the lure of slave owning once it became possible for them legally to own other men and women.[43] Ironically it was Johann Herder, the German philosopher of Lutheran persuasion, who created a theoretical framework for understanding the enslaved and the subaltern. While never having seen the New World, Herder, more than many of his European contemporaries, took the cosmopolitan impulse to one of its logical conclusions and articulated the principles upon which a sophisticated cultural ethnography could rest.[44]

By 1789 political events within Europe, and globally, were to make slavery a burning issue. More than any other event in Western history the French

Revolution galvanized international opinion against slavery and around the issue of universal human rights.[45] The British radical Helen Maria Williams effortlessly saw the linkage, "respecting the rights of man in Europe we shall always agree in wishing that a portion of those same rights were extended to Africa."[46] By 1791 even the translator of a vast collection of Moslem law was shocked by how much legal energy had been spent in Moslem countries defining slavery and the rights of owners.[47] Street-corner lecturers harangued London and provincial audiences about the evils of the slave trade, and Quakers and Methodists prayed in their chapels for the victims of enslavement. Young radicals thought in 1791 that "the time is fast approaching when [the slave trade] and the other abuses of government will be destroyed, and justice which is in the interest of the many will be admitted as the ruling principle."[48]

In these same radical circles the plight of African slaves fused with the issue of women's rights, and all became part of a seamless web of republican rhetoric.[49] Even Anne Larpent, a devout, educated Anglican woman of the 1790s who had never ventured into revolutionary Paris, spent endless hours reading Thomas Paine or in discussions about the meaning of the French Revolution. She also saw the link between the personal and the political and argued that an extreme distance between men and women had been one cause of the Revolution.[50] Seeing events in Paris at first hand, Helen Maria Williams described an undoing of gender mores: "women too, far from indulging in the fears incident to our feeble sex, in defiance of the cannon of the Bastille . . . with a spirit worthy of Roman matrons . . . mount[ed] guard in the streets . . . call[ed] out boldly." In the mind of Williams, "women have certainly had a considerable share in the French revolution . . . whatever the imperious lords of the creation may fancy."[51] Clubs of male reformers took up the feminist cause and embraced Mary Wollstonecraft as well as the women revolutionaries in France.[52] Irish republicans of Presbyterian origin, like Mary Ann McCracken, thought that "the present era will produce some women of sufficient talents to inspire the rest with genuine love of Liberty . . . I think the reign of prejudice is nearly at an end."[53]

As we are about to see, imbued with such utopian ideas, circles of young radicals and romantics, the generation of the 1790s, invented new forms of personal experimentation and attempted to create new genres of human affect and freedom. One of their prophets, and a seeker among many forms of sectarian Protestantism, William Blake sang of free love between the sexes.[54] Even animals had their moment of liberation, with John Oswald raising the issue of their humane treatment.[55] He too like Paine made his way to revolutionary Paris; a few years earlier he had been proclaiming the virtues of the revolutionary Dutch.[56]

As if this sort of incendiary writing and theorizing were not enough, the pied piper of the British radical and romantic left, William Godwin, gave the world a reasoned argument against marriage and monogamy and in favor of complete freedom in matters sexual.[57] In radical circles women married to brutal men could now describe themselves—in the spirit of Godwin—as property, in effect, as legal prostitutes.[58] A song of the day proclaimed, "Since Marriage an outrage on Nature we dream/We're determined to do the vile custom away/And each Man and each Woman shall then live in common/When once on the Shores of fam'd Botany Bay."[59]

Enemies of the Revolution spied all these reversals of traditional gender relations as deeply subversive. The mob that burned Priestley out of his home for supporting events in Paris, sang in condemnation: "While o'er the bleeding corpse of France,/Wild anarchy exulting stands/And female friends around her dance/with fatal lamp cords in their hands."[60] The anti-Jacobins could find no rhetoric too strong for the task of condemning the personal morality of Mary Wollstonecraft.[61] They hounded young radicals like John Thelwall who hid out in Wales, where he and his wife tried to raise their daughter to be freer, more independent, by putting her in trousers.[62] At every turn Thelwall, like his great contemporary and fellow poet William Blake, thought expansively across national boundaries and saw empire everywhere as the enemy. For them slavery became a condition that bound Africans as well as the "slaves of labour or of war."[63]

A Radical Consciousness

By the 1770s an ability to identify with political movements coming from abroad brought with it a consciousness about reform. This can be seen in many places, but we return continuously in this chapter to Great Britain. Where once in the 1690s, and for a few decades thereafter, England enjoyed pride of place in the political consciousness of the republic of letters, by the 1770s the action had passed to its rebellious American colonies. Then by the 1790s, the gaze of British reformers, who could still invoke the indigenous republican idealism of the 1650s, nevertheless turned increasingly toward Paris.

Government spies reported that in the early 1790s British supporters of the French Revolution assembled and gave toasts in the following, cosmopolitan order: loyalty to king and constitution, perpetual peace between Great

Britain, Ireland, and France, the universal rights of man, the virtues of United States of America, the happy prospect of revolution in Poland (in 1791), the wisdom of the English republican theorists of the seventeenth century, and, finally, the truth found among illustrious sages "who have enlightened mankind on the principles of civil society."[64] At this distance the logic of assembling all these causes may escape us unless we realize that it had become possible to imagine them as invisibly linked. The English republican tradition bore relevance to events in France and Poland, as well as to international peace and the American Revolution, because reformers could now think beyond national borders and interests and embrace a universalism they imagined as relevant to all Westerners. In Britain it was the cosmopolite who sang most vociferously for the cause of liberty.[65] In Paris his French counterparts championed the universal rights of man while pouring over English republican texts from the seventeenth century, writers like James Harrington, Algernon Sidney, and John Milton. They translated them and in the process sometimes made them more radical about pure democracy than the original texts argued.[66]

At the same moment, in British circles zealous for the cause of the French Revolution, a remarkable argument surfaced. It said that fraternizing in local political societies with ties to French revolutionaries should be seen as analogous to the international contacts needed for science. "Is there any impropriety in the *philosophical* Societies of London, Paris, or Stockholm, corresponding for the improvement of Chemistry, or experimental Philosophy?" Do we all not want these contacts because they are "the most effectual means of diffusing Information? Why then should societies instituted for the promotion of *political* Knowledge, be debarred from the common means of Improvement?" Thomas Cooper, chemist and educator, a friend to the Watt family of steam engine fame, made this telling point. It may go part of the way to explaining why the scientific circles around Priestley, Cooper, Thomas Beddoes, and Humphry Davy had been so warm for the American Revolution, then for the French. They saw themselves as doing in politics what had been done in science, and through international communication taking up "the common methods of communication permitted and adopted in every other branch of human science."[67] Pushing the boundaries through cosmopolitan communication in one area became a technique appropriated, used now to facilitate new and personal politics.

By late century a powerful new consciousness emerged. It was never exclusively British, despite the focus there. An essential ingredient of the cosmopolitan political consciousness, by definition, crossed national boundaries:

what had once seemed local and intractable came to be seen as similar to elsewhere, if approached with the multiple visions that an international conversation afforded. The cosmopolitan effect took on unprecedented personal
dimensions. With imaginations fired often by distant events, British men and
women sought not only to think, but also to live as reformers.

We remember the journeys to France, the famous border crossings of
the 1790s—undertaken by Mary Wollstonecraft, William Wordsworth, and
Helen Maria Williams—but there were countless others who less famously
became political cosmopolites.[68] Their revolutionary friends in France in turn
appealed directly to British sympathizers as "generous foreigners . . . who
applauded our courage . . . those compatriots of all countries who are friends
to humanity . . . who hope for the imminent destruction of all the prejudices that shatter the bonds of fraternity between individuals and between
peoples." We know about the language used in this particular appeal because
in 1791 the home of the pro-French Joseph Priestley in Birmingham was invaded by an antirevolutionary mob and letters sent to him by the Société
des amis de la constitution de Bordeaux were confiscated.[69] Predictably they
made their way to the Home Office. British members of societies formed in
imitation of their revolutionary French brethren said that both operated in
"the best Interest of Mankind," noting as proof of the assertion that everywhere, but especially in both France and England, they gave so much alarm
to the "pensioned Advocates of Aristocracy."[70]

There is as much continuity as there is rupture between the cosmopolitan Enlightenment as lived in the clubs, lodges, and salons and the political socializing of radicals and early romantics during the 1790s. In the last
decades of the century one theme seemed to dominate the conversation about
world events found in sociable circles: the meaning and nature of democratic republics and, after 1789, the kind of personal transformation needed to
create the democratic subject.[71] International republican conversation took
place in printed periodicals and private letters as well as in drawing rooms,
largely written or spoken in English or French (also used by Dutch and German correspondents, and readable by any English person with a decent education).[72] For a brief time, early in the 1790s, the conversation eclipsed national
identities, and like moths to the imported flame of revolution, some British
and Irish republicans even imagined reform, if not revolution at home, to be
inevitable.

In such exhilarating, yet dangerous times, consolation also came from
sensing that the like-minded could be anywhere. Strangers could be friends
just because they shared a set of republican ideals. In 1791 Helen Maria

Williams, the British expatriate and revolutionary loyalist, told her friends back home about the warmth of the reception she received for her pro-revolutionary writings, "La Société des amis de la Constitution at Rouen sent me a very flattering letter of thanks for my french journal, and ordered three thousand copies of an answer I sent them, to be printed." Still she felt home-sick and confided that all "the attentions of the Democrats [do not com-pensate] for this cruel separation from my friends at home."[73] Yet Williams's commitment to the new French republic ultimately won out, and the emo-tional radicalism of the 1790s so infected her that she became a permanent expatriate, a wanderer in a strange land even during her brief return visits to England.

Living as a Democrat

At a period when the Kingdoms of the earth are shook upon their settled founda-tions—when Kings are humbled to the dust by those they are born to govern . . . it is not very wonderful that the physical economy and organization of the human body should, in many instances, experience something of sympathetic and similar revo-lutions . . . however expedient the extermination of unnatural passions.[74]

Contemporaries warned that revolutions in the polity augured transforma-tions in personal manner and affect. The path-breaking French psychiatrist Philippe Pinel observed as early as 1790 that great revolutions in the politi-cal order transform the human passions, excite the imagination, and elevate people out of a long-felt lethargy.[75] Opponents of the French Revolution used graphic images to suggest that sexual depravity and unnatural passions ruled in the hearts of its sympathizers. In 1791 James Gillray produced engravings that suggested the rape of George III by the radical Horne Tooke.[76] Other opponents of the French further insinuated that women in particular were to blame for events in Paris. In his *Reflections on the Revolution in France* (1790), Edmund Burke insisted that the French Revolution had the capacity to unhinge all mores, undo patriarchal authority in church and home, and unleash the extremes of atheism and unnatural passions. The so-called anti-Jacobins accused the radicals of being relativists in their morals and mores and hinted darkly at sexual deviation.[77] Those whom by day were seen to be men could become—they implied—women of the night. The enemies of revolution expressed with particular nastiness an anxiety that we should take seriously. All the boundaries and borders established to police conduct and behavior now seemed breachable. So moved by this new freedom, the young

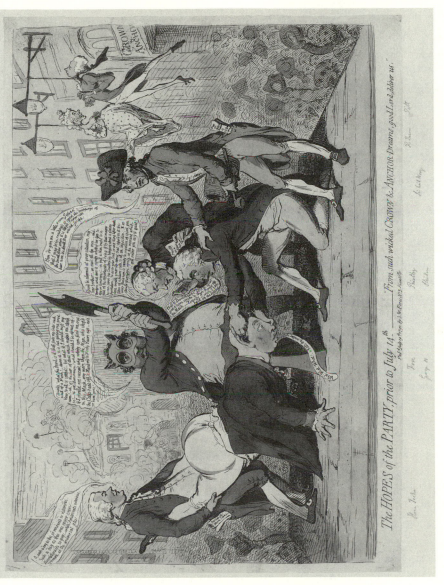

Figure 9. *The Hopes of the Party, prior to July 14th*—"*From such wicked Crown & Anchor dreams, good Lord deliver us.*" By James Gillray, published by Samuel William Fores, 10 July 1791. Images are of John Horne Tooke, Charles James Fox, King George III, Joseph Priestley, Richard Brinsley Sheridan, Sir Cecil Wray, Bt, Charlotte Sophia of Mecklenburg-Strelitz, William Pitt. Courtesy of the National Portrait Gallery, London.

William Wordsworth sang its praises: "once, Man entirely free, alone and wild,/ Was blest as free—for he was Nature's child./ He, all superior but his God disdained,/ Walked none restraining, and by none restrained."[78]

Being young in the 1790s meant coming of age in a new, unscripted world. The revolutions everywhere licensed revolt against patriarchy, in particular one's own father. A young British radical could only rush to Paris. Once there, James Watt, Jr—son of the famous perfecter of the steam engine, wrote back to his perplexed father in Birmingham to tie the warp of the Enlightenment to the woof of revolution: "The principles upon which the thrones [of kings] were founded are now disavowed by an enlightened age and mankind awakened from their lethargy are everywhere shaking off a system founded upon force and Priestcraft." Giddy with the power unleashed, young James cast his lot with the Jacobins, and in his letters from 1792 onward he took to lecturing his now long-suffering father on the evils of monarchy, and on his own hatred for the "crimes of tyrants."[79] His young friends shared this sense of empowerment, with Josiah Wedgwood, Jr. writing to his father, the famous porcelain manufacturer, "I have been too long in the habit of looking upon myself as the equal of everybody to bear the haughty manners of those who come into a shop."[80] These young rebels enjoyed plenty of company, and no social or political convention was sacrosanct.

When James Watt, Jr. arrived in Paris in March he brought greetings from the Manchester Constitutional Society to the mayor, and Robespierre presented him and his traveling companion, Thomas Cooper, to the Jacobin society. With Watt and Cooper went a letter from Thomas Walker that "hinted at the imminent collapse of the British monarchy and aristocratic society."[81] At the same moment the constitutional society in London wrote to the Paris Jacobins as "citizens of the world . . . engaged in the fraternity of human kind."[82] Enthused by the writings of Thomas Paine, and by the heady exaltation of a revolution in full throttle, Cooper would remember those months as the happiest of his life.[83] Fraternizing had become so intense—in Paris but also in radical circles in Manchester—that lives came to be shaped by it. During the 1790s the corresponding societies in England and the Jacobin clubs in France rested upon foundations created throughout the century by the civic life of enlightened sociability. If one single thread ran through the cosmopolitanism of these circles, it was their interest in utility, in the practical, in progress, and in the improvement of self and society. The cause of revolution had brought people together who would otherwise have been strangers and who had no common bonds except their causes.

In Britain, in one sense, the meaning of political revolt against all authority could only be intensely personal, and vicarious, as at the time no actual revolution had occurred. So the newly radicalized stuck together, even years after the revolution had led to disillusionment for some. By 1800 the King of Clubs in London constituted the fashionable club for liberal Whig reformers, and into the circle moved Tom Wedgwood, Gregory Watt (the son of James and half brother of James, Jr.), James Mackintosh (after 1803, Sir James), the Smith brothers, and the Scottish poet Thomas Campbell, confidant of Gregory Watt. Robert Southey, Samuel Taylor Coleridge, Humphry Davy, James and John Tobin—overlapping with Gregory Watt—made yet another related circle.[84] Ever present lay the influence and personal persuasion offered by William Godwin. At the height of the Napoleonic wars the young, but emotionally and physically ill Tom Wedgwood longed for the company of French republicans.[85] Among the members of these loose clubs or associations, many like Mackintosh became celebrated Whigs, while the Reverend Sydney Smith sealed his credentials by being one of the founders of the *Edinburgh Review* and a major contributor to it.

Smith's life nicely illustrates the linkage between the personal and the political. He had been deeply influenced by the principles of the French Revolution about which he learned, he said, while in 1798 accompanying on tour the son of his parish patron who had gone to study at the University of Edinburgh.[86] Smith's life embodied the meaning that could be extracted from revolutions lived vicariously. He believed that others too, like Godwin, had also been "impelled and directed" by the progress of the Revolution. "The fearful convulsion . . . agitated the world of politics and of morals . . . burst open the secret springs of imagination and of thought . . . roused [Godwin] not into action but into thought." Being young in 1790s Britain, and drawn to the radical politics of the age, required above all new and rebellious thinking.

Smith said that Godwin changed his life, and he discovered that "passions which have not usually been thought worthy to agitate the soul, now first seem to have their most ardent beatings, and their tumultuous joys."[87] If Smith knew joy and likened it to the effects of the French Revolution, he came to happiness by a most circuitous route. In contrast to the liberty he found in Godwin, Smith experienced what he called "the tyranny, trouble and folly" of his own father.[88] They had poisonous relations complicated by tension about money and ideology, with the freethinking Smith even defending the right to commit suicide. Eventually his father told him in 1797 to go away and never darken his door.[89]

While the father and son Watt eventually made their peace, the Smiths never reconciled. Conservative father and radicalized son sputtered on for years in an acrimonious vein. Significantly when the younger Smith and his wife finally established a family of their own they raised their children in an atmosphere of such freedom that one governess after another fled in despair. He "purposely indulged" his own children in "the liberty . . . [which will] accustom a young man gradually to be his own master." Husband and wife saw their marriage as companionate and sought to set a very different emotional tone in the household from that which Smith had known as a child.[90] Radicals like the Smiths, romantics like Wordsworth and Coleridge, dreamed of eliminating personal distance, of finding emotional transparency. In their youth they had learned one of the lessons of their liberal Protestantism well; in young adulthood, attained in the 1790s, they went to new emotional places.

Same-sex experimentation in intimacy, as well as intense friendships between the sexes, characterized these circles of radicals and romantics. The Wordsworth-Dorothy Wordsworth-Coleridge triangle has long defied any sort of simple characterization. To say that each in his or her way was in love with the other, while leaving open the nature of that love, is probably the

Figure 10. *Weird Sisters: Ministers of Darkness: Minions of the Moon. They should be Women!—and yet their beards forbid us to interpret, . . . that they are so.* Intaglio print. James Gillray, *The Genuine Works of James Gillray* (1830), 17. Courtesy of the Metropolitan Museum of Art, Gift of Paul F. Walter, 1980.

best that anyone at this distance can do.[91] Southey was also smitten by his male friends, particularly Coleridge. Long after they had abandoned their plan to migrate to Pennsylvania and join Priestley, who had left England in disgust—there to set up the utopian community on the egalitarian principles of what they called "pantisocracy"—Southey longed for Coleridge's company: "the man, to whom, in all the ups and downs of six years, my heart has clung with most affection, despite even its own efforts."[92] The anti-Jacobins mercilessly ridiculed their circle, depicting them as effeminate, infantile, sickly, and absurd.[93]

At the root of the utopian and (avant la lettre) socialist scheme known as pantisocracy stood the passionate figure of George Dyer. More than the other utopians who wanted to find personal and gender equality in Pennsylvania, Dyer possessed a deep concern for the poor and disadvantaged. Unlike so many within the circle that nevertheless embraced him, Dyer knew poverty firsthand, having seen his father committed to the poorhouse. Throughout his life he wrote and spoke about social conditions.[94] Yet Dyer also shared in the experimentally erotic milieu of these young romantics. For a time the circle of Dyer, Southey, Wordsworth, and Coleridge became intensely involved one with the other. In 1800 Dyer suppressed a book of poetry that contains these lines addressed to Robert Anderson: "But, no, my friend: I ready thy candid page,/. . ./ Oh! May I view again with ravish's sight,/ As when with thee, Anderson, I stray'd, /And all the wonder-varying scene survey'd."[95] Dyer also knew his Anacreon well, and the ancient poet had long been associated with same-sex intimacy.[96] A barely suppressed eroticism infused Dyer's memories of his youthful Cambridge days. In his "Ode to the River Cam" the picture evokes "nature's living power" and the "new-born joys" of "bard, the lover, and the jocund swain." Yet it also makes clear that "All must be left, tho' friendly to the Muse; / And man, poor man, lie down in cheerless gloom."

The revolutionary vision shared by Dyer and his circle of radical romantics held them together for a time in London and the Lake District, all bound by a labile affection. The circle endorsed both science and the English revolutionary tradition of the seventeenth century, to some extent learned in their university days at Cambridge. Dyer entered "in converse sweet with Locke, immortal sage; / So too by Cam with him, whose bosom glow'd / With thy pure raptures, and the Muse's rage [Milton]." Algernon Sidney also stood with them as they cursed "those murd'rers of the world," the Austrians and the Prussians. Whether in alliance with the French revolutionaries, or with the Poles led by Kosciusko, Dyer and his cosmopolitan friends wooed "Thee,

Liberty."[97] Even after 1800, when the Napoleonic Wars turned many a radical into a conservative, members of the Southey circle continued to discuss women's rights and to address schemes for enabling women to achieve economic independence.[98] A few years earlier Southey had been influenced by conversing with the great feminist Mary Wollstonecraft.[99]

Other, less disciplined seekers were drawn to the romantic flame, and Tom Wedgwood, the son of the famous potter and friend to the Watts, became Coleridge's bosom companion. Experimentation and the breaking of conventions gave purpose to their lives. They both shared an addiction to opium, as did Dorothy Wordsworth.[100] Aided by Coleridge, the young Wedgwood, and possibly his brother, also tried a form of hemp leaves known as "bang."[101] Tom had early on developed a disdain for "the pleasures of the family & having a great disgust to large mixed company."[102] After a series of male companions, many of them also associated with the King of Clubs,[103] Tom Wedgwood found little solace. He succumbed to tuberculosis and his addictions. Telling his brother in 1804 that his "present sufferings [are] too intolerable & they are beyond all alleviation . . . my pains & extreme feebleness & depression are now unceasing," Tom was dead by the summer of 1805.[104] His youthful dalliance with Godwin and radicalism, and with science, did not save him from the depression that stalked the Wedgwood family. It is little wonder that they also sought liberty in their personal lives, emboldened by their shared intimacies with poets and philosophers. By 1800 the politics found amid the sociability of republicans and radicals had become intensely personal, and they had given birth to a new, bohemian persona.

Experimentation with self and society seemed the only answer, at least in Britain where even the first generation of modern radicals, raised in the shadow of 1789, wanted to avoid its terror and violence. In 1800 Coleridge, Southey, Davy, Watt, and company sniffed nitrous oxide (what we call laughing gas), and Davy said of himself, "I seemed to be a sublime being, newly created & superior to other mortals." He described the gas as "joy-inspiring . . . [and it produced] a great sensation." Then echoing the language of the French Revolution, he added, "ça ira." Gregory Watt addressed Davy as my "dear Alchemist."[105] Robert Southey and his wife also enjoyed the pleasures of the gas, saying that it was transformative and must constitute the atmosphere in "Mohammed's Paradise."[106] Perhaps the liberation always promised by science, in this instance by the new chemistry of gases, had become far safer than the political ledge on which so many radicals had teetered during the 1790s. The inspiration drawn from revolutions on distant shores, or actual experience, led to a longing for safer places such as could be found in the private London clubs or chemical laboratories in which so many of these middle-aged radicals now found themselves.

Decades of sociability, politics observed or lived, had loosened old restraints but thrown up new cautions. In the midst of the Terror, Helen Williams shuddered, "the scenes which have lately been acting at Paris . . . have . . . been such that scarcely can my conviction that this temporary evil will produce permanent good at all reconcile my mind to that profusion of blood, that dismal waste of life of which I have been witness."[107] Living on the edge of a more democratic era, especially if trying to assist at its birthing, could bring exhilaration, as well as fear and foreboding. The cosmopolitan had given birth to the bohemian, but also to a deep uncertainty about where the borders and boundaries lay.

Epilogue

The nineteenth century opened with international warfare on a grand scale and the Napoleonic Wars offered few propitious moments for cosmopolitans. The French revolutionaries had appropriated the cosmopolite as one of their own, saying in the National Assembly that "zèle cosmopolite" propelled its willingness to admit foreigners as citizens of the new republic.[1] All the enemies of revolution, beginning with Edmund Burke, could now deride the cosmopolitan along with the revolution. Yet we make a mistake if we write the history of early modern cosmopolitanism that leads to a historical cul-de-sac. In the face of the nationalist onslaught so visible early in the nineteenth century, the cosmopolitan may have been less politically fashionable than it had been in the 1770s, most notably in the 1790s. But if we have learned anything about the behavior behind the words and affect of cosmopolites, we now know their protean qualities.

By the 1790s being cosmopolitan had come to mean crossing religious and national boundaries, or social ones, or being experimental, and embracing the socially different or eccentric as a mark of a commitment to liberty, equality, and fraternity. Within circles influenced by cosmopolitan mores, for example, the hostility toward slavery continued to burn brightly. In the 1840s the new World Anti-Slavery Convention held in London declared: "We are not merely Britons, but cosmopolites. We go to the east and to the west, to the north and to the south, to seek for misery and to endeavour to relieve it."[2]

By 1840 cosmopolites took on a wide range of human injustices without implying that they had renounced their national identity. But the anti-cosmopolites had long known the range, the implications and meanings that could be embraced under the cosmopolitan mantle, and historically they liked none of them. Let us recapitulate their dislikes. Recall that as representatives of the French state in the 1680s they closed down the dreamy alchemists with their questing for rejuvenation and elixirs. The royal officials told the Académie des sciences to get on with the business of measuring the size of France and testing the quality of its waters. Early in the eighteenth century the anticosmopolites witnessed with disdain the eccentric behavior of Jews and Christians in Avignon. They wanted such loose fraternizing stopped. At the same time in Britain the reformers of manners sought to imprison other loose livers who supposedly needed repression. Decades later in the 1780s, in France the anticosmopolites probably did not know about the freemasons in their midst eager to find a new universal religion. Had the old regime authorities known of them, they would have been spied upon and seen as promoting disorder. In the 1790s the habit of spying passed to the British Home Office and its agents collected information in London coffeehouses, Bristol, the Lake District—wherever transgressive men and women congregated. They also prosecuted seditious speech in the courts, not always with great success.

From the inquisitors in Avignon to Edmund Burke in Parliament, the proponents of church, nation, order, and orthodoxy knew that cosmopolitanism threatened authority. Without the border crossings of early modern Europe, the cosmopolitanism that turned political late in the eighteenth century could not have matured—indeed flourished, amid adversity, until well into the present. We have just witnessed a sampling of cosmopolite minority reports culled from diverse sources, long neglected, some experienced unselfconsciously by participants.

Perhaps the extremes of behavior witnessed in the 1790s made the anticosmopolites seem all too prescient. Certainly the nationalism that prevailed in Europe right up to 1945 insisted that citizens of the world were better off keeping a low profile. If their time has finally come, then they deserve the outlines of a history. The episodes described here have attempted to make a start at it. They are also offered as cautionary tales. There is nothing inevitable about people becoming cosmopolitan; they can just as easily in certain circumstances turn inward or hostile to all that is foreign. The case studies presented are addressed to every reader, everywhere, but especially to those who see the cosmopolitan threatened in a post-9/11 world. The events of that day, and the wars that have followed, challenge cosmopolites to hold to an ideal that zealots—from Islamic fascists to right-wing Christian bigots closer to home—would destroy, if they could turn the political order in their direction. The cosmopolitan acknowledges the common humanity of such people while repudiating their goals, and it seeks to give historical life to social habits, encounters, and practices that take the imagination beyond nation and creed.

Notes

Introduction

1. As cited in Thomas J. Schlereth, *The Cosmopolitan Ideal in Enlightenment Thought: Its Form and Function in the Ideas of Franklin, Hume, and Voltaire, 1694–1790* (Notre Dame, Ind.: University of Notre Dame Press, 1977), 47.

2. See Louis Charles Fougeret de Monbron, *Le Cosmopolite, ou, Le citoyen du monde* (London, 1761), 4. There is a 1751 edition of this work cited in the extremely useful summary of word usage in Gerd van den Heuvel, "Cosmopolite, Cosmopoli-(ti)sme," in Rolf Reichardt and Eberhard Schmitt, eds., *Handbuch politisch-sozialer Grundbegriffe in Frankreich 1680–1820* (Munich: R. Oldenbourg, 1986), 6: 41–55.

3. [Otto Hoffham], *De Kosmopoliet* (Amsterdam: Klippink, 1776–77). I owe this reference to Dr. Inger Leemans. See also Andre Hanou, "Beelden van de Vrijmetse-larij 4. Tempel of Tafel? De *Vrye Koks* van *De Kosmopoliet* (1776)," *Thoth* 43 (1992): 84–93.

4. Cosmopolite, *To the British Nation* (London: Printed & Sold by D.I. Eaton, 28 November 1795), 3, "it is obvious Parliament is nothing more than a register office for the crown."

5. Eusebe Philadelphe Cosmopolite, *Le reveille-matin des francois, et leurs voisins* (Edimbourg, 1574) (a false imprint, and without traditional accent marks).

6. Académie française, *Dictionnaire de l'Académie française* (Paris, 1762), vol. 1, entry for "cosmopolite." Cited in Andrea Albrecht, *Kosmopolitismus: Weltbürger-diskurse in Literatur, Philosophie und Publizistik um 1800* (Berlin: De Gruyter, 2005).

7. For the contemporary discussion of this phenomenon, see Steven Vertovec and Robin Cohen, eds., *Conceiving Cosmopolitanism: Theory, Context, and Practice* (New York: Oxford University Press, 2002), and summarizing positions held by Nussbaum, Hollinger, and Appiah, among others. See Pauline Kleingeld and Eric Brown, "Cosmopolitanism," in Edward N. Zalta, ed., *The Stanford Encyclopedia of Philosophy* (Fall 2002 ed.), <http://plato.stanford.edu/entries/cosmopolitanism/>.

8. See Schlereth, *The Cosmopolitan Ideal* and Albrecht, *Kosmopolitismus*. The latter offers a very useful and detailed summary of the early usages of the words "cosmopolite" and "cosmopolitan."

9. Paul Hazard, "Cosmopolite," in *Mélanges d'histoire littéraire générale et com-parée offerts à Fernand Baldensperger* (Paris: Champion,1930), 1: 354–64; A. Mathiez, *La révolution et les étrangers: cosmopolitisme et défense nationale* (Paris: Renaissance du livre, 1918). On the context within which Hazard wrote, see Austin Harrington, "Ernst Troeltsch's Concept of Europe," *European Journal of Social Theory* 7 (2004):

479–98. For Postel's use of the term, see his *De la Republique des Turcs: et là où l'occasion s'offrera, des meurs et des loys de tous Muhamédistes, par Guillaume Postel, cosmopolite* (Poitiers, 1560).

10. Seyla Benhabib, *Transformations of Citizenship: Dilemmas of the Nation State in the Era of Globalization* (Assen: Van Gorcum, 2001), 38.

11. Maxine Berg, "In Pursuit of Luxury: Global History and British Consumer Goods in the Eighteenth Century," *Past and Present* 182 (2004): 85–142.

12. See Simon Burrows, "The Cosmopolitan Press, 1760–1815," in Hannah Barker and Simon Burrows, eds., *Press, Politics and the Public Sphere in Europe and North America, 1760–1820* (Cambridge: Cambridge University Press, 2002), 23–47.

13. The Enlightenment also rested on a stinging critique of courts and their culture; see Jacob Soll, *Publishing* The Prince: *History, Reading, and the Birth of Political Criticism* (Ann Arbor: University of Michigan Press, 2005).

14. Stephen Eric Bronner, *Reclaiming the Enlightenment: Toward a Politics of Radical Engagement* (New York: Columbia University Press, 2004), 146–50.

15. See Robert Fine and Robin Cohen, "Four Cosmopolitan Moments," in Vertovec and Cohen, eds., *Conceiving Cosmopolitanism*, 138–39. For surveys of the ideal, see Derek Heater, *World Citizenship and Government: Cosmopolitan Ideas in the History of Western Political Thought* (New York: St. Martin's Press, 1996) and Schlereth, *The Cosmopolitan Ideal.* The historical record seems to bear out the approach to cosmopolitanism taken in Andrew Linklater, *The Transformation of Political Community: Ethical Foundations of the Post-Westphalian Era* (Columbia: University of South Carolina Press, 1998).

16. Siep Stuurman, "The Voice of Thersites: Reflections on the Origins of the Idea of Equality," *Journal of the History of Ideas* 65 (2004): 187.

17. For a helpful discussion of the terms as used in the early modern period, see Pamela H. Smith, *The Body of the Artisan: Art and Experience in the Scientific Revolution* (Chicago: University of Chicago Press, 2003), 17–18.

18. See Bernhard Giesen, "Cosmopolitans, Patriots, Jacobins, and Romantics," *Daedalus* 127, 3 (1998): 226. The article argues, improbably, that the state fostered the Enlightenment. Cf. Karen O'Brien, *Narratives of Enlightenment: Cosmopolitan History from Voltaire to Gibbon* (Cambridge: Cambridge University Press, 1997); Anthony Pagden, "The Genesis of 'Governance' and Enlightenment Conceptions of the Cosmopolitan World Order," *International Social Science Journal* 155 (March 1998): 7–15. I owe the phrase "de facto cosmopolitanism" to Austin Harrington; also helpful is van den Heuvel, "Cosmopolite, Cosmopoli(ti)sme," 41–43. For the criticism that Kant did not give every culture its due, see James Tully, "The Kantian Idea of Europe," in Anthony Pagden, ed., *The Idea of Europe: From Antiquity to the European Union* (Cambridge: Cambridge University Press, 2002), 331–58; for a kinder approach to Kant, see Sankar Muthu, *Enlightenment Against Empire* (Princeton, N.J.: Princeton University Press, 2003).

19. Sharon Anderson-Gold, *Cosmopolitanism and Human Rights* (Cardiff: University of Wales Press, 2001), 7, citing David Forsythe, *Human Rights and World Politics* (Lincoln: University of Nebraska Press, 1983); Charles Jones, *Global Justice: Defending Cosmopolitanism* (Oxford: Oxford University Press, 1999); Pauline Kleingeld, "Kant's Cosmopolitan Law: World Citizenship for a Global Order," *Kantian*

Review 2 (1998): 72–90. See also Kleingeld, "Six Varieties of Cosmopolitanism in Eighteenth-Century Germany," *Journal of the History of Ideas* 63 (1999): 505–24.

20. For men and women engaged in literary criticism in one such coterie during the Restoration in England, see Paul Trolander and Zeynep Tenger, "Katherine Philips and Coterie Critical Practices," *Eighteenth-Century Studies* 37 (Spring 2004): 367–87.

Chapter 1. Censors, Inquisitors, and Cosmopolites

1. Charles C. Noel, "Clerics and Crown in Bourbon Spain, 1700–1808," in James E. Bradley and Dale K. Van Kley, eds., *Religion and Politics in Enlightenment Europe* (Notre Dame Ind.: University of Notre Dame Press, 2001), 124–25.

2. The city of Avignon and the surrounding territory, which taken together make up the modern Department of the Vaucluse, actually formed two separate states prior to 1790, both under papal sovereignty. In the eighteenth century they were administered collectively by a vice-legate who lived in Avignon. In disputes with the papacy both Louis XIV and Louis XV briefly annexed the papal states, in 1662–64, 1688–89, and 1768–74. I owe these details to Eric Johnson.

3. Barbara de Negroni, *Lectures interdites: le travail des censeurs au XVIIIc siècle, 1723–1774* (Paris: Albin Michel, 1995), 13.

4. Bibliothèque de l'Arsenal, Paris, MS 10283. ff 1–9 Chev. Dubourg in 1725, his every movement and his meeting with the duc d'Orleans and also an Englishman described; f. 39 Prince Scarpin and a duchess, and see f. 42 where we learn they are seeing the envoy from Florence; they are watched for months; f. 81 ambassador of Malta also in the group; f. 108 letter to Brussels being opened because it is believed to be by a spy; f. 114 instructions to spy on the ambassador of Sardinia; f. 141 abbé D'aubigny from Liège—he is falsely representing himself as an envoy of William of Nassau; f. 149 he is doing business at rue Quinquampoix and at the Compagnes des Indes; hanging out with various merchants; f. 181 Schual Juif et Samuel Levi; they are brothers on business and not clear why they are being watched; f. 203 duc d'Aremberg "les vapeurs bachique qu l'on fut oblige de le monter dan sa chaise"; his secretary has stayed behind and his name is Violent; f. 249 on Jansenists printing books in Nancy; f. 307 one M de Macanas suspected of spying for Spain and seen in the company of the Spanish ambassador; two Italian singers are also involved, but they are actually 2 priests, see f. 312; 1729 f. 321 an English and Dutch meeting being observed, both Stanhope and Walpole are in Paris, f. 338 and seen talking with Russian ambassador. MS 10284 1730 f. 26 Walpole is ambassador and they are using an English banker; f. 35 contact between Lord Waldegrave and Spanish ambassador; Waldegrave described as ambassador; f. 43 they are really worried about spying for Spain with list of 5 spies living in Paris and one works for the pope, f.64; MS 10254, opens in 1723 and concerns sodomy; a priest from Flanders taken in the Luxembourg gardens and he is returned to Picardy; another abbé caught and described as incorrigible; MS 10293 resuming observations of foreigners, now in 1747, once again, all ambassadors; f. 220, English spy who hangs out in the cafes being followed by the

mouche and seen speaking to the domestic of the ambassador from Venice. By 1760 significant gaps appear in the records. For a fascinating account of spying in Venice, see Iain McCalman, *The Last Alchemist: Count Cagliostro Master of Magic in the Age of Reason* (New York: HarperCollins, 2003), 42–48.

5. For work on this episode, see L. J. Boon, ed. *"Dein godlosen hoop van menschen": Vervolging van homoseksuelen in de Republiek in de jaren dertig van de achttiende eeuw* (Amsterdam: De Bataffsche Leeuw, 1997). See note 4 for relatively light punishments for sodomy imposed in Paris. Theo van der Meer pioneered the study of the 1730–31 events.

6. Jean Schreuder, *Redevoering, Uytbesprooken door een Broeder Orateur . . . 27 December 1755*, 6–7.

7. See *Daily Advertiser*, London, December 1735, also *Europische Mercurius*, 1730, 1: 283–304; 2: 289–304.

8. W. M. Jacob, *Lay People and Religion in the Early Eighteenth Century* (Cambridge: Cambridge University Press, 1996), chap. 5.

9. Josiah Woodward, *An Account of the Rise and Progress of the Religious Societies in the City of London . . .* (London, 1701), dedicatory preface.

10. Clark Library, UCLA, MS D951Z M294 ca. 1720, from the rules of one such group, the Society of Romney in the hand of N. Durant.

11. S. D. Smith, ed., *"An Exact and Industrious Tradesman": The Letter Book of Joseph Symson of Kendal, 1711–1720* (London: Oxford University Press for the British Academy, 2002), 740.

12. Shelley Burtt, *Virtue Transformed: Political Argument in England, 1688–1740* (New York: Cambridge University Press, 1992), 43.

13. William E. Burns, "London's Barber-Elijah: Thomas Moor and Universal Salvation in the 1690s," *Harvard Theological Review* 95 (2002): 277–83.

14. Clark Library, MS D951Z M294, f. 9, "Peculier Orders of the Society of Romney."

15. John Barrell, "Coffee-House Politicians," *Journal of British Studies* 43 (April 2004): 228–29.

16. Clark Library, UCLA, MS M677M3 ca. 1720, [Anon.] "Miscellanea curiosa," f. 15.

17. For 's Gravesande's admission into the society that published the *Journal Littéraire*, see University Library, Leiden, Marchand MS 2, letter from St. Hyacinthe, 2 March 1713 and Marchand MSS 1, 16 September 1713, F. le Bachellé in Utrecht to the society saying he is afraid of writing for fear of revealing "the secrets of the society."

18. A copy of this document can be seen in the appendix to Margaret C. Jacob, *The Radical Enlightenment: Pantheists, Freemasons and Republicans*, 2nd ed. rev. (Morristown, N.J.: Temple Books, 2003), 289–91. A French translation will appear with L'Orient, Paris.

19. University Library, Leiden, Marchand MS 1, letters of 16 September 1713, 14 December 1713, from F. le Bachellé in Utrecht to the society. In the same collection, 18 9bre 1712, Fritsch in Paris to Marchand on seeing Douxfils in Brussels.

20. See University Library, Leiden, Prentenkabinet, boxes 1 through 9.

21. Bernard Picart, *The Ceremonies and religious customs of the various nations of the known world; together with historical annotations, and several curious discourses*

. . . Written originally in French, and illustrated with a large number of folio copper plates . . . designed by Bernard Picart . . . Faithfully translated into English, by a gentleman some time since of St. John's College in Oxford (London: Claude Du Bosc, 1733–39); the first edition appeared in French in 1723.

22. One of these can be found at Young Research Library, UCLA. See the Abraham Wolf Spinoza Collection, Department of Special Collections, 1990, item no. 307, *La vie et l'esprit de Mr. Benoit de Spinoza* (Amsterdam: Charles Le Vier, 1719).

23. See Margaret C. Jacob and Matthew Kadane, "Missing Now Found in the Eighteenth Century. Weber's Protestant Capitalist," *American Historical Review* 108, 1 (February 2003): 20–49.

24. Susan E. Whyman, *Sociability and Power in Late-Stuart England: The Cultural Worlds of the Verneys, 1660–1720* (New York: Oxford University Press, 1999), 87–96; see also Paul Langford, "Polite Manners from Sir Robert Walpole to Sir Robert Peel," *Proceedings of the British Academy* 94 (1996): 103–25.

25. For the classic study of these groups, see Wijnand Mijnhardt, *Tot Heil van 't Menschdom. Culturele genootschappen in Nederland, 1750–1815* (Amsterdam: Rodopi, 1987); cf. Margaret C. Jacob, "Polite Worlds of Enlightenment," in Martin Fitzpatrick, Peter Jones, Christa Knellwolf, and Iain McCalman, eds., *The Enlightenment World* (New York: Routledge, 2004), 272–87.

26. *A Supplement to Dr. Harris's Dictionary of Arts and Sciences . . . By a Society of Gentlemen* (London, 1744), arranged alphabetically.

27. Francisco Bethencourt, *L'Inquisition à l'epoque moderne: Espagne, Portugal, Italie, XVe–XIXe siècle* (Paris: Fayard, 1995), 416–17.

28. E. William Monter, *Ritual, Myth and Magic in Early Modern Europe* (Brighton: Harvester, 1983), chap. 4.

29. See Jonathan Israel, *European Jewry in the Age of Mercantilism 1550–1750*, 2nd ed. (Oxford: Clarendon Press), 1989.

30. See E. William Monter and John Tedeschi, "Toward a Statistical Profile of the Italian Inquisitions, Sixteenth to Eighteenth Centuries," in E. William Monter, *Enforcing Morality in Early Modern Europe* (London: Variorium Reprints, 1987), 130–57.

31. For a set of rules governing the Inquisition and much of Avignon's religious and clerical life, see *Constitutiones et decreta provincialis concilii avenionensis* (Rome, 1697); *Decreta dioecesan synodi avenionensis . . .* (Avignon, 1713), 11 for attention to bad books and their readers being prohibited.

32. René Moulinas, *Les juifs du pape en France: les communautés d'Avignon et du comtat venaissin aux 17e et 18e siècles* (Paris: Commission française les archives juives, 1981), 117.

33. Archives départmentales de Vaucluse, MS 1G 827, *Livre des conclusions des consulteurs du St-Office d'Avignon, des lettres patentes des inquisiteurs et de lettres de la congrégation de Rome sur les affaires portées devant le tribunal, 1698–1724*, f. 298, 16 April 1704, "pagus est ignobilis in provincia occitana . . . villa nova iuxta Rhodanum a secus avenionensem hanc civitatem ibi quidam Commesatoris et helluones Bachicum ordinem instituerunt, cuius leges praecipue sunt egregiae." The records of the inquisition primarily occupy two manuscripts, MS 1G 826 (1674–1789) and 1G 827 (1698–1724), unfoliated, but bound, and to be found in microfilms, 2MI 806 and 807. I numbered all the "pages" beginning with the first in MS IG 826, and continuing

with f. 253 commencing on the first page of MS 1G 827; numbers higher than 253 occur in the second microfilm and follow the manuscripts as bound. The dates of the two volumes overlap but the first—for reasons obscure—begins before the second and continues to 1789 (both cited as Avignon Inquisition). For an overview of these records, see L. Duhamel, L. Imbert, and J. de Font-Réaulx, *Inventaire-sommaire des Archives départementales . . . de Vaucluse* ser. G, vol. 2, 218–25.

34. Avignon Inquisition, f. 398, "ex hoc experimento creatus fuit magnus Magister, et electi [balliori] et Comendatores, aliquibus Indigni huius ac Impii ordinis [administri], intra fines oppidid se aliquandiu continerunt Bacchici commilitones."

35. Avignon Inquisition, f. 398, 12 August 1711.

36. Found in Bibliothèque municipale d'Avignon, no. 8 27.762, *Nouvelles de l'ordre de la boisson, avec Privilege du Grand Maître*, begins on 29 November 1703 and ends in 1734. But from the claim that it was published in Liège, to the names of members given, and the various cities where meetings occurred, nothing in the text can be taken as necessarily true.

37. Avignon Inquisition, 15 [February?] 1704, f. 299.

38. Avignon Inquisition, 15 [February?] 1704, f. 299. On the efforts of the French Church to stamp out Protestantism, see Joseph Bergin, *Crown, Church, and Episcopate Under Louis XIV* (New Haven, Conn.: Yale University Press, 2004), 246–52.

39. Bibliothèque municipale d'Avignon, #8 27.762, *Nouvelles de l'ordre de la boisson.* Cf. Arthur Dinaux, *Les sociétés badines bachiques littéraires et chantantes* (Paris: Librairie Bachelin-Deflorenne, 1867), 421–24, which describes a similar society, Ordre des Chevaliers de la Joye, founded in 1696.

40. The statutes can be found in *Journal de B.-L. Soumille, 1703–1774, prêtre bénéficier de l'église-collégiale de Villeneuve-les-Avignon* (Alais: J. Martion, 1880), 112. He was the equivalent of a provost, *un viguier royal*.

41. For the earliest example of the use of all these masonic terms on the Continent, as early as 1710, see Jacob, *The Radical Enlightenment*, appendix.

42. Bibliothèque municipale d'Avignon, MS 2559, f. 75, "Entretien de deux freres de l'ordre de la boisson sur les miseries d'Avignon en l'année 1709."

43. Avignon Inquisition, 19 August 1705, f. 311.

44. Ibid.

45. Duhamel et al., *Inventaire-sommaire*, 2: 224, summarizing the contents of MS G828, "Registre des noms de ceux et de celles qui abjurent l'hérésie font profession de la foy catholique entre les mains du Rme Inquisiteur."

46. Avignon Inquisition, 26 September 1708, f. 340, "I also do not doubt that You will understand this priest has been accused unjustly, or rather as the result of a conspiracy, and that he has been put in prison with malice aforethought."

47. Bibliothèque municipale d'Avignon, MS 2818, f. 150, dated 28 August 1750.

48. Avignon Inquisition, 5 June 1709, f. 345.

49. Richard Mowery Andrews, *Law, Magistracy, and Crime in Old Regime Paris, 1735–1789*, vol. 1, *The System of Criminal Justice* (New York: Cambridge University Press, 1994), 448–51.

50. Avignon Inquisition, 17 July 1709, ff. 346, 348.

51. Avignon Inquisition, 12 March 1710, f. 353.

52. Andrews, *Law*, 458–59.

53. Avignon Inquisition, 27 May 1716, f. 381.

54. Avignon Inquisition, 10 June 1716, f. 383.

55. Avignon Inquisition, 22 July 1716, f. 384.

56. Avignon Inquisition, 19 June 1720, f. 397.

57. Avignon Inquisition, 11 September 1766, MS 1G 826, f.106.

58. Avignon Inquisition, 14 August 1778, ff. 110–11.

59. Moulinas, *Les juifs du pape en France*, 382 citing MS 3091, piece no. 7 in Musée Calvet. Cf. July Julliany, *Essai sur le commerce de Marseille* (Paris: chez Renard, 1842), 1: 74.

60. Avignon Inquisition, 9 December 1766.

61. Avignon Inquisition, 16 July 1676, f. 125.

62. Avignon Inquisition, 24 April 1692, ff. 151–52.

63. Avignon Inquisition, 3 May 1704, f. 167.1. For a reproduction of a contemporary engraving of the *carcan*, see Andrews, *Law*, 313.

64. Avignon Inquisition, 7 March 1704, f. 167; the iron collar also threatened on 23 December 1709, f. 190.

65. Avignon Inquisition, 13 June 1705, f. 192.

66. Avignon Inquisition, 23 January 1704, f. 295.

67. Avignon Inquisition, response to letter from Lord Cardinal Marescot, prefect of the Sacred Congregation, of 5 May 1708, f. 193.

68. Avignon Inquisition, 10 June 1705, f. 303, to Father Commissioner Grales.

69. Avignon Inquisition, 4 July 1703, f. 334.

70. Ibid. "Suntne pauperes isti hebraei, qui induuntur vestibus pretiosis tum sericis tum laneis contexis, [num] in argento, et sic pompatice incedunt per plateas sicut nobiles iam notae cum quobus ludos choreas, cantus, convivia, deambulantes instiuunt quae omnia [fere o pni ?] sine magnis expensis quae reserva[nt] [indenni] ad solvenda sua debita. Suntne ita pauperes isti iniquissimi hebrei qui pro conficiendis memoria [libus] ad S. Cong. et sibi procurandis patronis ad eorum effectum obtinendum nimirum Licentian pernoctationum impendunt et vulgo dicitur quiquaginta et etiam millia duplionum. Tandem suntne pauperes isti nefandi hebreai qui coegerunt mercatores, artifices, operarios, occludere suas tabernas."

71. Avignon Inquisition, 22 May 1709, f. 345.

72. Avignon Inquisition, 11 July 1711, f. 361.

73. Avignon Inquisition, 7 January 1715, f. 378.

74. Avignon Inquisition, 1 May 1717, ff. 388–89.

75. Avignon Inquisition, margin gives the date 1734. In the case brought before the Holy Office of Avignon against "Israel de Valebregue, a Jew of this city, accused and convicted of possession of forbidden books associated with fortune-telling, which he was in the habit of lending to Christians. In a hearing held in the palace of the Holy Office on the 4th day of May, before the most reverend Father Joseph d'Albert, Inquisitor General, and the most reverend Lord Lupe de Sallieres de Fosseran, Vicar General of the most reverend and most excellent Lord Archbishop, at which were present the most illustrious Lords Advocates, and the lord Procurator and Counsel for the Fisc of the Holy Office, having first heard the arguments of the Lord Jeste, Counsel for the fore-named convict: The court ruled that the fore-named Israel de Valebregue be released having served the time he had already spent in prison,

given the length of his incarceration, under solemn admonition not to commit similar acts in the future, on pain of summary penalties including corporal punishment. Valebregue furthermore shall remain for one month under house arrest at the residence of his father, on pain of the same penalties. Finally, he is sentenced to pay all court costs, including the expenses of the investigation."

76. Avignon Inquisition, letter written by the Secretariat of State to M. the Vice-Legate of Avignon, 30 March 1757, f. 76.

77. See this author's review of Adam Sutcliffe, *Judaism and the Enlightenment*, *Jewish Quarterly Review* 94 (Summer 2004): 531–35.

78. Israel, *European Jewry*, 264. Note for the period of the Baroque: Avignon Inquisition, 26 March 1677, hearing held "in the Archbishop's palace in the presence of the most illustrious and excellent lord Archbishop and Father Inquisitor General of our holy faith and in the presence of the reverend and most illustrious lords advocates and also in that of the noble lord François de Garcin, it was concluded, given the situation, and whereas the tribunal's determination remains firm in the absence of evidence to the contrary, that the aforesaid Effraim is prohibited from employing Christians to light the fire in his home on Fridays and on the sabbath, or employing them to clean the house or wash cooking utensils or prepare food or perform similar servile works within his home, on pain of flogging at the first infraction without further warrant of the court. The aforementioned Effraim is also ordered to pay all and several expenses of this investigation as a penalty in accordance with the rates in force in this sacred tribunal."

79. Ran Halévi, *Les loges maçonnique dans la France d'Ancien Régime: aux origines de la sociabilité démocratique* (Paris: A. Colin, 1984); Daniel Mornet, *Les origines intellectuelles de la révolution française (1715–1787)* (Paris: A. Colin, 1934).

80. Bibliothèque nationale MS FM 2 153 bis, loge d'Ecosse de la Vertu, 1776 to the Grand Orient in Paris: "L'attentat commis par un Jacobin, se disant Inquisiteur, envers la R.Loge de meme envers toute la maconnerie, ce qui devoit d'autant plus fixer l'attention des Chefs de l'ordre." By 25 June 1776 the lodge had taken to calling itself "vertu persecutée." Its list of members included two Benedictine priests and a printer; accent marks are reproduced as they appear in the original.

81. BN, MS FM 1 13 letter from an Avignon lodge to the Provincial Grand Lodge in Aix en Provence, 16 October 1786—"C'est avec une veritable joie que nous apprenous que les malheurs de nos ff. d'avignon touchent a leur terme: connoisses nos sentimens pour tous les enfans de la veuve, et surtout pour ceux qui sont opprimer: nous avons depose dans votre sein les peines qui nous avons ressentier a la premiere nouvelles des disgraces qu'ils essayoient. . . . Heureusement la vertu a fait laise le fanatisme et l'envie; il ne nous rente quie nous feliciter avec vous du'un success debite et pour le quel nous faissons des vieux bien sincerer."

82. BN, MS FM 1 110, f. 58, 23 March 1786—the lodge in Aix to the Grand Lodge in Paris to beg for patience with the brothers in Avignon "que le malheur de nos ff d'Avignon est deva soumis a un autre Gouvernement que le notre . . . et quand ils sont en butte a ignorance our au fanatisme, ce sont de ces evenemens contre lesquels on ne peut que les enhorter a s'armer de Courage et de patience. L'homme vertueux triomphe enfin des menees sourdes de l'envie; nos ff des Naples en sont un example bien consolant pour la maconnerie. . . . Nous presummons que nos ff d'avignon ont

obtenu aupris de Cour du Rome, a la reparation des injustice et des violences qu'on a exercees contre eux, puisque nous n'avons recu de ces ff aucune planche posterieure a la votre:nous en acceptons evidence l'augure, et puisse le G.A de l'Un excuser les vieux sincerer que nous fasson pour leur tranquillite!" And see f. 71, 26 November 1787—some brothers in Avignon have suspended their work.

83. BN, FM 2 153 bis, Avignon, L' Parfaite Union, discourse of 1785 on the beauty of our institution and the causes of decadence: "Vainement nous fairions nous illusion sur cette pretendue liberte que L. homme apporte en naissanet et qu'il conserve jusqu'a sa mort! on la dit et repette avec trop d'affectation pour y croire serieusement, non, M.F. l'homme n'est pas ne libre rarement."

84. British Library, London, MS ADD 2422, f. 26, English translation, original from Avignon and dated 12 February 1787, f. 24.

85. For almanacs, see the collection at the Bibliothèque d l'Arsenal, call no. 8 S.13757.

86. David Sorkin, *"A Wise, Enlightened and Reliable Piety": The Religious Enlightenment in Central and Western Europe, 1689–1789*, Parkes Institute Pamphlet 1, University of Southampton, 2002.

87. Brijraj Singh, "'One Soul, tho' not one Soyl'? International Protestantism and Ecumenism at the Beginning of the Eighteenth Century," in Ourida Mostefai and Catherine Ingrassia, eds., *Studies in Eighteenth-Century Culture* 31 (Baltimore: Johns Hopkins University Press, 2002), 61–84.

88. See Bradley and Van Kley, *Religion and Politics in Enlightenment Europe*, passim, note 1.

Chapter 2. Alchemy, Science, and a Universalist Language

1. Paul A. David, "Reputation and Agency in the Historical Emergence of the Institutions of 'Open Science'" (Publication 261, Center for Economic Policy Research, Stanford University, 1994; rev. December 1998) summarizes this perspective; it relies on the work of Mario Biagioli, "Galileo's System of Patronage," *History of Science* (1990): 28 and Mordechai Feingold, *The Mathematicians' Apprenticeship: Science, Universities and Society in England, 1560–1640* (Cambridge: Cambridge University Press, 1984), among others. The point is summarized again by Paul A. David, "Patronage, Reputation, and Common Agency Contracting in the Scientific Revolution: From Keeping 'Nature's Secrets' to the Institutionalization of 'Open Science'" (working paper, Economics Department, Stanford University, March 2000).

2. Michael D. Gordin, "The Importation of Being Earnest: The Early St. Petersburg Academy of Sciences," *Isis* 91 (2000): 10.

3. See Harold Cook and David Lux, "Closed Circles or Open Networks? Communicating at a Distance During the Scientific Revolution," *History of Science* 36 (1998): 179–211.

4. Pierre Bourdieu, *Science of Science and Reflexivity* (Chicago: University of Chicago Press, 2004), 54–55.

5. Lynn K. Nyhart and Thomas H. Broman, eds., *Science and Civil Society, Osiris*

2nd ser. 17 (2002); for a general treatment of civil society without attention to science, see Frank Trentmann, ed., *Paradoxes of Civil Society: New Perspectives on Modern German and British History* (New York: Berghahn Books, 2000).

6. Cf. Bourdieu, *Science*, 52.

7. Further evidence of the cosmopolitan quest can be found in George Starkey, *Alchemical Laboratory Notebooks and Correspondence*, ed. William R. Newman and Lawrence M. Principe (Chicago: University of Chicago Press, 2004).

8. For one of many alchemical explications of "the universal spirit of Nature" see Eugenius Philalethes [Thomas Vaughan], *Anima magica abscondita; Or Discourse of the Universall Spirit of Nature* (London, 1650). The tract begins by attacking the scholastics and then proceeds to describe the universal spirit. For a clear statement of the principles, see J. Malbec de Tresfel, *Abrege de la theorie et des veritables principes de l'art appellé chymie qui est la troisième partie ou colomne de la vraye medecine hermetique . . . dedié a M. Valot, Conseiller du Roy* (Paris, 1671), 15–28 on the principles; 40, "la Chymie a la connoissance des elemens inferieurs, du Sel, du Soulfre, & du Mercure"; and 43, where the goal is "great and admirable remedies that conserve health, reestablish lost energy (les forces perduës), . . . and prolong life." Paracelsus is also invoked (51).

9. See, for example, George Acton, *A Letter in Answer to certain Queries and Objections made by a learned Galenist against the theorie and practice of Chymical Physick* (London, 1676).

10. For background on this support, see Daniel Garber, "Defending Aristotle/ Defending Society in Early Seventeenth Century Paris," in Wolfgang Detel and Claus Zittel, eds., *Ideals and Cultures of Knowledge in Early Modern Europe* (Berlin: Akademie-Verlag, 2002), 135–60.

11. Prefecture of the Police, Paris, MS Aa/5/218 arrest of Marie Magnan "pour travailler a des distilation en congellations de Mercure pour faire d'Or."

12. A. Everaerts used "cosmopolitiae"; Michael Sendivogius (1566–1636) had his works collected under the title, *Les oeuvres du Cosmopolite*—see the catalogue of the Bakken Library, Minneapolis. The National Medical Library in Washington, D.C., lists a work by Sendivogius as *Cosmopolite; ou Nouvelle lumiere chimyque* (Paris, 1669).

13. For one such fanciful journey, see *Les avantures du philosophe inconnu, en la recherche & en l'invention de la Pierre Philosophale . . .* (Paris, 1646), esp. 46–47.

14. *Otto Tachenius his Hippocrates Chymicus. Discovering the Ancient Foundations of the Viperine Salt*, trans. J .W., unpaginated introduction; [John Frederick Houppreght] *Aurifontina Chymica; or a Collection of Fourteen small Treatises Concerning the First Matter of Philosophers, For the discovery of their Mercury . . . for the benefit of Mankind in general* (London, 1680).

15. Quoting Pamela H. Smith, *The Body of the Artisan: Art and Experience in the Scientific Revolution* (Chicago: University of Chicago Press, 2004), 147.

16. For good illustrations of these points, see the account in William R. Newman, *Gehennical Fire: The Lives of George Starkey, an American Alchemist in the Scientific Revolution* (Cambridge, Mass.: Harvard University Press, 1994) and J. T. Young, *Faith, Medical Alchemy, and Natural Philosophy: Johann Moriaen, Reformed Intelligencer, and the Hartlib Circle* (Brookfield, Vt., Ashgate, 1998).

17. Robert Boyle, *The Correspondence of Robert Boyle*, ed. Michael Hunter,

Antonio Clericozio, and Lawrence M. Principe, vol. 1, *1636–61* (London: Pickering and Chatto, 2001), 46; Robert Boyle to Francis Tallents, 20 February 1647, emphasis in original.

18. See Harold J. Cook, "Medical Communication in the First Global Age: Willem ten Rhijne in Japan, 1674–76," in *Disquisitions on the Past and Present* (Taipei: Academia Sinica, forthcoming); read before publication by the kindness of the author.

19. Deborah E. Harkness, "Maps, Spiders, and Tulips: The Cole-Ortelius-L'Obel family and the Practice of Science in Early Modern London," in Randolph Vigne and Charles Littleton, eds., *From Strangers to Citizens: The Integration of Immigrant Communities in Britain, Ireland and Colonial America, 1550–1750* (Brighton: Sussex Academic Press, 2001), 184–96.

20. The concluding sentence in Alexandra Walsham, *Providence in Early Modern England* (Oxford: Oxford University Press, 1999), 334.

21. Paracelsus, *Paracelsus: His Archidoxis, Comprised in Ten Books*, ed. J. H. (London, 1660), unpaginated epistle.

22. Boyle, *Correspondence*, 1: 42, Boyle to Marcombes on usefulness in 1646; 46, Boyle to Tallents in 1647.

23. For the importance of events in the 1640s, see David Cressy, "Revolutionary England, 1640–1642," *Past and Present* 181 (November 2003): 35–72.

24. Boyle, *Correspondence*, 1: 51, Boyle to Hartlib, presumed to be early 1647.

25. Boyle, *Correspondence*, 1: 82–83, Boyle to Lady Ranelagh, 31 August 1649.

26. Samuel Hartlib, *A further Discoverie of The Office of Publick Addresse for Accommodations* (London 1648), 2; on Jews, Turks, etc., see 26. Cf. Charles Webster, ed., *Samuel Hartlib and the Advancement of Learning* (Cambridge: Cambridge University Press, 1970), and Webster, *The Great Instauration: Science, Medicine and Reform, 1626–1660* (London: Duckworth, 1975).

27. Boyle, *Correspondence*, 1: 5.

28. Boyle, *Correspondence*, 1: 13.

29. Boyle, *Correspondence*, 1: 52–53, Boyle to Hartlib, 1647.

30. Cf. Klaus Vondung, "Millenarianism, Hermeticism, and the Search for a Universal Science," in Stephen A. McKnight, ed., *Science, Pseudo-Science, and Utopianism in Early Modern Thought* (Columbia: University of Missouri Press, 1992), 118–40; Antonio Clericuzio, "New Light on Benjamin Worsley's Natural Philosophy," in Mark Greengrass, Michael Leslie, and Timothy Raylor, eds., *Samuel Hartlib and Universal Reformation: Studies in Intellectual Communication* (Cambridge: Cambridge University Press, 1994), 234–46.

31. Smith, *The Body of the Artisan*, 175–76.

32. Boyle, *Correspondence*, 1: 49.

33. Boyle, *Correspondence*, 1: 104, Boyle to John Mallet.

34. Boyle, *Correspondence*, 1: 58, Boyle to Hartlib, 1647, "we may evidently observe those commonwealths (as the *Hollanders* and the *Venetians*) to be the most happy and the most flourishing, where ingenuity is courted with the greatest encouragements."

35. *Enchyridion physicae restitutae, or The Summary of Physics Recovered* (London, 1651), epistle, copy in Clark Library, UCLA, QD25 E77E 1651. He is usually identified as Jean d'Espagnet. I owe this information to Rafal Prinke.

36. Ibid., p. 19; emphasis in the original. See Lawrence M. Principe and William

R. Newman, "Some Problems with the Historiography of Alchemy," in William Roy-
all Newman and Anthony Grafton, eds., *Secrets of Nature: Alchemy and Astrology in
Early Modern Europe* (Cambridge, Mass.: MIT Press, 2001), 411–12. They argue that
vitalism is of minimal importance in the alchemical tradition. The evidence presented here suggests that is not quite the case.

37. Eugenius Philalethes [Thomas Vaughan], *Anthroposophia theomagica; or, A
Discourse of the Nature and Man and his state after death. Grounded on his Creator's
Proto-Chemistry* . . . (London, 1650), dedicated to the Fraternity of the Rosie Cross;
attacking Aristotle (see preface), condemns atheists, and then says "I speak of Celes-
tial hidden Natures known only to Magicians. . . . The Sun and Moon are two Magical principles the One active, the other passive, this masculine, that Feminine"
(22–24). Bound with, by the same, *Anima Magica abscondita; or, A Discourse of the
universall Spirit of Nature.* . . . The threat of naturalism in alchemical circles had
been visible in sixteenth-century Italy; see William Eamon, *Science and the Secrets of
Nature: Books of Secrets in Medieval and Early Modern Culture* (Princeton, N.J.: Princeton University Press, 1994), 158–59.

38. Clericuzio,"New Light on Benjamin Worsley's Natural Philosophy," 240–42.

39. William Chamberlayne, *Pharonnida: A Heroic Poem* (London, 1659), "epistle to the reader."

40. See Christopher Hill, *The World Turned Upside Down: Radical Ideas Dur-
ing the English Revolution* (Harmondsworth: Penguin, 1972); James R. Jacob, *Robert
Boyle and the English Revolution* (New York: Burt Franklin, 1977); Patrick Curry,
Prophecy and Power: Astrology in Early Modern England (Cambridge: Polity, 1989).

41. [Houppreght], *Aurifontina Chymica.* For what could be found in book
stores during the Restoration, see William Cooper, *William Cooper's A Catalogue of
Chymicall Books, 1673–88*, ed. Stanton J. Linden (New York: Garland, 1987).

42. Acton, *Letter in Answer to certain Queries*, 2.

43. See Boyle, *Correspondence*, 5: 45 for mention of Du Clos, who can now be
identified.

44. See Deborah E. Harkness, *Talking with Angels: John Dee and the End of Nature*
(Cambridge: Cambridge University Press, 1998) and Lawrence M. Principe, *The Aspiring Adept: Robert Boyle and His Alchemical Quest* (Princeton, N.J.: Princeton University Press, 1998), 194–95.

45. Betty Jo Teeter Dobbs, *The Janus Faces of Genius: The Role of Alchemy in
Newton's Thought* (Cambridge: Cambridge University Press, 1991), 170–85.

46. See Royal Commission on Historical Manuscripts, *Report on the Correspondence and Papers of Samuel Hartlib (c. 1600–1662)* (London: Reproduced for Sheffield
University Library by the Commission, 1980).

47. Eirenaeus Philalethes Anglus, Cosmopolita, *An Exposition Upon Sir George
Ripley's Epistle to King Edward IV* (London, 1677), title page.

48. Philalethes, *Exposition Upon Sir George Ripley's Epistle*, 1.

49. Wilhelm ten Rhyne, *Dissertatio de arthritide: Mantissa schemata: de Acupunctura et Orationes . . . De Chymiae & Botaniae antiquitate . . . Londini impensis
R Chiswell & apud Arnoldum Leer* (The Hague, 1683). For a translation and commentary, see Robert W. Carrubba and John Z. Bowers, "The Western World's First
Detailed Treatise on Acupuncture: Willem Ten Rijne's *De Acupunctura*," *Journal of*

the History of Medicine and Allied Sciences 29 (1974: 371–98 and Roberta E. Bivins, *Acupuncture, Expertise and Cross-Cultural Medicine* (New York: Palgrave, 2000), chap. 3.

50. Bivins, *Acupuncture*, 76, citing the relevant passage from Bayle's *Nouvelles de la république des lettres* (Paris, 1686), 1013.

51. Groenevelt attached a tribute to Ten Rhyne on his engraving; see Harold J. Cook, *Trials of an Ordinary Doctor: Joannes Groenevelt in Seventeenth-Century London* (Baltimore: Johns Hopkins University Press, 1994). I am grateful to Harold Cook for the point about the pneuma.

52. See Alice Stroup, *A Company of Scientists: Botany, Patronage, and Community at the Seventeenth-Century Parisian Royal Academy of Sciences* (Berkeley: University of California Press, 1990), chaps. 1, 2. Cf. Adrian Mallon, "Science and Government in France, 1661–1699. Changing Patterns of Scientific Research and Development" (Ph.D. thesis, Queen's University, Belfast, 1983), esp. 36–38, 42–44.

53. For biographical information on them, see the invaluable David J. Sturdy, *Science and Social Status: The Members of the Académie des Sciences, 1666–1750* (Rochester, N.Y.: Boydell Press, 1995), chap. 6.

54. Archives de l'Académie royale des sciences (hereafter Ads), Procès-verbaux, vol. 1, Registre de physique, 22 Décembre 1666-Avril 1668, "Project d'Exercitations Physiques, proposé a l'assemblée, par le Sr. Du Clos," ff. 3–5. Similar language about mercury, sulfur, and salt (but without mention of hermetic philosophy) appears in MS Codex 783, attributed to George Barrett, 1680 and found at Rare Book Room, Van Pelt Library, University of Pennsylvania.

55. On the importance of distillation in alchemy, see Bruce T. Moran, *Distilling Knowledge: Alchemy, Chemistry, and the Scientific Revolution* (Cambridge, Mass.: Harvard University Press, 2004).

56. BN, MS français 1333, "Remarques sur le livre des Essais Physiologiques de Mr. Boyle. Faites par le Sr du Clos et tenu en l'assemblée, au Moys de Juillet 1668."

57. Principe, *Aspiring Adept*, 70–71.

58. Du Clos, *Dissertation sur les principes des mixtes naturels . . . 1677* (Amsterdam: Elsevier, 1680), 46–47, 59.

59. For elaboration on the point see Smith, *Body of the Artisan*, 226–33.

60. Principe, *Aspiring Adept*, 49–50.

61. BN MS français 1333, "Dissertations physiques du Sr. Du Clos . . . 1677," f. 6 and read by Blondel, Flamel, Perrault, and Mariotte.

62. "Dissertations physiques du Sr. Du Clos . . . 1677," ff. 6–9.

63. "Dissertations physiques du Sr. Du Clos . . . 1677," f. 296, from the separate essay on Boyle bound with "Dissertations physiques. . . ."

64. Philalethes, *Anima magica*, 6.

65. Du Clos, *Dissertation sur les principes des mixtes naturels*, 6, "En travaillant à la resolution chymique des Planets, je me suis vainement occupé à reduire ces Mixtes en quelques matieres simples, qui pussent estre reputées premieres, & passer pour Principes. Le Feu des founeaux saisoit separer de toutes les Plantes de l'Eau, de l'Huyle, du Sel & de la Terre."

66. Du Clos, *Dissertation sur les principes des mixtes naturels*, 33–35; 44 for nature as the soul and for transmutation; 67 for God's power; BN MS français 1333 for his pious theism.

67. For a look at how this worldview worked around the emotions and litera-ture, see Gail Kern Paster, *Humoring the Body: Emotions and the Shakespearean Stage* (Chicago: University of Chicago Press, 2004).

68. Samuel Du Clos, *Observations on the Mineral Waters of France, made in the Royal Academy of the Sciences, Now made English* (London, 1684).

69. BN MS français 1333, Du Clos's essay on Boyle's *Essays Physiologiques*, f. 1.

70. Du Clos's essay on Boyle's *Essays Physiologiques*, f. 22.

71. Dobbs, *The Janus Faces of Genius: The Role of Alchemy in Newton's Thought* (Cambridge: Cambridge University Press, 1991), 174–81.

72. On the finances for later in the seventeenth century, see Alice Stroup, *Royal Funding of the Parisian Académie Royale des Sciences During the 1690s*, Transactions of the American Philosophical Society 77, part 4 (Philadelphia: American Philo-sophical Society, 1987).

73. For his knowledge see Bibliothèque d l'Arsenal, MS 2517, "Recueul du Mr. Du clos sur la transmutation du metaux"; cf. Mallon, "Science and Government in France," 149.

74. Mallon, "Science and Government," ff. 38–39.

75. ADS, Procès-verbaux, Reg.11, ff..157r–158r, cited and translated in G. G. Mey-nell, *The French Academy of Sciences, 1666–91: A Reassessment of the French Académie royale des sciences Under Colbert (1666–83) and Louvois (1683–91)*, http://www.haven.u-net.com/6text_7B2.htm#Utilite.

76. Meynell, *The French Academy of Sciences*, "L'autre recherche plus convenable a cette Compagnie et qui seroit plus du goust de Monseigneur de Louvois regarde tout ce qui peut illustrer la Physique et servir a la Medecine, ces deux choses estant presque inseparables parceque la medecine tire des Consequences et profite des nouvelles decouvertes de la Physique." In 1694 the word "physique" was defined as "Science qui a pour objet la connoissance des choses naturelles; La Physique fait partie de la Philoso-phie. la physique est necessaire à un Medecin. estudier en physique. il est sçavant en physique. la physique d'Aristote" in *Dictionnaire de l'Académie française*, 1st ed. (1694).

77. ADS, Cartons (1666–1793), carton 1, found in individual notebooks.

78. *Nouvelles de la République des Lettres* 8 (October 1685): 1152–55.

79. William Lewis, *A Course of Practical Chemistry. In which are contained All the Operations described in Wilson's Complete Course of Chemistry. With Many new, and several uncommon Processes. To each Article is given, The Chemical History, and to most, an Account of the Quantities of Oils, Salts, Spirits, yielded in Distillation* (Lon-don: J. Nourse, 1746).

80. "Recueil du Mr. Du Clos," ff. 3–4.

81. "Recueil du Mr. Du Clos," ff. 59 et seq., "Remarques de Mr. Du Clos sur le livre des essayes philosophiques de Mr Boile faittes par M. Du Clos et lires en l'assem-blee de l'academie au mois du Juillet, 1668."

82. "Recueil du Mr. Du Clos," ff. 187–90.

83. Moran, *Distilling Knowledge*, passim. For background on Lemery's text, see Bernard Joly, "De l'alchimie à la chimie: le développement des 'cours de chymie' au XVIIe siècle en France," in Frank Greiner, ed., *Aspects de la tradition alchimique au XVIIe siècle: actes du colloque international de l'Université de Reims-Champagne-Ardenne (Reims, 28 et 29 novembre 1996)* (Paris, SÉHA, 1998), 85–94.

84. [N. Lemery], *Modern Curiosities of Art & Nature. Extracted out of the Cabinets of the most Eminent Personages of the French Court. Together with the choicest Secrets in Mechanicks . . . composed and experimented by the Sieur Lemery Apothecary to the French King. Made English from the Original French* (London: Matthew Gilliflower, 1685).

85. ADS, Procès-verbaux, vol. 11, 1683–86.

86. Ibid., ff. 15–16.

87. Douglas McKie, "James, Duke of York, F.R.S.," *Notes and Records of the Royal Society of London* 13, 1 (1958): 6–18.

88. Stroup, *Royal Funding*, 56.

89. James D. McClellan, III, "The Académie Royale des Sciences, 1699–1793: A Statistical Portrait," *Isis* 72 (1981): 566.

90. Quoted in Elmo Stewart Saunders, "The Decline and Reform of the *Academie des sciences a Paris,* 1676–1699" (Ph.D. dissertation, Ohio State University, 1980), 177. Appendix B contains a transcript of the 1699 rules.

91. ADS, dossier Truchet, *Eloge du P. Sébastien Truchet, Carme, Histoire de l'Académie des Science, 1729.*

92. ADS, dossier des billettes, notes that begin with Agriculture.

93. Found in appendix in Saunders, "Decline and Reform," 267. On the expansion and list of new members see Sturdy, *Science and Social Status.*

94. See *Journal d'Angleterre,* 1668–1670.

95. Jean-François Dubost and Peter Sahlins, *Et si on faisait payer les étrangers? Louis XIV, les immigrés et quelques autres* (Paris: Flammarion, 1999).

96. Archives nationales, Paris, O o 41, f. 190.

97. Philippe Minard, *La fortune du colbertisme: état et industrie dan la France des Lumières* (Paris: Fayard, 1998), 218–24.

98. Summary taken from Manfred Kracht and Erwin Kreyszig, "E. W. von Tschirnhaus: His Role in Early Calculus and His Work and Impact on Algebra," *Historia Mathematica* 17 (1990): 16–35.

Chapter 3. Markets Not So Free

1. For the contemporary debate on the issue of nationalism, globalization, and cosmopolitanism, see http://www.aworldconnected.org/article.php/570.html. In at least one classic study of urban space the category of the cosmopolitan figures not at all; see Mark La Gory and John Pipkin, *Urban Social Space* (Belmont, Calif.: Wadsworth, 1981).

2. For plans he received from his Italian colleague Francesco Fontana, 1732, see François Fossier, *Les dessins du fonds Robert de Cotte de la Bibliothèque nationale de France: architecture et décor* (Paris: Bibliothèque nationale, 1997), 459–62.

3. Helen Tangires, *Public Markets and Civic Culture in Nineteenth-Century America* (Baltimore: Johns Hopkins University Press, 2003), 4.

4. Jean-Jacques Rousseau, among others, offered such criticisms; see Sophia Rosenfeld, "Citizens of Nowhere in Particular: Cosmopolitanism, Writing, and Political

Engagement in Eighteenth-Century Europe," *National Identities* 4 (2002): 25–43. For another discussion of Rousseau's views, see Andrea Albrecht, *Kosmopolitismus: Welt-bürgerdiskurse in Literatur, Philosophie und Publizistik um 1800* (Berlin: De Gruyter, 2005), chap. 2.

5. "L. Grenade, *Les Singularitéz de Londres, 1576*," trans. Derek Keene, Gill Healey, and Ann Saunders in Ann Saunders, ed., *The Royal Exchange*, Publication 152 (London: London Topographical Society, 1998), 48–49. Cf. *Comune Concil tentum in Camera Guildhall civitas London*, 16 March 1703, extending the hours to four a day. For an account of the financial side of the London Exchange from the 1690s onward, see Ranald C. Michie, *The London Stock Exchange: A History* (Oxford: Oxford University Press, 1999).

6. Liah Greenfeld, *The Spirit of Capitalism: Nationalism and Economic Growth* (Cambridge, Mass.: Harvard University Press, 2001), 34–40.

7. This sketch is reproduced in Margaret C. Jacob, *The Enlightenment: A Brief History with Documents* (Boston: Bedford Books, 2001), 115. The original can be found at École des ponts et chaussées, Paris.

8. Oscar Gelderblom, "De economische en juridische positie van buitenlandse looplieden in Amsterdam in de zestiende en zeventiende eeuw," in Leo Lucassen, ed., *Amsterdammer worden: Migranten hun organisaties en inburgering, 1600–2000* (Amsterdam: Vossiuspers, 2004), 169–88.

9. Perry Gauci, *The Politics of Trade: The Overseas Merchant in State and Society, 1660–1720* (New York: Oxford University Press, 2001), 40.

10. For the negative connotation in literature, see M. Lafont, *Les trois frères rivaux, comédie en un acte* (Amsterdam: Pierre Marteau, près la Bourse, 1771), 7: "Je fais un magasin de bourses dans ma poche: / Je ne crois pas qu'au monde il soit d'Agioteur, / De Notaire, de Juif, même de Procureur / Qui porte aux louis d'or une plus tendre estime." For the imagined history, see *De Volmaakte Koopman: Hande-lende van alles wat in de koopmanschap voorvalt door de Heer Savary* (Amsterdam, 1683), 1–2. See also Wyndham Beawes, *Lex Mercatoria Rediviva; or, The Merchant's Directory. Being a Compleat Guide to all Men in Business . . .* (London: R. Baldwin, [1751]), 410, where the bill of exchange is invented by the Hebrews and the Romans. This is largely a translation of Savary des Brulons, *Dictionnaire de commerce*; he in turn was the son of the author of the most popular guide to commercial life, pub-lished in multiple editions and from French translated into every major language; Jacques Savary, *Le Parfait negociant. ou. instruction générale pour ce qui regarde le commerce des Marchandises de France, & les Pays Etrangers*, augmented by Jacques Savary des Bruslons, 8th ed. (Paris: Estienne, 1777), 805–6, "si le Change a été inventé en 640 ou en 1316, & autre côté le bannissement des Juifs étant la punition de leurs rapines & leurs malversations, qui avoient attiré la haine de tout le monde." This language does not appear in the English translation. Cf. Frank Felsenstein, *Anti-Semitic Stereotypes: A Paradigm of Otherness in English Popular Culture, 1660–1830* (Baltimore: Johns Hopkins University Press, 1995).

11. Samuel Hayne, *An Abstract of All the Statutes Made Concerning Aliens Trad-ing in England . . . With Observations thereon, proving that the Jews . . . break them all* (London, 1685).

12. Beawes, *Lex Mercatoria Rediviva*, 455. In Amsterdam the number was limited

to 375 Christians and 22 Jews. On the establishment of Jewish brokers in Amsterdam, see Daniel M. Swetschinski, *Reluctant Cosmopolitans: The Portuguese Jews of Seventeenth-Century Amsterdam* (London: Littman Library of Jewish Civilization, 2000), 142–48.

13. See Oscar Gelderblom, "The Political Economy of Foreign Trade in England and the Dutch Republic (1550–1650)," in Oscar Gelderblom, ed., *The Political Economy of the Dutch Republic*, forthcoming.

14. The Mercers' Company, Ironmonger Lane, London, EC2, Gresham Repertory, Reel 93, ff. 183–84, 1676. Sometimes in money matters the committee invoked a "Grand Committee," f. 207.

15. Ibid., f. 188, 1676.

16. Ibid., ff. 192–93, 29 April 1676.

17. Ibid., f. 203, 1677.

18. The committee meeting records supply much of this account. See Mercers' Company, 1723–39, for lease to a notary public on 22 May 1723 and the leasing of pepper cellars to the East India Company; 27 Nov. 1723, 1 and 18 May 1724 leases to women, and see ff. 180–89 for those behind in their rent, of which approximately one-sixth are women. The first lease to the Company appears on Reel 93, f. 12, December 1678. See also Ann M. Carlos and Larry Neal, "Women Investors in Early Capital Markets 1720–1725," March 2004, unpublished paper kindly transmitted by the authors.

19. Mercers' Company, f. 200, 1689.

20. On the repairing and maintaining the clock, Mercers' Company, Reel 93, see f. 74, 1681.

21. Mercers' Company, 16 November 1730 meeting of committee.

22. Ibid., December 6, 1734; and on beggars and short-loaners, 14 October 1726; 16 November 1730 on fruitsellers and disorderly persons petitioned against by the tenants.

23. Laura Gowing, "'The Freedom of the Streets': Women and Social Space, 1560–1640," in Paul Griffiths and Mark S. R. Jenner, eds., *Londinopolis: Essays in the Cultural and Social History of Early Modern London* (Manchester: Manchester University Press, 2000), 143–44.

24. Mercers' Company, 16 August 1723; complaints from the poor in the almshouse.

25. Ibid., 28 June 1728 on seizure; 5 June 1730 on forgiveness.

26. Corporation of London Records Office (hereafter LR), Repertory Court of Aldermen, Rep. 27, f. 344, Wednesday 11 February 1606, f. 344r, rep. 27, and 5 August, 1607, f. 75r, rep.28. For fire see Tuesday, 1 December 1635, f. 38r, rep.50. For the regulating of the times see Tuesday, 24 January 1631/2, f. 70r, rep. 46. I am indebted to Deborah Harkness for these citations.

27. LR, Thursday 23 November 1639, f. 26r, rep 52.

28. Blair Hoxby, *Mammon's Music: Literature and Economics in the Age of Milton* (New Haven, Conn.: Yale University Press, 2002), 50.

29. For background on Clayton and his politics in the 1680s, see Gary S. De Krey, *London and the Restoration, 1659–1683* (Cambridge: Cambridge University Press, 2005), 135 et seq.

30. Mercers' Company, Reel 93, f. 199, 21 June 1689.

31. Ibid., f. 201.

32. See Douglass C. North and Barry W. Weingast, "Constitutions and Commitment: The Evolution of Institutions Governing Public Choice in Seventeenth-Century England," *Journal of Economic History* 49 (December 1989): 803.

33. *The Spectator,* Sunday 19 May 1711, reprinted in Saunders, ed., *The Royal Exchange,* 206–7.

34. Readily found in *Letters concerning the English Nation,* in Jacob, *The Enlightenment,* 119.

35. *The Court Broker: A description of an Anti-Patriot* (London: T. Fox, 1747), 11.

36. I have benefited from seeing an advance copy of the chapter, "Staging Commercial London: The Royal Exchange," from Jean Howard, *Theater of a City: Social Change and Generic Innovation on the Early Modern Stage* (forthcoming).

37. Stanley Chapman, *Merchant Enterprise in Britain: From the Industrial Revolution to World War I* (Cambridge: Cambridge University Press, 1992), 55–56.

38. Gauci, *Politics of Trade,* 67–68.

39. Mercers' Company, f. 118, 2 April 1736 on keeping the clock in good working order and 12 August 1736 on making it "more butifull."

40. Kroniek van de beurs van Antwerpen, vanaf 1485, from Stadsarchief Antwerpen, Gebodboek A., f. 79.

41. See in general Geert de Clercq, ed., *Ter Beurze: Geschiedenis van aandelenhandel in België, 1300–1990* (Bruges: Van de Wiele; Antwerpen: Tijd, 1992). Cf. Jos Marechal, *Geschiedenis van de Brugse beurs* (Bruges: De Anjelier, 1949).

42. Eddy Stols, "Mercurius met een exotische maraboet: De Antwerpse koloniale handelsmetropool in de zestiende en zeventiende eeuw," in Johan Verberckmoes, ed., *Vreemden vertoond: Opstellen over exotisme en spektakelcultuur in de Spaanse Nederlanden en de Nieuwe Wereld* (Leuven: Peeters, 2002), 7–8.

43. Stadsarchief Antwerpen, Gebodboek A (1489–1539), f. 179.

44. Gebodboek A, f. 213, in 1536; in 1538, f. 224 on "blood being let" on the floor of the bourse; Gebodboek B, in 1542, f. 40, on prohibiting fighting, weapons, etc. on the floor.

45. Lowijs Guicciardijn, *Beschrijvinghe van alle de Nederlanden . . . ,* in Nederduytsche spraecke door Cornelium Kilianum,* with a historical notice by Petrum Montanum (Amsterdam, 1612); originally published in Italian in 1567, and done in a modern facsimile edition by Zwager in the 1950s.

46. Jan van der Stock, ed., *Antwerp: Story of a Metropolis, 16th–17th Century, Hessenhuis 25 June–10 October 1993* (Ghent : Snoeck-Ducaju, 1993), 234.

47. Frederik Clijmans, *De beurs te Antwerpen: Beknopte aanteekeningen* (Antwerp, 1941), 9–29; Roelof van Gelder and Renée Kistemaker, *Amsterdam, 1275–1795: de ontwikkeling van een handelsmetropool* (Amsterdam: Meulenhoff Informatief, 1983), 93.

48. Stadsarchief Antwerpen, Gebodboek A, 3 November 1540, 236.

49. De Clercq, ed., *Ter Beurze,* 69.

50. Floris Prims, *Geschiedenis van Antwerpen* (Brussels: Standaard Boekhandel, 1927–49), 5: 218.

51. Stadsarchief Antwerpen, Gebodboek A, f. 116, April 1525. For the Spanish and English, see J. A. Goris, *Étude sur les colonies marchandes méridionales (portugais, espagnols, italiens) à Anvers de 1488 à 1567* (Louvain: Librairie Universitaire, 1925), 109.

52. Stadsarchief Antwerpen, Gebodenboek B, 1542, f. 40, 17 October.

53. P. Génard, *Antwerpsch Archievenblad* (Antwerp, 1864–), 9: 379–90.

54. Ibid., 404–27.

55. Ibid., 14: 1–99.

56. Ibid., 16: 330–31.

57. I owe the reference to the architecture of the temple to Jonathan Sheehan, Center for the Study of Religion, Princeton, and his paper "The Space of Ritual: Inside the Temple of Solomon in Early Modern Europe," given at the conference Knowledge and Its Making in Northern Europe (1500–1800), Pomona College, 11 April 2003.

58. Stadsarchief, Antwerp, MS PK 2224, passim.

59. Ibid., MS PK 2206, 1599–1600, written in French and coming from all the nations in the town and opposed to the constant ringing of the bell in the Bourse.

60. Ibid., MS PK 919, passim for ordanances for the 1620s.

61. Pieter Scheltema, *De Beurs van Amsterdam* (Amsterdam: Portielje, 1846), 47–48.

62. P. Génard, *Bulletin des archives d'Anvers* (Antwerp: Van Merlen, 1864–65), 2: 68.

63. MS PK 303, 21 March 1696 letter from Maximilien Emanuel, governor of the Low Countries, to the magistrates.

64. Cited in De Clercq, ed., *Ter Beurze.*

65. Jean Pierre Ricard, *Le Négoce d'Amsterdam, Contenant tout ce que doivent savoir. . .* (Amsterdam, Etienne Lucas, 1722), 5–6. The full title page of *Confusion de confusiones. Dialogos Curiosos Entre un Philosopho agudo, un Mercaderdiscreto, y un Accionista erudito. Descriviendo el negocio de las Acciones, sa origen, su ethimologia, su realidad, su juego. Y su enredo, Compeuseto po Don Josseph de la Vega, que con referente obsequio lo dedica al Merito y Curiosidad Del muy Ilustre Senor Duarte Nunez da Costa* (Amsterdam, 1688).

66. For Lyon, see BN Estampes, microfilm frame H148083, an engraving from 1749.

67. Savary, *Le Parfait negociant*, 595.

68. See Peter M. Garber, *Famous First Bubbles: The Fundamentals of Early Manias* (Cambridge, Mass.: MIT Press, 2000).

69. Bibliothèque de l'Institut de France, MS X 388, f. 1 A good place to start on the Paris Bourse is the classic essay, George V. Taylor, "The Paris Bourse on the Eve of the Revolution, 1781–89," *American Historical Review* 67, 4 (1962): 951–77. For a succinct account of Law's scheme, see Mark Potter, *Corps and Clienteles: Public Finance and Political Change in France, 1688–1715* (Burlington, Vt.: Ashgate, 2003), 185–88.

70. Daniel Roche, ed., *Almanach parisien en faveur des étrangers et des personnes curieuses* (Paris: Universitaire de Saint-Étienne, 2001), 122–23, editions in 1761 and 1766.

71. See Amalia Deborah Kessler, "From Virtue to Commerce: The Parisian Merchant Court and the Rise of Commercial Society in Eighteenth-Century France" (Ph.D. dissertation, Stanford Law School, 2003), 194–200.

72. See Beawes, *Lex Mercatoria Rediviva*, 454–57.

73. See *Manuel des agens de change et des courtiers de commerce, contenant les Édits . . .* (Paris: Chez Mme. Ve. J Decle, 1823), 1–6, "pour retrancher la confusion qui

autrement pourroit advenir . . . de ne faire ny exercer ledit estat de courtier de change, banque et vente en gros des marchandies estrangères en aucunes villes et lieux de ce royaume."

74. Ibid., 7, edict of Louis XIII, 1629.

75. Ibid., 21–33, 1705, 1706, 1708, 1709, 1711, 1713; 37 for the phrase.

76. *De Volmaakte Koopman: Handelende van alles wat in de koopmanschap voorvalt door de Heer Savary* (Amsterdam, 1683), 694–95.

77. *Manuel des agens*, 59–60.

78. Ibid., 67–69.

79. Charles Carrière, *Négociants marseillais au XVIIIe siècle*, 2 vols. (Marseille: Institut historique de Provence, 1973), 1: 228.

80. See A. Genevet, *Compagnie des agents de change de Lyon: histoire depuis les origines jusqu'a l'établissement du parquet en 1845* (Lyon: Imprimerie de Pitrat, 1890), 37.

81. Archives municipales, Lyon, MS BB 180, f. 72

82. Chambre de Commerce, Lyon, "Repertoire du premier Registre, ou sont incerees des deliberations, memoires et autres titres concernant la Chambre de Commerce de la ville de Leon, commencé le 21 aoust 1702," f. 2 (1703): The Chamber of Commerce shall be composed of 9 merchants, "tous néz catholiques," subjects of the king and "negociant actuellement"; 2 shall be merchants of "drapiere"; 2 bankers or merchants of silk, "un epicier, un toillier, et un mercier." All were to be called directors; they would meet Monday of each week and serve *gratuit*. Accented as in the original.

83. Savary, *Le Parfait negociant*, 611.

84. Ibid., 599

85. Genevet, *Compagnie des agents de change de Lyon*, 67–86.

86. Archives municipales, Lyon, MS BB 314 1, f. 35, Soufflot is to be architect, carpenter and mason are also appointed; the engineer of the city is responsible for solidity. A more ambitious plan to hire Robert de Cotte had to be scrapped. See *L'Art baroque à Lyon: Actes du colloque (Lyon 27–29 Octobre 1972)* (Lyon: Institut d'histoire de l'art de l'Université Lyon II, 1975).

87. Archives municipales, Lyon, MS DD 295 book 50 gives all the expenses for outfitting the new *loge du change*; over 121,000 livres spent; on 20 June 1750 Louis XV agreed to purchase the house where the loge is located. On the top parapet are the words "Regnante Lud XV Victore Fac. Anno Dom 1749." This manuscript also lists the contents of the building.

88. On rue de Gadagne; two statues by Perrache, one of Europe, the other of Asia; two others represent Africa and America; J.-C. Bellicard did engravings of them and 4 drawings survive. Ibid., ff. 50–53,

89. Archives Patrimoine-culturel de la Chambre de Commerce et d'Industrie Marseille-Provence (hereafter CCI), Marseille, MS B 8, "Deliberation de la chambre du commerce de Marseille," 1698 to 1726, 3 vols.; demonstrated by a list of those approved to live abroad, a few hundred in every decade living in Smyrne, Alexandria, Seyde, Constantinople, Cairo, Tripoli, Alep, Tunis, Acre, Cyprus, etc.

90. Carrière, *Négociants marseillais*, 1: 232; in 1662 the merchants got permission to hold a "bourse de commerce" at the entrance of Pavillon Puget, the avant-corps of the actual hôtel de ville. See also Paul Giraud, *Marseille: L'Hôtel de ville: la Loge, les deux Maisons du roi* (Marseille: Chez l'auteur, 1962).

91. *Lettres d'un négociant de Marseille à un des ses amis a Paris, concernant le commerce*, 3rd letter, 1726, 7.

92. Daniel Panzac, "International and Domestic Maritime Trade in the Ottoman Empire During the 18th Century," *International Journal of Middle East Studies* 24, 2 (1992): 193–94.

93. CCI, MS B 8 "Deliberation de la Chambre," 20 February 1720.

94. Archives municipales, Marseille, HH 295, dated 11 March 1713.

95. From *Nouvelles lettres instructives et amusantes*, 126, quoted extensively in Carrière, *Négociants marseillais*, 233. I have not been able to find a copy of the original.

96. For a discussion of this complex financial environment, see François-Xavier Emmanuelli, *Vivre à Marseille sous l'Ancien Régime* (Paris: Perrin, 1999), 108–14.

97. *Arrest du conseil d'etat du roi, qui fait défenses à tous Faillis & Banqueroutiers, de fréquenter la Salle de la Loge, si ce n'est après qu'ils auront entiérement payé leur Créanciers*, Marseille, 17 January 1730.

98. Archives municipales, Marseille, FF 203, 6 June 1766.

99. CCI, found in MS D 51, "Loge du Bourse (Batiment et police 1674–1793)," undated and unfoliated; the document begins, "Monseigneur Les Negocians soussignés" but the signatures are lost.

100. Ibid., same dossier as above, unfoliated and undated: the document begins "La détermination de faire fermer la Loge à une heure preçise."

101. Archives municipales, Marseille, FF 203, 18 February 1774.

102. Ibid., MS AA 7 4f, ff. 199–201, dated January 1767.

103. Ibid., FF 203, 6 June 1766.

104. CCI, MS D 51, "Loge du Bourse (Batiment et police 1674–1793)," unfoliated, dated 1765 with signatures. And next document dated in a different hand, the vote for and against.

105. Ibid., same dossier, letter dated Bordeaux, 12 April 1759.

106. L. M. Cullen, "History, Economic Crises, and Revolution: Understanding Eighteenth-Century France," *Economic History Review* 46, 4 (1993): 640–41.

107. CCI, MS D 51, letter dated Bordeaux, 18 October 1773, "il est deffendu à tous faillie et Banqueroutiers de frequenter notre Bourse, ou place de change, avant d'avoir satisfait aux Pactes et conventions . . . en Génerales doit etre interpretté ainsi contre les faillies Etranger; cependant comme ils ne portent pas avec eux un caractere distinctif ce ne peut étre que sur la denonciation d'un creancier qui les Reconnoîtrois dans la place du change ou Bourse . . . obliger les faillis de faire enregistrer au Greffe de la Jurisdiction consulaire leur concordats et les quittances de leurs creanciers pour mettre par la les Juge et Consuls en état de connoître ceux qui seroient dans le cas de l'Exclusion."

108. Ibid., same dossier, letter of 22 October 1773, Dunkirk, sending a copy of the decree against bankrupts; and one the next day from Bayonne; 26 October 1773, from Amiens; 6 November 1773 from Rouen, and on the 14th of the month, letter from Lyon, etc.

109. For English moralizing, see Julian Hoppit, *Risk and Failure in English Business, 1700–1800* (Cambridge: Cambridge University Press, 1987), 164.

110. CCI, MS L v 29, where we are told that the courtiers rented 20 "bureaux" in "une grand salle au dessous de la maison de Ville qu'on appelle vulgairement la

Loge et ou les negociants rassembleur tour les jour on y fit construire vingt petits bureaux qui entourent de la salle . . . les courtiers affin dy resoudre les ventes et achapter secretement."

111. Ibid., 2 September 1712, where there is fighting with the notaries as to who can sell insurance and make payments to the king; 27 September 1712, on the secrecy employed by the courtiers; 1 August 1712, "quand les notaires sevoient fondes a faire des assurances ce qui n'est qu'une partie des fonctions des courtiers royaux." And again, "cette qualite des notaires dans des boutiques ou ils doivent naturelement faire tout ce qui depend de leur profession et les assurance." On the importance of the notaries in Paris, see Philip T. Hoffman, Gilles Postel-Vinay, and Jean-Laurent Rosenthal, "Information and Economic History: How the Credit Market in Old Regime Paris Forces Us to Rethink the Transition to Capitalism," *American Historical Review* 104, 1 (1999): 69–94.

112. A detailed account of these events can be found in Louis Bergasse, *Histoire du commerce de Marseille* (Paris: Plon, 1954), 4: 621–30.

113. The most important tract on the topic by the trader, Journu, and entitled *Essai sur les causes de la cherté de l'argent et des lettres de change a Marseille* (Nîmes, 1774), is discussed in Louis Bergasse, *Histoire du commerce de Marseille* (Paris: Plon, 1954), 621–46; see *Essai*, 7, "Nous avons un Corps de Courtiers de change, qui sont l'office d'une banque publique. Ils payent les dettes d'un Négociant par son crédit sur un autre Négociant . . . Marseille, seule au monde, a des Courtiers de cette espece."

114. For the printed text, Le Sieur Roland, *Mémoire à consulter et consultation par le sieur Simon Roland, ancien premier échevin de la ville de Marseille et l'un des membres de la chambre de commerce.*

115. Journu, *Essai*, 37; on foreigners, 20; for nationalism, 27; for these events see also Bergasse, *Histoire*, 645–46.

116. See the discussion of the attempts at reform in the 1770s in Potter, *Corps and Clienteles*, 162.

Chapter 4. Secrecy and the Paradox at the Heart of Modernity (the Masonic Moment)

1. See Margaret C. Jacob, *Living the Enlightenment: Freemasonry and Politics in Eighteenth-Century Europe* (New York: Oxford University Press, 1991), passim.

2. See Ann Thomson, "Joseph Morgan et le monde islamique," *Dix-huitième siècle* 27 (1995): 349–63.

3. For a more extended discussion, see Margaret C. Jacob, *The Origins of Freemasonry: Facts and Fictions* (Philadelphia: University of Pennsylvania Press, 2005).

4. University Library, Leiden, Marchand MSS 2, f. 36, item 8, Rousset writing to Marchand.

5. Douglas Smith, *Working the Rough Stone: Freemasonry and Society in Eighteenth-Century Russia* (DeKalb: Northern Illinois University Press, 1999), 148–49.

6. *Lettre de M. L'abbé DF . . . à Madame La Marquise de*** Contenant le véritable Secret des Francs-Maçons* (Anvers, 1744), 3–4.

7. *Essai sur les Mysteres et le veritable objet des Franc-Maçons* (Paris, 1771; 2nd ed. Amsterdam, 1776), 14–18.

8. See, for example, *Almanach des francs-massons pour l'année . . . 1772*, 24–25; another version, same title page but with year given as 1777, describes the reception in a London lodge of that year of the eldest son of the Nabob of Carnatica, Madras; cf. Cecil Adams, "The Freemasons' Pocket Companions of the Eighteenth Century," *Ars Quatuor Coronatorum* 45 (1934): 165–231. Yet note on p. 165 that a copy of Anderson's *Constitutions* (London, 1723) in 1738 cost 10s. 6d. On the almanacs see Jacob, *Origins of Freemasonry*, chap. 2.

9. For an early example of French masonic rule giving, see BN MS FM 94, "Manuscrit devoirs en joints aux maçons libres," 1735.

10. Jacob, *Living the Enlightenment*, 92 .

11. Helen Berry, "Rethinking Politeness in Eighteenth-Century England: Moll King's Coffee House and the Significance of 'Flash Talk,'" *Transactions of the Royal Historical Society* 6th ser. 11 (2001): 65–81.

12. Patricia Meyer Spacks, *Privacy: Concealing the Eighteenth-Century Self* (Chicago: University of Chicago Press, 2003).

13. See the lists assembled by the police at the Prefecture of the Police, Paris, MS AA/7/297–303, f. 541.

14. For an excellent overview of masonic practices of inclusion (and exclusion), see Pierre-Yves Beaurepaire, "Fraternité universelle et pratiques discriminatoires dans la Franc-Maçonnerie des Lumières," *Revue d'histoire moderne et contemporaine* 44–42 (1997): 195–212. On women in French freemasonry, see James Smith Allen, "Sisters of Another Sort: Freemason Women in Modern France, 1725–1940," *Journal of Modern History* 75 (2003): 783–835.

15. For a more detailed account, see the entire issue of *L'Histoire* 256 (July–August 2001). I am deeply grateful to the librarians of the Grand Orient and especially to Pierre Mollier. I owe the point about bartering with the Germans to my colleague, Arch Getty.

16. Library of the Grand Orient of France (hereafter GODF), Paris, MS 113.2.96.

17. For a general survey of lodges throughout Europe, see my *Living the Enlightenment*.

18. GODF, MS 113.2.96, 6 February 1746.

19. Ibid., 29 August 1742, "Ordre adressée au f. Arthur Cope, Ven . . . ble M. en Titre de la Loge Anglaise, de la part de l'Intendant de la Guienne pour fermer le local où se tient la Loge . . . Je vous défends de la part du Roi d'y tenir à la venir aucunes assemblées sans prétexte de. . . . Sur l'intimation de cet ordre, la Loge décide quelle ne s'assemblera plus dans le même local."

20. Bibliothèque historique de la ville de Paris, MS 665 from 1729 to 1743 (at the latest) contains anti-Fleury, antimonarchical, anticlerical sentiments and masonic songs. Indeed, only the freemasons are seen as innocent. No author given in the text or in printed catalog.

21. See my *Living the Enlightenment*, chap. 5.

22. GODF, MS 113.2.96, 6 February 1746. "Le f. . . . dénonce au R. Atel des Loges de Franche Maçonnes ditte des Soeurs de l'Adoption, qui se tiennent en ville; La Loge décide dans san sagesse de prévenir." All quotations about the lodge's meetings are from this source.

23. Metropolitan Museum of Art, New York, Prints Room, no. 61.621.5, *Sun Foundry* (Glasgow, n.d. but early nineteenth century), 379 for text and engraved pictures that promised the lavatories were "chaste in style."

24. BN, FM 4 1249, no place or date but clearly from the late eighteenth century and entitled "Statutes des dames."

25. GODF, MS 113.2.96, 30 November 1747. "Proposition d'affiliation du S. Cappadoce Juif se disant *Franc-Maçon* reçu à Amsterdam; non seulement la Loge décide de ne point admettre cet individu dans now assemblées maçoniques, mais encore de ne point le reconnâitre pour frère." The following decision was made, "Le 11 Fevrier 1749 . . . La Loge décide que *jamais Juifs* ne serait admis parmi nous."

26. Beaurepaire, "Fraternité universelle et pratiques discriminatoires," 205.

27. See Jacob, *Living the Enlightenment*, chap. 6.

28. BN, 161 H 506 (1–2); *Discours prononcé a la loge de *** par le Frere Orateur* (1740), 11–12. Note similar sentiment, but in a time declared to be one of crisis, Bibliothèque municipale d'étude et d'information, Grenoble, MS Q 50, "Discours de M. Barral," 24 June 1779.

29. For examples, see GODF, MS 113.2.96, "Le 13 Juillet 1747. Dans . . . de 60 frs. a été accordé à un.f. nécéssiteux outre 32 livres produit de la boëte des pauvres. Le Fevrier 1750. Secours accordé a deux FF. De notre Loge . . . detenu pour dettes à Paris f. 150:- Le 23 Mars 1751. Secours de f. 60:- donné par la Loge pour un f. Visiteur se trouvant dans le besoin." On 22 June 1751 one F. Durant from Pons and a member of the lodge, detained in prison in London for debt, is given 50 francs. In 1756 all members gave 9 francs each for a banquet.

30. Smith, *Working the Rough Stone*, 166–67.

31. For an early copy of his teachings, see Bibliotheca philosophia hermetica, Bloemstraat, Amsterdam, MS c 1780, "Traité de la réintegration des Etres"; cf. Gérard van Rijnberk, *Martines de Pasqually* (Lyon: Raclet, 1938).

32. *La Loge Rouge devoilée*, new ed., July 1790, 16; pamphlet found at Bibliothèque historique de la ville de Paris.

33. Greater detail on these tensions can be found at the BN, MS FM 86, records from Bordeaux in the 1780s.

34. Charles Porset, *Les Philalèthes et les convents de Paris: une politique de la folie* (Paris: Champion, 1996), 139.

35. GODF, MS 113.1.602, f. 1, no. 395, 2nd Circulaire, February 1785. Some of these documents are reprinted in the Porset volume, which has a wealth of primary source material. See no. 360, "le monde sait des operations theurgiques et pneumatologi, ques des Sraepher, des Srhedder [?], même du Comte de Cagliostro, pasoissent réunir a la Maçonnerie, et mème indiquer poiur la veritable science, le moyen de mettre l'homme en relation avec des êtres intellectuels intermediaires entre Dieu et lui." On Willermoz, see Catherine Amadou, "Inventaire du fonds Jean-Baptiste Willermoz," *La Renaissance Traditionnelle, Revue d'études maçonniques et symboliques* 123–24 (July–October 2000): 186–210.

36. GODF, MS 113 f. 12. For the range of learning and reading that an educated person of this decade could experience, see Bibliothèque de l'Arsenal, Paris, MSS 7581–89, an anonymous diary that begins in 1774.

37. GODF, MS 113.1.602, f. 13, no. 361, art. 5. And see art. 7, "les Chefs ou Maitres qui ont prétendu posse de la vraie science, tels que Martines Pasqualis, Kukumus [?], de Jonsthon, de Hunt Dictus-Eques-Ab-Ense, De Weéler, de Sraepher, Casetier à Leipsic, et autres."

38. Ibid., f. 15, no. 396, art. 1.

39. See also Pierre-Yves Beaurepaire, "'Une école pour les sciences: le collège des Philalèthes et la tentation académique des élites maçonniques lilloises à la fin de l'Ancien Régime," *Revue du Nord* 81 (1999): 723–44. Cf. Charles Porset and Cécile Révauger, eds., *Franc-maçonnerie et religions dans l'Europe des Lumières* (Paris: Champion, 1998).

40. GODF, MS 113.2.96, 9 November 1788. "Banquet que donne ce jour la L..Angl. pour célébrer l'heureux retour du parlement de Bordeaux en exil à Libourne et rendre hommage à des . . . Magistrats qui sont rendu an Siège de la Justice."

41. GODF, MS 92.2.53, 17 August 1788.

42. BN, FM 2 76, records of La fidelité from the 1780s, item no. 38.

43. For a description of the festival, see Lynn Hunt, *Politics, Culture, and Class in the French Revolution* (Berkeley: University of California Press, 1984), 35.

44. GODF, MS 92.3.141

45. GODF, MS 92.3.53, "Discours du F. Mailleres membre et deputé de la loge la vrais anglaise . . . 15 juillet 1790," f. 32.

46. Ronald Schechter, *Obstinate Hebrews: Representations of Jews in France, 1715–1815* (Berkeley: University of California Press, 2003), 28.

47. GODF, MS 92.3. f. 33.

48. BN, MS 4996, on microfilm, on constituting lodges in Belgium, in Huy and Liège, 1809–12, under the auspices of the Grand Lodge of France; f. 20 for social tensions.

49. See Pierre-Yves Beaurepaire, "Les véritables auteurs de la révolution de France de 1789 démasqués: Discours de persécution et crimes d'indifférenciation chez F. N. Sourdat de Troyes," *Dix-huitième siècle* 32 (2000): 403–21.

50. GODF, MS 92.2.53, f. 49, discourse of 24 June 1788. Cf. Steven C. Bullock, *Revolutionary Brotherhood: Freemasonry and the Transformation of the American Social Order, 1730–1840* (Chapel Hill : University of North Carolina Press, 1996) and Mark Tabbert, *American Freemasons: Three Centuries of Building Communities* (New York: New York University Press, 2005), 36–47.

51. See Margaret Ó hÓgartaigh, "Making History and Defining the Nation: Nineteenth-Century Interpretations of 1798," in Philip Bull, Frances Devlin-Glass, and Helen Doyle, eds., *Ireland and Australia, 1798–1998: Studies in Culture, Identity and Migration* (Sydney: Crossing Press, 2000), 24–33.

52. Henry Joy and the Rev. William Bruce, *Belfast Politics* (Belfast, 1794; reprint Belfast: Athol Books, 1974), 16.

53. Jean Agnew, ed., *The Drennan-McTier Letters, 1776–1793* (Dublin: Women's History Project in Association with the Irish Manuscripts Commission, 1998), 29, letter of 1777. Cf. Ian R. McBride, *Scripture Politics: Ulster Presbyterians and Irish Radicalism in the Late Eighteenth Century* (Oxford: Clarendon Press, 1998).

54. Patrick Fagan, "Infiltration of Dublin Freemason Lodges by United Irishmen and Other Republican Groups," *Eighteenth-Century Ireland* 13 (1998): 68.

55. Agnew, ed., *Drennan-McTier Letters*, 202, from the mid-1780s; 210, 252–53 for Newry being very disagreeable in 1786.

56. Ibid., 321–22.

57. Ibid., 356, William Drennan to Sam McTier, 5 February 1791.

58. Ibid., 357, William Drennan in Dublin to Sam McTier, in Belfast, 21 May 1791.

59. Ibid., 358, same letter.

60. Ibid., p. 364, Sam [McTier] to W. D. [William Drennan], 9 July 1791.

61. Ibid., 361, same to same, 3 July 1791.

62. Ibid.

63. See Lian Swords, ed., *Protestant, Catholic and Dissenter: The Clergy and 1798* (Blackrock, Dublin: Columba Press, 1997).

64. National Library of Dublin, MS 13176 (2), Frances Edgeworth to Dr. D. Beaufort, 17 April 1797, writing from Ireland to her father in London.

65. For a more detailed account, see the excellent work by Nancy J. Curtin, *The United Irishmen: Popular Politics in Ulster and Dublin, 1791–1798* (Oxford: Clarendon Press, 1998), with reference to freemasonry, 245–46.

66. National Library, Dublin, MS 13176 (2), Frances Edgeworth to Dr. D. Beaufort, Cork, 18 September 1798.

67. Public Record Office, Northern Ireland, Belfast, cited in Mary McNeill, *The Life and Times of Mary Ann McCracken, 1770–1866: A Belfast Panorama* (Dublin: Allen Figgis, 1960), 127, writing in 1797.

68. Library of the Grand Lodge of the Netherlands, The Hague, MS 41:8, f. 26.

69. The lodge La Bien Aimée, MS 41:6, found in the Grand Lodge of The Netherlands; discussed in Jacob, *Living the Enlightenment*, 163–64.

Chapter 5. Liberals, Radicals, and Bohemians

1. The aspect of this chapter that concerns the bohemian first received articulation in Lynn Hunt and Margaret C. Jacob, "The Affective Revolution in 1790s Britain," *Eighteenth Century Studies* 34 (2001): 491–521. On the wars see Fred Anderson, *Crucible of War: The Seven Years' War and the Fate of Empire in British North America, 1754–1766* (New York: Knopf, 2000), 114, 541, 599.

2. Nicholas Canny, *Europeans on the Move: Studies on European Migration, 1500–1800* (Oxford: Clarendon Press, 1994), 279.

3. Linda Colley, *Britons: Forging the Nation 1707–1837* (New Haven, Conn.: Yale University Press, 1992), 132.

4. For the impact on British masonic lodges, see Peter Clark, *British Clubs and Societies, 1580–1800: The Origins of an Associational World* (Oxford: Clarendon Press, 2000), 331–37.

5. American Philosophical Society, Lee MSS, BL 51, 1: 71, Samuel Adams to R. H. Lee, 10 April 1773.

6. Patrick M. Geoghegan, *Robert Emmet: A Life* (Montreal: McGill-Queen's University Press, 2002), 264.

7. Huntington Library, San Mariono, Calif., MS BN 454, Jun 16 1815, Helen M. Williams to her friend Ruth Baldwin Barlow in America, 16 June 1815.

8. Ghislaine de Boom, *Les ministres plénipotentiaires dans les pays-bas autriciens principalement Cobenzl*, Académie royale de Belgique Mémoires 10th ser. 31 (Brussels: Lamertin, 1932), 63–66; cf. for the later period Simon Burrows, "The Cosmopolitan Press, 1759–1815," in Hannah Barker and Simon Burrows, eds., *Press, Politics and the Public Sphere in Europe and North America, 1760–1820* (Cambridge: Cambridge University Press, 2002), 31.

9. See Jacob, *The Radical Enlightenment.*

10. Library of the Grand Lodge of the Netherlands, The Hague, MS 41:10 for 1795 and discussed by me in "Radicalism in the Dutch Enlightenment," Margaret C. Jacob and Wijnand W. Mijnhardt, eds., *The Dutch Republic in the Eighteenth Century: Decline, Enlightenment, and Revolution* (Ithaca, N.Y.: Cornell University Press, 1992), 234.

11. See Janet L. Polasky, *Revolution in Brussels, 1787–1793* (Hanover, N.H.: University Press of New England, 1987).

12. Peter D. G. Thomas, *John Wilkes: A Friend to Liberty* (Oxford: Clarendon Press, 1996), 63.

13. American Philosophical Society, Lee MSS, BL 51 vol. 1, p. 39, A. Lee to R. H. Lee, December 27, 1768, "I have dined with Mr. Wilkes in the King's Bench; he speaks very warmly in favor of America and Highly applauds their proceedings."

14. See Michael Heyd, *Be Sober and Reasonable: The Critique of Enthusiasm in the Seventeenth and Early Eighteenth Centuries* (New York: E.J. Brill, 1995).

15. For an example from a text originally in Dutch, then translated out of French into English and appearing in Ireland, see John Stinstra, *An Essay on Fanaticism, Addressed to the People of his own Persuasion*, trans. Rev. Isaac Subremont (Dublin: Thomas Ewing, 1774).

16. Phillis Wheatley, *Poems on Various Subjects, Religious and Moral* (London: A. Bell, 1773), 46.

17. [Hester Chapone], *Miscellanies in Prose & Verse by Mrs. Chapone, Author of Letters on the Improvement of the Mind. To which is added, The Temple of Virtue, A Dream. By James Fordyce* (Dublin: J. Williams, 1775), 15; 40–50 on enthusiasm and indifference.

18. Jayne E. Triber, *A True Republican: The Life of Paul Revere* (Amherst: University of Massachusetts Press, 1998), 20.

19. Raymond Williams, *Culture and Society, 1780–1950* (Harmondsworth: Penguin, 1958), 48.

20. Horace Walpole, *Horace Walpole's Correspondence with Thomas Gray, Richard West and Thomas Ashton*, ed. W. S. Lewis, George L. Lam, and Charles H. Bennett, Yale Edition of Horace Walpole's Correspondence 13–14 (New Haven, Conn.: Yale University Press, 1948), 138, Gray to Walpole, 30 December, 1764, on burning; for the opposite impulse, see Walpole, *Correspondence with Thomas Chatterton, . . .* , Yale edition 16 (1951), 191 n, Michael Lort to Walpole, for the opposite impulse, 8 September 1779.

21. See the discussion of the philosophes in Gerd van den Heuvel, "Cosmopolite, Cosmopoli(ti)sme," in Rolf Reichardt and Eberhard Schmitt, eds., *Handbuch*

politisch-sozialer Grundbegriffe in Frankreich 1680–1820 (Munich: R. Oldenbourg, 1986), 6: 43–45; 46–47 for Rousseau.

22. Helena Rosenblatt, *Rousseau and Geneva* (Cambridge: Cambridge University Press, 1997).

23. See Dale K. Van Kley, *The Religious Origins of the French Revolution: From Calvin to the Civil Constitution, 1560–1791* (New Haven, Conn.: Yale University Press, 1996), 296–97.

24. Library of the Grand Lodge, The Hague, MS 41:8, f. 26.

25. Cf. Robert M. Ryan, *The Romantic Reformation: Religious Politics in English Literature 1789–1824* (Cambridge: Cambridge University Press, 1997).

26. James E. Bradley, *Religion, Revolution and English Radicalism: Non-Conformity in Eighteenth-Century Politics and Society* (Cambridge: Cambridge University Press, 1990).

27. John Rylands Library, Manchester, MS Box 2/12, letters of William Turner to his son Billy, f. 35, 1776, and passim. Living in Wakefield, the family reads French (f. 38) and admires the physico-theological writings of William Derham.

28. Ibid., f. 65, n.d. but placed in order from 1777.

29. Harvard University, Houghton Library, Thelwall MSS Eng 947.2 (21).

30. See *A Liturgy on the Universal Principles of Religion and Morality* (London, E and C. Dilly, 1776), x-xi; at the John Rylands Library, B 787B. See the advertisement, "A Liturgy . . . used at a Chapel in Margaret-street, Cavendish-square. Price 2s." See also J. Dybikowski, *On Burning Ground: An Examination of the Ideas, Projects and Life of David Williams* (Oxford: Voltaire Foundation, 1993), 38–43. And on these circles see Anthony Page, *John Jebb and the Enlightenment: Origins of British Radicalism* (Westport Conn.: Praeger, 2003).

31. *A Liturgy*, 21–26. The Rylands copy was owned by the Pollock family in Newry, County Down.

32. Nicholas A. Hans, *New Trends in Education in the Eighteenth Century* (London: Routledge and Kegan Paul, 1951), 164–65.

33. Jack Fruchtman, Jr., *Thomas Paine and the Religion of Nature* (Baltimore: Johns Hopkins University Press, 1993), 10. Note that Mayhew was an opponent of enthusiasm; see John Rylands Library, Benson MSS, f. 102 Mayhew to Benson, 28 August 1761. He is also afraid his ministry will be taken away from him by Trinitarian "Athanasian & Calvinistic"orthodoxy; see f. 101, 1754. Cf. Thomas Paine, *Common Sense and Other Writings*, intro. Joyce Appleby (New York: Barnes and Noble, 2005).

34. G. J. Barker-Benfield, *The Culture of Sensibility: Sex and Society in Eighteenth-Century Britain* (Chicago: University of Chicago Press, 1992), 224–35.

35. Rebecca Larson, *Daughters of Light: Quaker Women Preaching and Prophesying in the Colonies and Abroad, 1700–1775* (Chapel Hill: University of North Carolina Press, 1999), 221–22.

36. See Clifford D. Conner, *Jean Paul Marat: Scientist and Revolutionary* (Atlantic Highlands, N.J.: Humanities Press, 1997), 23–24.

37. Michael Turner, "The Limits of Abolition: Government, Saints and the 'African Question,' c. 1780–1820," *English Historical Review* 112 (April 1997): 319–57.

38. E. V. Goveia, *The West Indian Slave Laws of the 18th Century* (London: Caribbean Universities Press, 1970), 20–21, 44–45.

39. P. J. Marshall and Glyndwr Williams, *The Great Map of Mankind: Perceptions of New Worlds in the Age of Enlightenment* (Cambridge, Mass.: Harvard University Press, 1982), 300–301.

40. Geoghegan, *Robert Emmet*, chap. 4.

41. *Northern Star*, Belfast, 25 April 1792, "The Negroe's Complaint."

42. Mitchell Library, Glasgow, MS 73, poems of William Campbell.

43. See Seymour S. Cohen, "Thomas Cooper," *American National Biography* (New York: Oxford University Press, 1999), 5: 462–64; brought to my attention by the author.

44. Sankar Muthu, *Enlightenment Against Empire* (Princeton, N.J.: Princeton University Press, 2003).

45. See Lynn Hunt, ed., *The French Revolution and Human Rights: A Brief Documentary History* (Boston: Bedford Books, 1996). Cf. Michael Durey, *Transatlantic Radicals and the Early American Republic* (Lawrence: University of Kansas Press, 1997), 282–85.

46. John Rylands Library, MS 570, 26 February 1792, to Mrs Piozzi.

47. Ali Ibn Abi Bakr, Burhan al-Din, al-Marghinani, *The Hedàya, or Guide: a Commentary on the Mussulman Laws*, trans. Charles Hamilton (London: T. Bensley, 1791), xlii–xliii.

48. Keele University Library, Wedgwood MSS, W/M 1460, 18 March 1791, Josiah, Jr., to his father.

49. See *The Cabinet, by a Society of Gentlemen*, 3 vols. (London: J. March, 1795).

50. Huntington Library, see MS HM 31 201, ff. 15 passim, Mrs Larpent's Diary for the period. She was the wife of the Licenser of the London stage; see entry for 2 December 1796, on French men and women too separate; she sees Montaigne as the culprit.

51. Helen Maria Williams, *Letters Written in France, in the Summer of 1790, to a Friend in England* (Dublin: G. Burnet, 1791), 27–38. She is speaking of Madame Sillery who became Brulart and renounced her title.

52. See throughout *The Cabinet, by a Society of Gentlemen*.

53. Mary McNeill, *The Life and Times of Mary Ann McCracken, 1770–1866: A Belfast Panorama* (Belfast: A. Figgis, 1960), quoting a letter of 16 March 1797.

54. William Blake, *For the Sexes: The Gates of Paradise* (London, 1793), Huntington Library # 57439.

55. John Oswald, *The Cry of Nature; or, An appeal to Mercy and to Justice on behalf of the Persecuted Animals* (London, 1791).

56. David V. Erdman, *Commerce des Lumières: John Oswald and the British in Paris, 1790–1793* (Columbia: University of Missouri Press, 1986), 52–73, 68.

57. William Godwin, *An Enquiry concerning Political Justice, and its Influence on General Virtue and Happiness . . .* , vol. 2 (London, 1793), 844–51.

58. Huntington Library, MSS of Charlotte [Turner] Smith, HM 10836, to Sarah Farr Rose, 15 June 1804 Charlotte Smith refers to herself as nothing more than "a legal prostitute," that she was in effect sold to her husband, "This monster." On marriage as making people into property, see Godwin, *An Enquiry*, 849–50.

59. Mitchell Library, Glasgow, MS 73, f.61, for a copy.

60. Birmingham City Library, MS 281, "Church and King (A Song)"

61. Harriet Jump, ed., *Lives of the Great Romantics III: Godwin, Wollstonecraft and Mary Shelley by Their Contemporaries*, vol. 2, *Mary Wollstonecraft* (London, Pickering & Chatto, 1999), xiii–xiv.

62. Houghton Library, Thelwall MSS Eng 947.2 (21), 3 March 1798 to Dr . . . , "With respect to ourselves . . . Maria in particular grows a very stout and vigorous girl . . . we have daily and hourly proofs of the advantages of the stile of dress we have adopted for she bounds along in her trousers in all the romping vivacity of independence." Letter contains a mention of Coleridge.

63. Michael Scrivener, *Seditious Allegories: John Thelwall and Jacobin Writing* (University Park: Pennsylvania State University Press, 2001), 138 and chap. 7.

64. Public Record Office, UK, MS HO/42/19/396–97, celebration toasts in Birmingham at the meeting to mark 14 July 1791. This account is in manuscript but it conforms to published accounts in the same dossier.

65. By a Cosmopolite, *The Political Harmonist; or, Songs, and Poetical Effusions, sacred to the Cause of Liberty* (London: T. Williams, 1797).

66. Rachel Hammersley, "English Republicanism in Revolutionary France: The Case of the Cordelier Club," *Albion* 43 (October 2004): 464–81.

67. Thomas Cooper, *A Reply to Mr Burke's Invective* (London: J. Johnson, 1792), 10. Cf. Margaret C. Jacob and Larry Stewart, *Practical Matter: Newton's Science in the Service of Industry and Empire, 1687–1851* (Cambridge, Mass.: Harvard University Press, 2004), chap. 4.

68. Public Record Office, MS HO 42/19/522–3, Birmingham, 15 August 1791, spy report by James Ward on Presbyterian minister, Hobson, who has gone off to Paris.

69. Ibid., HO 42/19/59, letter dated 21 May 1791.

70. Cooper, *Reply to Mr. Burke's Invective*, 9.

71. On the Spanish colonies and rebellion in the late eighteenth century, see Anthony McFarlane, "Identity, Enlightenment and Political Dissent in Late Colonial Spanish America," *Transactions of the Royal Historical Society* 6th ser. 8 (1998): 325–27.

72. On the teaching of French for reading and writing in a boy's school in Bolton, Yorkshire in the 1760s—by a master who could not however speak it—see John Rylands Library, Sedden MSS, box 1/4, Rev. Holland to James Nicholson about his son at the school in the 1760s.

73. John Rylands Library, MS 570, 12 October 1791, Orleans, Williams to Mrs. Piozzi. Now printed in Hester Lynch Piozzi, *The Piozzi Letters: The Correspondence of Hester Lynch Piozzi, 1784–1821 (formerly Mrs. Thrale)*, vol. 1, *1784–1791*, ed. Edward A. Bloom and Lillian D. Bloom (Newark: University of Delaware Press, 1989), 371.

74. *Modern Propensities; or, an essay on the Art of Strangling, etc . . . with Memoirs of Susannah Hill and A Summary of her Trial at the Old-Bailey . . . 1791, On the Charge of Hanging Francis Kotzwarra . . .* (London, c. 1791). A copy can be found in the Lewis Walpole Library, Farmington, Conn.

75. *Journal de Paris*, 18 January 1790, article entitled "Variété" and signed by Pinel. I owe this reference to Dora Weiner.

76. See Marcus Wood, *Radical Satire and Print Culture, 1790–1822* (Oxford: Clarendon Press, 1994), 61.

77. Lewis Walpole Library, print no. 789.10.18 1p, October 18 1789, *Female Furies or Extraordinary Revolution*, depicts women completely out of control in Paris, killing

the king's bodyguards and firing muskets; print no. 793.3.7 2 *False Liberty Rejected*, by I. Cruikshank, depicts Condorcet and Phillippe Egalité naked from the waist down. Cf. Charles Edmonds, *Poetry of the Anti-Jacobin: comprising the celebrated political and satirical poem . . . of . . . George Canning . . . with notes by Charles Edmonds . . . Etchings by James Gillray* (London: G. Willis, 1854), 5; reprinting texts from the 1790s. Burke was not alone in seeing the immediately radical potential of the French Revolution and especially of the doctrine of the "rights of man." A rare anonymous satirical tract from 1792, *Buff or, a Dissertation on Nakedness: A Parody on Paine's Rights of Man* (London: J. Mathews, 1792), Bancroft Library, University of California, argues that Paine's notion of the rights of man might as well include an attack on any system of dress. It concludes, "I have discoursed most wisely on the propriety of Nakedness . . . In this manner it would be no difficult matter to prove that ignorance was preferable to knowledge, nastiness to cleanliness, that eating and drinking were abominable customs, and not to be endured; that Religion, Literature, the liberal Professions, the Arts, Sciences, manufactures, and every species of accumulative improvements should be abolished," 26–27. In addition a hostile, easily available biography of Paine claimed that he was degenerate in morals as well as politics, everything from a wife-beater to a false husband who would refuse his wife her sexual due; see Francis Oldys, *The Life of Thomas Pain* (London, 1793), 171: "Paine has no moral character."

78. *Descriptive Sketches* . . . , composed 1791–92, published 1793; here quoted from William Wordsworth, *Poetical Works*, ed. Thomas Hutchinson, new ed. rev. Ernest de Selincourt (New York: Oxford University Press, 1936), 14; cf. Stephen Gill, *William Wordsworth: A Life* (Oxford: Clarendon Press, 1989), 56–65, 71–72, where Wordsworth's largely private radicalism is discussed. On Wordsworth and Coleridge "in love with one another," see Gill, 122.

79. Birmingham Public Library (hereafter BBL), JWP, W/6, James Watt, Jr., writing from Nantes to his father, 17 October 1792.

80. Keele University Library, Wedgwood MSS, W/M 1460, Josiah, Jr., to his father, 13 April 1791.

81. I quote Durey, *Transatlantic Radicals*, 34, who is paraphrasing Godwin. The groundbreaking work on James Watt, Jr., was done by Eric Robinson, "An English Jacobin: James Watt, Junior," *Cambridge Historical Journal* 2 (1953–55): 349–55. Cf. Erdman, *Commerce des Lumières*, 50–55.

82. *Adresse de la Société Constitutionnelle de Londres à la Société des Amis de la Constitution, séante aux Jacobins, à Paris* (Paris, 1792).

83. Durey, *Transatlantic Radicals*, 33.

84. John Ayrton Paris, *The Life of Sir Humphry Davy* (London: Colburn and Bentley, 1831), 62; William Clayfield was also in this circle.

85. Keele University Librry, Wedgwood MSS, W/M 1112, Tom Wedgwood to his brother Josiah, 5 November 1804, "I have an excessive desire to see Mme Stael . . . I feel as if I could taste in her society for the first time in my life, some kinds of spiritual enjoyment. I mean, that she would call into being in me some energies which have yet life for want of sympathy and reaction."

86. Sydney Smith, *The Works of the Rev. Sydney Smith*, 3 vols. in one (New York: Appleton, 1871), preface. On the club see R. B. Litchfield, *Tom Wedgwood: The First Photographer* (1903; New York: Arno Press, 1973), 97. On conversations in this

circle, see *The Letters of Sydney Smith*, ed. Nowel C. Smith (Oxford: Clarendon Press), 1953), 1: 63; letter of June 1801.

87. Smith, *Works*, 3: 16, from the *New Monthly Magazine*.

88. Smith, *Letters*, 1: 103, letter of April 1805 to Francis Jeffrey.

89. Huntington Library, Sydney Smith MSS, HM 30430, 26 June 1796 to his father, Robert Smith, wanting money. It is clear there has been an estrangement: "I hope my dr father you will do me the favor of writing to me—as it will be a proof that you begin to feel a returning regard for me." HM 30431 July 9 1796, protesting his love and that his father has mis-remembered if he attributes such sentiments, or lack thereof to him. HM 30433, 5 November 1797, Smith to his brother, Bobus, saying that his father has told him to go away and stay away; 25 November 1797 to his father A I hope the conversation upon suicide which pass'd between us, has produced no other unpleasant sensation in your mind than the want of respect to you, of which I am sorry to say, you have a right to accuse me." He says that they have quarreled about metaphysical "nonsense." HM 30449, from Edinburgh, 25 December 1801, Sydney has had it with the insults from his father and wishes to terminate their correspondence; HM 30453, 1804, "you have for years treated me with the great cruelty and injustice."

90. Smith, *Letters*, 1: 69, letter to Mrs. Beach, wife of his patron, March 1802.

91. Certainly contemporaries were made uneasy by the attachment between Wordsworth and Coleridge; British Library MSS ADD 35345, Josiah Wedgwood, Jr., to Tom Poole, 1 February 1799, hoping that Wordsworth and Coleridge will remain separated; Coleridge will benefit from "mixed society."

92. Huntington Library, HM 4829, 27 July 1800, Southey to William Taylor.

93. Alison Hickey, "Coleridge, Southey, 'and Co.' Collaboration and Authority," *Studies in Romanticism* 37 (Fall 1998): 328–39.

94. New York Public Library, uncataloged Dyer letter, no. 101, 5 February [no year]. Dyer to the Rev. Mr. . . .

95. George Dyer, *Poems* (London, 1800); preface, xxxvii "the principles of freedom are too sacred, to be surrendered to trifles"; ode addressed to Dr. Robert Anderson, 2: 91. The Huntington Library's copy belonged to Southey.

96. Dyer, *Poems*, 1: 17. My thanks to Bernie Frischer on matters classical and Anacreon.

97. Ibid., 1: 44–45, *Ode on Liberty. Written on a Public Anniversary*, and at the time of the Polish uprising.

98. Huntington Library, Box 10, Southey-Rickman correspondence, John Rickman, from Christchurch to Southey 4 January 1800, RS 746; Southey on the subject of Beguinage and what to do to employ women. See MS 771, 5 August 1802, in which Rickman is returning to England from Ireland, "I think (if I become vacant) I shall resume my old train of thought about aiding the Ladies—the Monastico-Politico-Beguinage—which I think would take, if well recommended."

99. Letter of 16 January 1800, S. to C., in *New Letters of Robert Southey*, 2 vols., ed. Kenneth Curry (New York: Columbia University Press, 1965), 215, "Mary Wollstonecraft told me [Baboeuf] was the most extraordinary [man] she had ever seen—and in the orgasm of the Revolution the system of total equalization would have been wise."

100. Kathleen Jones, *A Passionate Sisterhood: The Sisters, Wives and Daughters of the Lake Poets* (New York: St. Martin's Press, 2000), 226–27, 240.

101. Keele University Library, Wedgwood MSS, W/M 1112, f. 159, Coleridge to Wedgwood (possibly Josiah), 17 February 1803; on Tom's addictions see same call number, 24 June 1804, Tom to Josiah, Jr.; on the family's reserve, see Sarah to Tom, 3 July 1804, her unworthy letter to him attributed "to the inveterate bad habit of not expressing our feelings which so many of our family have & I amongst the rest . . . my taciturnity has really been owing partly to the family infirmity."

102. Ibid., MS W/M21, 27 April 1790, Tom to his brother, Josiah, Jr., on his going off to live with John Leslie.

103. Ibid., same to same, 18 November 1800 and 1 April 1802, "I am just going to the King of Clubs."

104. Ibid., 12 November 1804, on his suffering; Thomas Campbell, 16 July 1805, letter of condolence to Josiah, Jr.

105. Quoting from Davy MSS at the Royal Institution HD 20B, and discussed in greater detail in Margaret C. Jacob and Michael J. Sauter, "Why Did Humphry Davy and Associates Not Pursue the Pain-Alleviating Effects of Nitrous Oxide?" *Journal of the History of Medicine* 57 (April 2002): 161–76.

106. Huntington Library, MS HM 4823, 5 September 1799, Southey to William Taylor, on Davy's gas, "the last symptom is a feeling of strength & an impulse to exert every muscle. For the remainder of the day it left me with increased hilarity & with my hearing, taste and smell certainly more acute. I conceive this gas to be the atmosphere of Mohammeds Paradise." On the use of the gas, see also Jones, *Passionate Sisterhood*, 83.

107. John Rylands Library, Manchester, MS 570, 4 September 1794 to Mrs. Piozzi.

Epilogue

1. *Moniteur*, no. 261 (18 IX. 1793), 673.

2. Quoted in David Turley, *The Culture of English Anti-Slavery, 1780–1860* (London: Routledge, 1991), 205; brought to my attention to Jenna Gibbs. Citing *Proceedings of the General Anti-Slavery Convention . . . 1840* (London: British and Foreign Anti-Slavery Society, 1841); and *Proceedings of the Convention . . . 1843* (London: J. Snow, 1843), 120ff, 14.

Index

Page numbers in *italics* indicate illustrations

Acknowledgments

So many libraries and their staff helped with this project: Bibliothèque municipale, Avignon, the British Library, the John Rylands in Manchester, the archives of the Mercers' Company; the Library of the Grand Orient, Paris, the library of the Académie des sciences, Paris; the Huntington Library, San Marino, the New York Public Library, and, never least, the Young Research Library and the Clark Library, both at UCLA. At UCLA its History Department, and the chair from 2002 to 2005, Teo Ruiz, facilitated all my endeavors. A major aspect of Chapter 5 first took shape in conversations and writing with Lynn Hunt, who must share any praise or blame.

As always and with a rare humanity, Jerry Singerman at Penn Press has guided and assisted. Deborah Harkness proved to be a superb reader; Joyce Appleby, as always, shared her wisdom. Part of Chapter 2 was delivered as the University Research Lecture, 2004, at UCLA, and its audience asked many thoughtful questions. Various and wonderfully competent graduate students have helped with research and translations: Nancy Llewelyn, Inger Leemans, Eric Casteel, Jenna Gibbs, and Naomi Taback.

This book is dedicated to the memory of Lynn Hunt's father, who died in 2005. He was a beloved friend.